THE FIFTH DIMENSION

THE FIFTH DIMENSION

An After-School Program Built on Diversity

Michael Cole and the
Distributed Literacy Consortium

Russell Sage Foundation • New York

The Russell Sage Foundation

The Russell Sage Foundation, one of the oldest of America's general purpose foundations, was established in 1907 by Mrs. Margaret Olivia Sage for "the improvement of social and living conditions in the United States." The Foundation seeks to fulfill this mandate by fostering the development and dissemination of knowledge about the country's political, social, and economic problems. While the Foundation endeavors to assure the accuracy and objectivity of each book it publishes, the conclusions and interpretations in Russell Sage Foundation publications are those of the authors and not of the Foundation, its Trustees, or its staff. Publication by Russell Sage, therefore, does not imply Foundation endorsement.

Library of Congress Cataloging-in-Publication Data

The fifth dimension : an after-school program built on diversity / The Distributed Literacy Consortium.
    p. cm.
    Includes bibliographical references and index.
    ISBN 10: 0-87154-084-3
    ISBN 13: 978-0-87154-084-3
    1. After-school programs—United States.   2. Community and school—United States.
    I. Distributed Literacy Consortium.

LC34.4C74 2006
371.19—dc22

    2006040873

The paper used in this publication meets the minimum requirements of American National Standard for Information Sciences—Permanence of Paper for Printed Library Materials. ANSI Z39.48-1992.

Text design by Genna Patacsil.

RUSSELL SAGE FOUNDATION
112 East 64th Street, New York, New York 10021
10 9 8 7 6 5 4 3 2 1

Contents

CONTENTS

Preface

This volume describes and analyzes a long-term effort to address a number of recalcitrant issues that affect children's welfare in the contemporary United States. These issues are located at the intersection of theories of human development, the changing institutional organization of children's lives, concern over the role of new computer and communication technologies in shaping children's experiences, and the debate over appropriate ways to study children's learning and development. As if these were not enough issues to bundle into one book, we found it impossible to ignore the role that institutions of higher learning might play in resolving these issues while also seeking to fulfill their commitments to their own students and faculty.

Such an ambitious agenda could not have been carried out by one person, or even by a few people. It has required the active engagement and cooperation of scores of people willing to commit themselves to the effort over many years. On the university side, this agenda has involved a wide range of scholars from anthropology, education, linguistics, psychology, and sociology. Participating in the communities have been people who work in the institutions responsible for caring for and nurturing children. These community participants have also been active in obtaining resources that not only create new ways to foster children's development but help address the entrenched barriers (intellectual, social, institutional) that frustrate their efforts at creating healthy environments for such development.

The research reported in the chapters to follow began in the early 1980s at the Laboratory of Comparative Human Cognition as a collaboration between Michael Cole and Peg Griffin. The early phases of the work were supported by the Carnegie Corporation of New York and the Spencer Foundation. When the project upon which the bulk of the research reported here began in the early 1990s, only Cole remained to provide continuity with the project's early beginnings. Thanks to funding provided by the Mellon Foundation and administered by the Russell Sage Foundation it became possible to participate in a broad-based and long-lasting collaboration among incredibly diverse people. When it came time to decide on the authorship of this book, we recognized that the collective nature of its production made it inappropriate to designate any one individual as "the author," or even as "the editor." Cole, owing to the longevity of his involvement and institutional responsibilities as director of the Laboratory of Comparative Human Cognition, served as the coordinating author and editor, but the final product was by no means his individual responsibility. Our collaboration in recent years and our responsibility as scholars to report on our findings to the community at large had led us to think of ourselves as a single, albeit loosely knit community that we called "the Mellon Patch," in recognition of that foundation's central role in supporting our efforts. This was not, of course, a name we could seriously consider for "the author" of this volume, not only because the Carnegie, Spencer, and Russell Sage Foundations played such key roles in shaping and assisting our effort, but also because "the Mellon Patch" hardly gives any appropriate indication of the objective of our research collective. When addressing our colleagues, we referred to ourselves as the Distributed Literacy Consortium, a name that reflects our focus on literacy, broadly conceived, and on the various means we have pursued in promoting it. Those means have prominently featured new computer technologies including computer networking, which were coming into their own as educational media just as our work began. Significantly, the same technique we used to promote literacy among the children with whom we worked enabled and facilitated the existence of our geographically distributed research consortium.

In spite of the collective nature of this volume, individuals contributed to the writing and editing by submitting drafts of sections of chapters; these drafts were used to stimulate the discussion that helped other individuals produce the final text. Some contributors focused only on those chapters that described work in which they themselves had been involved; others volunteered to work on chapters to which they had no such connection in order to help those writing about their own work avoid getting so caught up in the details as to lose sight of whole. Hence, it seemed appropriate that the authorship of this book be credited jointly to Cole as the long-term organizer in collaboration with, and as a part of, the Distributed Literacy Consortium. It seemed important, in addition, to recognize the primary writers of some of the chapters. Such recognition is essential for junior members of the Consortium seeking to establish their credentials, but it is equally appropriate in cases where only a small subset of the overall group was primarily involved in producing the text.

And finally, we want to acknowledge by name the more than one dozen academics who were responsible for implementing activities for children; the three teams of academics who conducted research on the various implementations in the role of evaluators; and the many staff members who labored to make their work possible:

Program Implementers

William Blanton: University of Miami. While at the College of Education, Appalachian State University, Blanton initiated several programs simultaneously in local schools and on the university campus with children from a variety of home backgrounds. His training is in literacy education.

Don Bremme, Department of Education, Whittier College—Bremme created a Fifth Dimension at a Boys and Girls Club in Whittier, California, frequented by children from a variety of backgrounds. His training is in ethnographic research in educational settings.

Michael Cole, Laboratory of Comparative Human Cognition (LCHC), University of California at San Diego—Cole conducted his program at a Boys and Girls Club. He is trained as an experimental psychologist but brought experience in cross-cultural, ethnographically based research to the project.

Richard Duran, Gevirtz Graduate School of Education, University of California at Santa Barbara—Duran initiated his program at a Boys and Girls Club serving mainly working-class Latino children. His training is in psychology and education, with a special focus on Latino children. He was later joined by Mary E. Brenner, whose background is in the anthropology of education.

Margaret Gallego, School of Education, San Diego State University—Gallego created a program while at Michigan State University in collaboration with an East Lansing community center. Her background is in literacy education and anthropology, with a focus on Latino children and their families.

Catherine King, Psychology Department, University of New Orleans—King initiated a program while she was at the University of New Orleans. She subsequently moved it to Elon, a small college in North Carolina where the activity was conducted at a local YM/YWCA. Her training is in experimental and developmental psychology.

Gillian McNamee, Erikson Institute for Advanced Study in Child Development, Chicago—McNamee conducted her Fifth Dimension in a Chicago housing project. Her training focused on language, literacy, and school issues among young children from various ethnic backgrounds.

Miriam Schustack and Patricia Worden, Psychology Department, California State University at San Marcos—Schustack and Worden created their program at a Boys and Girls Club. Both are trained as experimental psychologists.

Olga Vásquez, Communication Department, University of California at San Diego—Vásquez has conducted her Fifth Dimension, dubbed La Clase Mágica, in a local mission since 1989. A former teacher, Vásquez earned a degree in education and anthropology, with a focus on Latino children in their family and community settings.

Program Evaluators: Quantitative Evaluation Team

Richard Mayer, University of California at Santa Barbara—Both Mayer's background as an educational psychological methodologist and his long-term involvement in the school system contributed to his importance in the current work.

William Blanton, while at Appalachian State University—His project was located within the College of Education as a central part of its reorganization efforts, Blanton played a major role in the evaluation of the programs from the perspective of the state and was thus highly motivated to focus on this line of research.

Miriam Schustack, California State University at San Marcos—Schustack was trained as a psychological methodologist, and her program was run out of the Psychology Department, which strongly favored high levels of reliable quantitative evidence of any claims that might arise from the program's apparent effects. Carefully grounded quasi-experiments are her forte.

Program Evaluators: Process Evaluation Team

Ray McDermott, School of Education, Stanford University—McDermott headed a group of participants focused on the microgenetic level of analysis of children's interactions with each other and with undergraduates in the cultural medium that characterized each site. He worked closely with Shelly Goldman, Mimi Ito, and other colleagues at the Institute for Research on Learning (IRL) in this work. None had any responsibility in running the site.

Don Bremme, Whittier College, and Michael Cole, University of California at San Diego—Bremme and Cole shared the methodological concerns of the people from IRL. They took responsibility for filming or otherwise recording interactional events, added their recordings to the filming and taping done by the IRL group, and made their data open for analysis.

Program Evaluators: Language and Culture Evaluation Team

Luis Moll, School of Education, University of Arizona, and Robert Rueda, School of Education, University of Southern California—Moll and Rueda, the two outside researchers who headed the "language and culture" evaluation teams, both have a long history of engagement in the investigation of bicultural and multilingual programs in school and nonschool settings. They brought their own bilingual/bicultural experience and appreciation of both quantitative and qualitative data to the evaluation process.

This "outside" group had "internal" participants who shared their research interests and provided information from the perspective of implementers for whom issues of language and culture were paramount in the organization of their sites: Betsy Brenner and Richard Duran, University of California at Santa Barbara; Margaret Gallego, who started as an insider at Michigan State University and moved to the role of outsider at San Diego State University; and Olga Vásquez, University of California at San Diego.

The Laboratory of Comparative Human Cognition (LCHC) was the "responsible unit" that administered most of the grant monies received for the project. LCHC staff members Peggy Bengel, Katherine Brown, Michael Cole, Karen Fiegener, and Honorine Nocon took responsibility for communication among Consortium members, organized the overall project data archive, and ensured that progress reports were written and edited and that budgetary accounts were sent in on time.

Finally, a special debt of gratitude is owed to Nancy Casey, then program officer at the Russell Sage Foundation, who recognized the unity in the broad diversity of our individual efforts and who worked tirelessly to promote the success of our work.

A LOOK BACK, A LOOK AHEAD

Those of us in this cast of characters shared an interest in literacy, some theoretical ideas about what literacy promotes and what promotes literacy, a great deal of concern about the role of literacy in heightening social inequalities, and a willingness to conduct research to see whether we were smart enough to come up with new ideas and new literacy practices that might temper, if not transform, literacy's less attractive consequences while amplifying its more attractive ones.

Our approach to the investigation of literacy development brought together several related intellectual issues, each of which could be the focus of an entire monograph. Can new literacy practices that go beyond "time on task" to provide children with powerful knowledge-generating resources be constructed for use in the after-school hours? Do new communication technologies offer any substantial opportunities to create such practices, or do they turn out to be simply one more way in which the "haves" attain more while the "have-nots" attain less? Can researchers from not only different universities and departments but different social institutions cooperate with each other to produce genuine, visible, excess profits vis-à-vis their task of creating the intellectual resources of subsequent generations?

Readers may judge the answers to these questions for themselves in the chapters to come. When we began investigating these issues twenty years ago, constructing new forms of literacy practices in the after-school hours and outside of the direct control of the educational establishment (as the representative of the state) was sufficiently deviant that it was the computer and telecommunication practices, not the fact that these activities took place after school, that won the interest of our sponsors. In the ensuing decades, after-school time has become a compelling topic in its own right for many educators and developmentalists, as has the nature and quality of higher education. Our fondest hope is that in some small way our efforts will be of use to those charged with improving the lives of the children in their care.

For those who are interested in finding out more about the activities described in this book and as a visual aid to accompany descriptions of activities discussed in the text, web pages have been constructed to which access is free. The major website describing this project is available at http://communication.ucsd.edu/5thd.manual. Two websites that are currently being used by those who carry on the activities described in the text may be found at www.uclinks.org and http://5d.org. We welcome readers' participation and commentary.

Foreword

When Mike Cole and I met about five years ago in a diner in San Diego, I felt simultaneously wrapped in a warm, fuzzy blanket and refreshed by a blast of crisp New York autumn air. Warm and fuzzy because Mike's conversation was infused with concern about the young people attending the Fifth Dimension–UC Links programs, and refreshing because he took such an open, critical, and intense view of the programs he had spawned. This book, which reflects more than twenty years of experience, is a treasure trove for all of us who are interested in helping the after-school field grow and flourish.

Learning about the Fifth Dimension—the Distributed Literacy Consortium (DLC) initiative in which undergraduates staff after-school programs for elementary school kids—has broadened our perspective on the possibilities for enriching kids' lives. An animating force for Mike Cole and his colleagues who make up the Distributed Literacy Consortium was their interest in creating an educational activity that would bring theory and practice together in a single course. The consortium looked at after-school programs primarily through the lens of the university. Their goals are to provide a worthwhile practicum course for undergraduates and to conduct research on the development of successful after-school programs, while our focus at The After-School Corporation is more on social policy: TASC strives to increase the quantity and quality of after-school programs with the goal of making after-school programs a public responsibility as well as universally available and sustainable. When I first was introduced to the Fifth Dimension, some of the goals that TASC was just dreaming about—leveraging the resources of universities, making work in after-school programs a recognized and legitimate part of an undergraduate's education, and engaging kids with technology—were ones that the Fifth Dimension was already seriously pursuing.

Although TASC and the DLC approached the question of building engaging after-school programs from different perspectives, we shared a common vision of creating warm, supportive, child-centered environments where learning would be fun and would reflect the children's community and culture. The consortium's emphasis on the possibilities for encouraging children's development through the motivational power of games played alongside undergraduates with whom they have developed relationships created the kind of environment that TASC programs also strive for: one in which kids have choices, learn by doing, and are able to build relationships with peers and adults.

The Fifth Dimension has not only tackled some of the challenges that we at TASC have found most elusive but created a model for leveraging the resources of universities: both faculty and students bring their skills and experience to the after-school setting and introduce new theory and rigor to a field that is still developing. It is enticing to consider what new resources for after-school programs could be garnered if all of New York City's one hundred colleges and universities were to adapt the Fifth Dimension model.

Fifth Dimension programs have also succeeded in integrating challenging technology into after-school programs. The philosophy that undergirds the Fifth Dimension—that children will benefit from a learning environment that is not simply "more school" but that does support what is learned during the school day—is reflected in the computer activities, which are less structured and more fun than those in school and yet are not just games. Kids write to whimsical characters that live in the Internet and together with their instructors work in teams to solve problems and engage in critical thinking.

TASC, in turn, has resolved some of the challenges presented by the Fifth Dimension model. By creating a citywide system and tapping into multiple public funding streams, the programs that TASC supports have achieved more stability than many of the Fifth Dimension programs. In addition, TASC has had the resources to strengthen the capacity of the community organizations that run the programs, thereby providing a more secure foundation for the after-school programs.

This book documents an approach to the burgeoning field of after-school programs that points to other possible collaborations with the vast resources of the higher education system. As the authors point out, if the 2,200 colleges and universities in this country mandated courses in education, human development, sociology, psychology, linguistics, and communication that would require students to get real-world experience, these students could thus staff a wide variety of youth-serving projects. Such an undergraduate workforce could become a significant and dependable source of labor for high-quality after-school programs and other community services. The medical and social work internship models are examples of what could work for after-school programming.

The beauty of this approach is the benefit to both children and undergraduates when the latter make up a portion of the after-school workforce. And in fact, working in a community and school setting would have educational value for all college students, not just those studying social sciences. The flexibility in structure and content offered by after-school programs gives undergraduates myriad opportunities to be creative, to take initiative, and to acquire important job skills by learning to function in a complex, multigenerational, multicultural environment. Most universities and colleges cannot afford to offer students this kind of experience, but the reciprocal arrangement of the Fifth Dimension model can make it possible.

The after-school experience can also change how undergraduates understand and process what they are learning in class, and not just in teaching courses. The data provide strong and consistent evidence for the conclusion that we learn more when we teach others, when we are engaged in the material, and when we have to absorb and integrate knowledge. Teaching math reinforces our own math skills. Teaching a language improves our fluency. And the challenge of keeping a group of children engaged for two or three hours is undoubtedly an effective way to learn how to be a successful manager in a wide variety of fields.

The Fifth Dimension initiative raises the bar for after-school programming and therefore is an approach that students, teachers, community leaders, and political leaders should embrace as we seek ways to better prepare young people for life in the twenty-first century.

Lucy N. Friedman
President
The After-School Corporation

Chapter 1

Introduction

For the past decade, a group of college professors and their students have been gathering several days a week with elementary school children at various after-school centers to take part in an unusual educational experience. They play games and puzzle over homework problems. They write to each other and to whimsical characters that live in the Internet, and they chat about what it is like at college and what they think about the latest Harry Potter movie. The official reason the college professors are engaged in these pursuits is to provide undergraduates with a rich practicum course related to their course of study and to conduct research on developing successful after-school programs for school-age children. The college students are on hand to learn how to apply the lessons from their lecture courses to the lives of real children whose well-being during these sessions is in their hands. The children are there to have fun.

This program has been implemented by universities in a variety of communities not only across the United States but also in other countries. We call the activity carried out in the community the Fifth Dimension, and the overall system of university-community collaboration to create after-school activities for children the UC Links Project. It is our belief that the Fifth Dimension–UC Links Project is now a proven success in reaching its most basic goal: to provide a workable model of after-school activities that advance the academic achievement—and particularly the literacy abilities—of elementary school children while providing college students with sorely needed practicum experiences to supplement their lecture classes. We also believe that our strategy for implementing, evaluating, and sustaining this project contains important lessons for educators, researchers, and policymakers interested in the development of after-school activities for children. And perhaps our experience with this program will be generally helpful to all those concerned with promoting the education and welfare of children as they face the challenges of a newly "globalized" economy.

We believe that our work has implications for realizing the potential (but by no means automatic) efficacy of new information technologies in promoting children's learning and development. The use of such technologies in university-community collaborations may also contribute, we believe, to improving higher education. Finally, our research addresses the difficult problem of finding ways to sustain successful educational innovations.

AFTER-SCHOOL PROGRAMMING FOR CHILDREN—AN OLD IDEA

In the 1980s, when the current line of research was initiated, only a small proportion of school-age children attended institutionalized after-school programs; national attention was focused on the absence of supervision for "latchkey" children who were left alone at home or in the care of a sibling under the age of thirteen while parents were at work. Although there was little actual research on the consequences for children of spending time alone at home after school, the general sentiment in magazine and newspaper articles was that such an arrangement put children at risk. Subsequent research has suggested that children left alone or with older siblings are not necessarily harmed by the experience in any measurable way (Padilla and Landreth 1989). Nevertheless, the popular press still casts a skeptical eye on the practice of leaving children at home after school, even as parents continue to do so. Today about one-third of all school-age children, an estimated five million between ages five and thirteen, are latchkey children. What has changed is the importance attached to after-school programs.

THE NEW CLIMATE FOR AFTER-SCHOOL EDUCATION

As Robert Halpern (2003) makes clear in his comprehensive review of after-school programs dating from the late nineteenth century, implementers have drawn on a wide variety of social concerns and ideological commitments to justify their advocacy of adults and children participating in organized after-school settings. The earliest beginnings of the after-school care movement are nicely captured by one of the many origin stories to be found on the Web pages of various boys and girls club organizations, of which the following is representative:

> The origins of Boys and Girls Clubs are traced back to 1860 in Hartford, Connecticut. Three compassionate ladies invited a group of street boys into their home for tea or coffee and cake. The positive behavior and obvious appreciation of the boys completely surprised the ladies, so they extended their hospitality several more times with the same supportive response from the

2

boys. Along with several other supporters, the ladies resolved to find an available facility where the boys could come regularly throughout the day. They called this the Dashaway Club, the first Boys Club.

In 1878 the Boys Club of New York was established in much the same way as the Dashaway Club. One day a woman worker at the Wilson Mission in Manhattan's Tompkins Square invited some of the boys in for coffee and cake. An immediate rapport was established. The boys returned the next day, asking if they could come in and play some more. After a short while, an empty storefront was found, and the Boys Club of New York was established. This was the first organization with the actual words "boys club" in its name. The movement then began to spread westward.

As can easily be seen, this organizational history presents the initial impulse for creating after-school organizations devoted to children as the benevolent concern of middle-class women about the fate of children left to the streets. This impulse was institutionalized primarily through church-based organizations, but over time it became secularized as it spread into a variety of institutions. Boys were not the only focus of these kinds of concerns; a variety of out-of-school programs sprang up during the late nineteenth century whose special focus was the welfare of girls (Murolo 1997). Unspoken, but carefully documented by Halpern (2003), is the close connection between the development of after-school institutions and restrictions on child labor, attempts to keep children in school for more years, and the social disruption caused by children who either did not attend compulsory schools or were unsupervised during the hours between school dismissal and the return of their parents from work in an era when the eight-hour workday was still only a gleam in the eye of labor leaders.

In recent years, national interest in expanding after-school programs has increased dramatically, and concern about social order and children's safety remains a major motivation behind these efforts, as nicely captured by the title of one such organization—Fight Crime: Invest in Kids California. This organization, with ties to like-minded groups, has recently issued reports with titles such as *America's Child Care Crisis: A Crime Prevention Tragedy* (Newman, Brazelton, et al. 2000) and *America's After-School Choice: The Prime Time for Juvenile Crime or Youth Enrichment and Achievement* (Newman, Fox, et al. 2000). These and similar reports feature evidence that children are most likely to be the victims or perpetrators of crime between 3:00 and 4:00 in the afternoon and that children attending after-school programs are more likely do well in school (see, for example, Lauer et al. 2004).

The titles of these reports reveal two other factors that are motivating the push for after-school care for children. First, these programs provide a supervisorial bridge between the end of the school day and the parents' return from work. (In two-thirds of married-couple families with children between ages six and seventeen, both parents work outside the home, a figure that increases to 78 percent for female-headed households; U.S. Bureau of Labor Statistics 2003.) Second, after-school programs offer cultural enrichment, including opportunities to develop various talents and increase educational achievement (Belle 1999; Eccles and Gootman 2002; Granger and Kane 2004; Heath 1994).

The latter motive has been the more significant driving force behind recent efforts to expand after-school care. For example, Robert Granger and Thomas Kane (2004, 72) note that, "over the last half-decade, after-school programs have moved from the periphery to the center of the national education policy debate. It happened very quickly. Between 1998 and 2002, federal funding for the 21st Century Community Learning Centers program grew from $40 million to $1 billion."

A multitude of programs, financed not only by federal, state, and local governments but also by several large philanthropic foundations, have been put in place.[1] In addition, prestigious institutions of higher learning, such as Harvard University and Wellesley College, which displayed no particular interest two decades ago in the after-school hours in their programs related to child development and education, have set up programs devoted to the promotion of widely available and high-quality after-school educational programs.

With this increased interest and investment has come closer scrutiny of the quality of after-school programming, the means for evaluating that quality, and the measures to be taken if quality is found to be lacking. Evaluators have found themselves working somewhere along a continuum between two analytic poles. At one end are compelling examples of individual programs that, according to the local organization or an outside evaluator, appear to work (see, for example, Halpern 2003, ch. 5). At the other end are studies of uniformly implemented, large-scale evaluation efforts based on randomized assignment of children to treatments. At present, there appears to be a consensus that evaluations should balance compelling accounts of individual local programs with discussion of generalizable principles in order to provide information that others can use for program design and policymaking.

Evidence that this balancing act is not easy comes from a report prepared for the National Research Council by Jacquelynne Eccles and Jennifer Gootman (2002). Focusing on studies in which evaluators placed a premium on random assignment of large numbers of children, with clear experimental designs and quantifiable outcome measures, these researchers "learned that many programs can effectively promote healthy development," although, they added, "we learned much less about why"

(Eccles and Gootman 2002, 189). Their conclusion is worth quoting at length, not only because it reflects the current "state of the art" of evaluation, but because it provides a yardstick against which to evaluate our own efforts, begun two decades earlier.

> Through consideration of our review of various programs, the basic science of evaluations, and a set of experimental evaluations, quasi-experimental evaluations, and non-experimental studies of community programs for youth, the committee agreed that no specific evaluation method is well suited to address every important question. Rather, comprehensive evaluation requires asking and answering many questions using a number of different evaluation models. What is most important to agree to, and rely on, is a set of standards that help determine the conditions under which different evaluation methods should be employed and to evaluate programs using the greatest rigor possible given the circumstances of the program being evaluated. (Eccles and Gootman 2002, 204)

BASIC GOALS: A PRELIMINARY SUMMARY

A decade and a half ago, when the issues associated with designing after-school programs to be effective supplements to schools and families as contexts for social and intellectual development were becoming visible on the social horizon but were not yet being studied as systemic problems, we began to develop, investigate, and evaluate the Fifth Dimension, a program with several goals:

1. To meet the need for enhanced educational achievement by providing a rich setting for school-age children in the after-school hours based on appropriate theorizing about the design of age-appropriate, development-enhancing environments for children.

2. To use the emerging computer technologies to invite the inclusion of girls and minorities in the program, so as to address the underrepresentation of these constituencies in positions of authority in society at large and in technological professions in particular.

3. To create a structure for ongoing interaction that capitalizes on diversity and brings together children and adults of various ages and from various cultural, economic, religious, and racial groups, as well as special needs children.

4. To create settings where the staff implementing the program and the participating university faculty and students stand to benefit as much

5

as the children as they learn ways to improve their own intellectual development and professional practices related to promoting children's intellectual, social, and academic development.

5. To develop programs that can be incorporated into the ongoing operations of local community organizations and their university partners and sustained over time.

We identified two needs that were critical to accomplishing these goals: a prototype activity system to serve as a common source of reference for researchers, and a research team no less diverse—in departmental affiliation, ethnicity, and research interests—than the sites and populations we studied.

THE PROTOTYPE SYSTEM

The prototype we used to pursue these goals was a model system of activity conducted during the after-school hours in a community institution concerned with children (a Fifth Dimension) combined with a college or university with an interest in having students learn about conducting research in such settings; together the activity model and the academic connection constituted a UC (University-Community) Link. We understood that if we were to accomplish our goals, an essential feature of each Fifth Dimension and UC Link would be adaptability to local conditions: the ideas and design features provided by the original Fifth Dimension–UC Links Project (LCHC 1982) would need to be changed and modified each time they were implemented in a new socio-ecological context. This need for local modifiability would be just as important as adherence to a basic set of design principles.

It is useful to begin with a description of the original prototype Fifth Dimension activity system and UC Links Project as a framework for understanding this educational intervention and as a benchmark against which to interpret local modifications. What follows is a description of an "ideal type" that serves that purpose.

The Fifth Dimension is an educational activity system that offers school-age children a specially designed environment in which to explore a variety of off-the-shelf computer games and gamelike educational activities during the after-school hours. The computer games are part of a make-believe play world that includes noncomputer games like origami, chess, and Boggle and a variety of other artifacts designed to enhance the quality of children's social interactions and the development of their intellectual skills. For example, project staff members design "task cards" or "adventure guides" to help participants (both children and undergraduate students) orient to the game, form goals, and chart their progress toward becoming an expert. In addition to accomplishing the tasks written into the software or game activity, the children are also asked to externalize their thought processes by reflecting on and criticizing information, writing to someone, looking up information in an encyclopedia, and teaching someone else what they have learned.

To keep the children distributed among the various games and activities, the Fifth Dimension staff typically display a chart in the form of a maze consisting of some twenty rooms. Sometimes this chart is displayed on a wall, and sometimes it is a physical maze made of cardboard or plywood. Each room provides access to two or more games, so the children choose which game to play as they enter a room.

The Fifth Dimension also includes an electronic figurehead—variously referred to as "the Wizard," "the Wizardess," "Maga," "Proteo," or "Golem"—who is said to live in the Internet and who writes to (and sometimes chats with) the children and undergraduates via the Internet. In the mythology of the Fifth Dimension, this figure acts as the participants' patron, the provider of games, and the mediator of disputes—as well as the sometimes irritating source of computer glitches and other misfortunes.

The Fifth Dimension is implemented as a partnership between a local institution of higher education and a local community institution. The involvement of university students is a major feature of the project. Enrolled in a course focused on fieldwork in a community setting, they serve not only as a draw for the children but as much-needed personpower for conducting the activities. The University of California at San Diego, the first UC Link where the first Fifth Dimensions were created, is an institution that emphasizes research, so the participating undergraduate students take an intensive, six-unit class that focuses on deep understanding of basic developmental principles, the use of new information technologies for organizing learning, and the mastery of field research methods. The students write papers on such topics as the development of individual children, the educative value of different games, differences in how boys and girls participate in the play world, variations in language use and site culture, and other topics that bring together conceptually oriented coursework and field observations. Participating faculty make the Fifth Dimension and the development of their local UC Link a focus of their research.

Because the Fifth Dimension activities are located in a community institution, a local site coordinator must be present to greet the participants as they arrive and to supervise the flow of activity. The site coordinator is trained to recognize and support the pedagogical ideals and curricular practices that mark the Fifth Dimension as "different"—a different way for kids to use computers, a different way of thinking about intellectual challenges, a different way of playing with other children, and a different way for adults and children to interact.

A key design feature that serves several functions is the ready access of all Fifth Dimension participants to each other within and across sites. Thus, depending on the interests of participants at any level of the system, they can communicate with and involve others in their after-school experience. Experience shows that some sites cultivate relationships with one another, while other sites focus on intrasite activity and communication with participants or other institutions in their community.

THEORETICAL ROOTS OF THE FIFTH DIMENSION

A set of common theoretical ideas has guided the design of local implementations of the Fifth Dimension; like the program itself, these ideas share key features but differ and are developed according to local needs and preferences. At the broadest level, we admire theoretical orientations that place culture and social interaction at the center of attempts to understand human learning and development. These theoretical ideas are discussed in more detail in later chapters, but a brief orientation here is appropriate.

The work of Lev Vygotsky (1978) has inspired new ways of thinking about the role of culture in learning and development; in the chapters to come, the reader will encounter some of his seminal ideas, such as "mediation" and "zones of proximal development," and be reminded of the importance he places on various tools ("mediational means") and forms of activity, such as play, as resources for learning and development. All of us in the field have also been influenced by theorists who argue that if an environment is to be conducive to development, social participation in activities that are meaningful to the participants must play a role. Within this broad orientation, which can be traced back to John Dewey, analysts have taken approaches with somewhat different core concepts and orientations, such as sociocultural studies (Wertsch 1991), cultural-historical activity theory (Cole and Engeström 1997), communities of learners (Brown and Campione 1998; Rogoff 2003), and communities of practice (Lave 1988; Lave and Wenger 1991). Whatever our particular theoretical emphases, our common roots lead us to think simultaneously about the social organization of activity, the various tools used to carry out the various tasks (computers, pencils, paper, task cards, wizard, modems), social roles, modes of participation, and the relation of the activity to its context. These common theoretical roots also influence our strategies for evaluating the effectiveness of the systems we design and implement.

PARTICIPATING RESEARCH GROUPS

The second major part of our strategy was to build diversity directly into the social organization of the research group that undertook the study. In the preface, we identified the heads of the nine research sites that participated in the larger group project, which we called the Distributed Literacy Consortium. We describe the individual sites and histories in chapter 3.

Initially we paired sites according to the research interests of the implementers, such as a desire to focus on writing or an interest in promoting bilingual/biculturalism. We discovered rather quickly, however, that these pairings restricted rather than expanded collaboration. What the full complement of participants in the Distributed Literacy Consortium manifestly did achieve was very wide representation of the kinds of institutions, subject populations, research foci, and institutional collaborations we sought to develop and understand (see table 1.1).

THE ROLE OF UNIVERSITY COURSES

As noted earlier, a basic design feature of the programs in each locale was collaboration between an institution of higher learning and a community institution. The college and university courses presented in conjunction with the programs were centrally important to the design strategy, and we present here a brief overview of what they entailed (for a more detailed examination of these courses, see chapter 7).

The common element in all of the college courses was that they linked students taking courses rich in theory to a community setting where those theories could be tested in practice. A great variety of academic departments offered courses for student participants in local Fifth Dimensions, including psychology, education, communication, human development, and linguistics. Common to them all was a theoretical portion conducted on campus (the usual book-reading and report-writing activities) and an inquiry-based laboratory portion conducted at the Fifth Dimension site. There the undergraduates were encouraged to link theory with practice, to explore concepts from their readings, to create their own knowledge, and to confront, analyze, and reflect on their conceptions of teaching, learning, and development as scientific and professional activities. In all their courses, students wrote detailed clinical field notes describing their experiences at the Fifth Dimension research site. Through these field notes students not only linked academic concepts to community-based practice but learned methods of ethnographic documentation. For several members of the research team, the field notes provided a crucial source of data about the workings of the system.

Table 1.1 Fifth Dimension Sites of Implementation

College or University	Site	Location	Community Center Type	Years Hosting Fifth Dimension	Age of Child Participants	Dominant Language	Culture or Ethnicity	SES
University of California at San Diego (UCSD)	Solana Boys and Girls Club	Solana Beach, Calif.	Boys and Girls Club of America	1986 to present	Five to eleven	English	Anglo	Middle- and working-class
UCSD	La Clase Mágica	La Colonia, Solana Beach, Calif.	Catholic mission	1989 to present	All ages, adults	Spanish, bilingual	Mexicano	Working-class
California State University at San Marcos (CSUSM)	Escondido Boys and Girls Club (Baker branch)	Escondido, Calif.	Boys and Girls Club of America	Seven	Six to twelve	English	Anglo, Latino	Lower-middle- and working-class
Michigan State University (MSU)	Cristo Rey Community Center	North Lansing, Mich.	Catholic Charities Community Center	Four	Six to twelve	Spanish, bilingual	Latino	Working-class
Erikson Institute	Le Claire Community Center	Chicago, Ill.	State-funded school-age day care	Five	Five to six	African American English	African American	Working-class

University of New Orleans (UNO)	Claiborne Elementary School	New Orleans, La.	Elementary school after-school program	Four	Six to eleven	Black English dialect, English	African American	Middle- and working-class
Appalachian State University (ASU)	ASU and several elementary schools	Boone, N.C.	Elementary school after-school program	1991 to present	Seven to twelve	English	Anglo	Middle- and working-class
Whittier College	Boys and Girls Club of Whittier	Whittier, Calif.	Boys and Girls Club of America	1993 to present	Six to twelve	English, Spanish	Chicano, Mexicano	Working-class
University of California at Santa Barbara (UCSB)	Boys and Girls Club	Goleta, Calif.	Boys and Girls Club of America	1994 to present	Five to twelve	Spanish, English	Mexicano, Anglo, African American Asian origin	Working-class

Source: Author's compilation.

In our initial work and reports on the Fifth Dimension, we tended to take the UC Links structure for granted and to focus on issues of pedagogy and sustainability connected with the community half of the system (LCHC 1982; Nicolopoulou and Cole 1993; Vásquez 1994). Over time, however, we began to recognize that both the nature of the interactions at the site and the nature of education at the university depended a great deal on the particular institution of higher learning involved, the department supplying the students, and the ways in which course instructors related to the use of community sites as laboratories for their students' learning. This point was driven home for us in many ways, but none more dramatically than in the failure of some of the initial participating institutions of higher learning to provide a steady flow of students; the subsequent lack of students was a major cause of the demise of some otherwise successful systems.

The sites we focus on in this volume are connected to a variety of university departments and thus differ in how they incorporate questions of learning, development, teaching, technology, and institution building. Another source of variation can be found in the individual courses, which naturally vary in focus as a function of their institutional setting. In chapter 9, where we consider the overall lessons learned, we discuss what we learned about the importance of these varying features.

TRYING NOT TO REINVENT THE WHEEL: OUR EMPHASIS ON SUSTAINABILITY

Central to our undertaking of creating a network of after-school programs using the resources of both universities and neighboring community sites for the mutual benefit of both was the goal of learning what it would take to sustain this new innovation, and then doing so. When we began the current project, we were especially mindful that because putatively successful educational innovations routinely fail (Sarason 1988, 1991), generations of well-meaning educators have repeated, often unknowingly, the efforts of their predecessors. Consequently, the problem of sustaining successful educational innovations has received too little attention from social scientists. The same lack of attention to sustainability is a characteristic of current discussions of successful after-school programs. Thus, even as we review specific questions concerning the implementation and evaluation of the various programs we created, we do so with an eye on the issues associated with the routine disappearance of even valued educational activities.

In our implementation of Fifth Dimensions, we decided to address the question directly, using the program as our candidate for "successful innovation." Our plan was quite simple: we would initiate Fifth Dimensions in a variety of institutions to study the dynamics of their change—and possible demise—beginning with the period of their initiation and continuing at least to the end of their initial funding. We would rely on neither single anecdotes nor single cases. Instead, we would create a relatively large number of programs, and we would design both quantitative measures to monitor the relative success of the innovation in terms of the children's development and qualitative measures to index the dynamics of change. We would pay special attention to the periods of transition—particularly the period of implementation and then the dreaded day when regular funding came to an end—while remaining alert to the crises that could develop at any stage of the process.

With these goals in mind, we undertook an initial round of prototype design and research that preceded the research discussed here and helped to shape the organization of the current research (LCHC 1982; Cole 1996). During a year of planning begun in the fall of 1986, four community institutions (a school, a day care center, a boys and girls club [BGC], and a library) were exposed to a variety of potential after-school activities. All chose to initiate Fifth Dimensions. Three years later, when funding was greatly reduced and these four institutions had to take over greater responsibility for the activities, two of the four had already closed, a third was unwilling to take on the extra responsibilities and withdrew, and the fourth not only continued but expanded its activities. After a researcher who initiated a new version of the Fifth Dimension was hired as a faculty member at UCSD in 1991 (Vásquez 2003), arrangements were made for two departments to offer the required university practicum course for three quarters each year. In conjunction with an entirely different project, new Fifth Dimensions had also sprung up in Chicago, New Orleans, and Moscow, and a Fifth Dimension that served as a computer literacy class for a school was opened in a San Diego suburb in 1988 (for a review of these events, see Cole 1994).

At this point, the focus of interest had shifted and the current project began. We knew that Fifth Dimensions could attract children and that adults in charge of the activities found them useful. But we had too few cases to be able to make educated guesses about the range of community institutions that could put such activities together, the kinds of institutions of higher learning that would find them attractive for their students, and the combination of such factors that might lead to sustainable programs in some cases but not in others. We also had failed to solve to our satisfaction the problem of evaluating the consequences of participation for individual children. These became the critical issues that would engage us for the ensuing decade, at the end of which broader understandings emerged from the expanded collective of scholars who have contributed to this book.

OVERVIEW OF THE BOOK

The chapters that follow present the intellectual foundations and organizational work that have gone into our research on building, evaluating, and sustaining a system of effective after-school activities. Chapter 2 provides an overview of the general theoretical principles that guided our work. Brief descriptions follow in chapter 3 of each of the university-community partnerships, their joint experimental after-school activities, and their history over the life of the project and slightly beyond. Chapter 4 discusses the methodological challenges that confronted us, as they would any group of researchers who seek to design, evaluate, and sustain developmentally rich after-school activities.

Chapter 5 provides one set of responses to the challenges of evaluation. We summarize a series of experimental and quasi-experimental studies of changes in children's intellectual performance on a variety of specially designed and standardized tests conducted at a number of the consortium sites where such evaluations were possible. Chapter 6 focuses on the changes that occurred in interactions within a number of the local systems; these changes provide a close-up look at the proximal dynamics of change that can be plausibly linked to "cognitive outcomes," as measured by the psychological tests described in chapter 5.

Chapter 7 presents our studies of the Fifth Dimension as a form of educational activity for undergraduates in which theory and practice are wedded in a single course. This chapter provides, from a different perspective, usable methods for describing the changes that occur on the university side of the university-community system.

UC Links has spread well beyond the initiating group, and chapter 8 documents this transformation of the original idea into a worldwide effort that is no longer restricted to the after-school hours but has moved "back into school" in many locales. In this discussion, we review the status of the initial systems, providing a longer-term view of the factors that permit sustainability well beyond the expiration of external funding from project sponsors.

Chapter 9 returns to first questions. What began as an almost eccentric interest in after-school activities and their sustainability has now become a major issue at the national, state, and local levels. Our hope is that our experience of more than a decade of research, combined with the unusual diversity of the individual settings we created, can help to inform both the decisions of local communities that believe their children might benefit from after-school activities and policy debates about whether and when such efforts make a difference in the lives of children.

Chapter 2

The Intellectual Foundations of the Fifth Dimension

A s noted in chapter 1, the disciplinary backgrounds we brought to the design of our local after-school systems varied considerably, but we all adhered to a core set of concepts that placed a premium on the idea that individual development is a part of, and depends on, participation in a culturally organized social context viewed within its larger socio-ecological context. Within this family of theories, some theorists have focused on analyzing institutionalized educational activities for children and determining which tools are most effective for deliberate instruction, while others have approached learning as a natural by-product of the collective activity of adults who are engaged in any valued cultural practice. These different foci and theoretical concerns, not surprisingly, have led researchers to employ different methods and to deploy somewhat different concepts concerning processes of change.

All researchers can agree, however, that educational activities and cultural practices need to be conceptualized as social systems with several elements: the interplay among persons as active subjects; their competing or complementary objectives; the tools (mediational artifacts) they deploy; the social rules they formulate and debate; the communities they form and inhabit; and the divisions of labor that govern the configurations of their joint actions (Engeström, Miettinen, and Punamaki 1999; Lave 1988; Leontiev 1981; Moll et al. 1992; Rogoff 2003). This general perspective informs the design, implementation, and evaluation of all the systems we designed and implemented.

A natural correlate of theorists' use of settings, contexts, social ecologies, and practices as units of analysis is that instead of focusing on individual abilities and actions, they view human cognition, to use Jean Lave's (1988, 1) felicitous phrase, as "stretched over, not divided among, mind, body, activity, and culturally organized settings (including other actors)." This is not to say that we should never focus on individuals and individual change, but rather that we should strive always to conduct such analysis in relation to features of the system of which they are a part (Rogoff

2003). Jay Lemke (1997, 38) makes this relational view explicit when he links activity, modes of participation, processes of learning, and individual identities:

> Our activity, our participation, our "cognition" is always bound up with the participation and activity of Others, be they persons, tools, symbols, processes, or things. How we participate, what practices we come to engage in, is a function of the whole community ecology. . . . As we participate, we change, our identity-in-practice develops, for we are no longer autonomous Persons in this model, but Persons-in-Activity.

THE CENTRALITY OF CONTEXT

Given our emphasis on the study of learning and development within particular settings, situations, and activities, it is only natural that our analysis of the similarities and differences between Fifth Dimension programs should begin with the notion of context. However, we do so somewhat cautiously because, as many scholars sympathetic to this perspective have noted, notions such as context, activity, setting, and situation are used in a variety of ways by contemporary social scientists, any one of which can lead to misunderstandings (Chaiklin and Lave 1993; Duranti and Goodwin 1992). Mindful of such potential for misunderstanding, we are as explicit as possible here about our use of these terms.

Depending on the purposes at hand, we have found it useful to adopt two somewhat different notions of context. The first is what we call a "social-ecological" concept of context, ordinarily represented as a set of concentric circles in which the focal activities are at or near the center; context is constituted by and constitutes the levels ranging outward from the center (Bronfenbrenner and Morris 1998; Cole 1996) (see figure 2.1).

The image of concentric circles is helpful in capturing the embeddedness of an after-school program in a larger social ecology that influences its specific character and the conditions it must meet to be sustainable. The innermost circle symbolizes the interactions of children and undergraduates as they engage in joint activities with computers and games at a specific time, in a specific place, and as part of an inclusive setting—the activity we call the Fifth Dimension. This micro level of the system is symbolized by two people interacting with each other using an artifact—in this case, a computer game. This level routinely includes three- and even four-party interactions. At the next level is the relation of these two-, three-, or four-party interactions to the ensemble of such interactions that constitutes the local program, whether a Fifth Dimension, a Club Proteo, or a La Clase Mágica. At the next level, we look at the program as one ele-

Figure 2.1   A Bronfenbrenner-Style Picture of a Child and Undergraduate in a Fifth Dimension Activity System

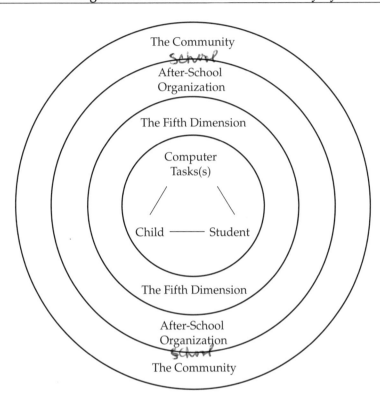

The Community

After-School
Organization

The Fifth Dimension

Computer
Tasks(s)

Child ——— Student

The Fifth Dimension

After-School
Organization

The Community

Source: Authors' compilation.

ment within a larger institution—for example, a youth club, a church, or a school. At the next level, we consider the program and its institutional context as part of a neighborhood ecology—a school district that channels children into after-school clubs, for example, or a community served by the school district.[1] Depending on which issue we are addressing, different levels of the system become the focus of our attention, but we need to stay aware of all the other levels as much as possible.

For example, an important common feature of the Fifth Dimension program considered at the third level of context—as a coherent system of activity in a community setting—is that the program runs after school.[2] As Robert Halpern (2002, 180) has pointed out, historically "after-school hours emerged gradually as discretionary time, a counterpoint to the rigid schedule and adult agenda of schools, and from the perspective of adult-child relations, as negotiated time." In middle-class culture, music and dance lessons, seasonal sports, and scouting are standard fare for children with the family resources (Larson and Verma 1999). For many children, the late afternoon after school is a time to attend one of a variety of loosely structured care programs designed to keep them safe, active, and engaged in satisfying activities until their parents can pick them up (Belle 1999).

The location of Fifth Dimensions in the context between home and school points immediately to an important design requirement. The program must provide a variety of sources of motivation for children's participation or they will not come. The opportunity to play is, of course, one such motivation, but affiliation, peer interaction, and learning are also obvious candidates (Griffin and Cole 1984; Leontiev 1978).

Promoting play was a particularly prominent objective in Fifth Dimension design, both for the practical reason that it would attract elementary-age children after school and for the theoretical reason that play promotes and creates essential resources for development (Vygotsky 1978). Computer games and other playful Fifth Dimension artifacts were included in the design in part for both of these reasons.

However, the particular way in which play is incorporated into a Fifth Dimension requires that we pay attention to a different level of context—the relationship of the Fifth Dimension to its local institutional context. For example, play is likely to be introduced into an after-school program at a youth center in a way somewhat different from its use in a program offered through a library, school, or for-profit tutoring company. A Fifth Dimension in a library, for example, is conducted both more quietly than a Fifth Dimension in a boys and girls club and more noisily than other activities happening elsewhere in the library at the same time (Nicolopoulou and Cole 1993).

A second conception of context has proven its value in designing and implementing Fifth Dimensions: the weaving together of many elements over time. Context conceived of in this way helps to capture the dynamics of interaction that change from day to day in what would otherwise be viewed as "the same context" in the concentric-circles representation. On a day-to-day basis, it makes a difference which children and undergraduates, and how many of them, are present and in what order they appear at the activity, because the particular pairings of children and undergraduates are shaped by the relationships they build over time, by the availability of particular undergraduates, and by the needs of particular children at any given moment. Those social arrangements, in turn, must be woven together with the availability of particular games and with the condition and occupancy rate of the equipment needed to run them. (Computers are amazingly unreliable in this regard, and checkerboards and chessmen have a way of disappearing at odd times as well.)

Of course, such weaving together involves different levels of context, as interpreted within the concentric-circles model. When undergraduates arrive sleepless from all-night study sessions before a midterm, or children's attendance is greatly reduced because the school had a teacher conference day, the overall qualities that emerge from the weaving together of the program's elements differ in noticeable and often unpredictable ways. It is not uncommon, for example, for undergraduates to indicate in their field notes that they arrived exhausted and anxious but ended up having a great time with the kids and left energized. Alternatively, an eleven-year-old boy who has been at a Fifth Dimension all day because his school is closed may express his boredom by showing an eighteen-year-old girl that she is beneath notice owing to her lack of knowledge of "Sim City." In the latter case, the initial interaction may be confrontational but the outcome may be amicable, with that day's interaction providing an important learning experience for both the child and the undergraduate. Obviously, however, the context creates a very different emotional tone than on a normal day, when the child would have been at the Fifth Dimension program for only one to two hours after school. The "weaving together" notion of context keeps the designer of a Fifth Dimension program alert to the constant and daily need to deal with the heterogeneous and changing mix of factors that influences the implementation of a Fifth Dimension and the need to plan for contest and confrontation as well as for playfulness and affection.

Despite its manifest usefulness, there are limits to how far the concept of context can take us in designing Fifth Dimensions. The metaphors of circles and levels and threads are helpful in the abstract, but we also need a more concrete set of concepts to guide the design of precisely *how*, for example, play and learning are combined as a routine part of an activity. Such deliberate interweaving requires more than mixing play with educational games and having undergraduates present in an after-school program. Would that it were that simple! There is nothing automatic about mixing play, educational games, and college-age companions in a manner that not only is appropriate to the institutional context but also promotes a successful program.

This point was driven home to us in a study by Bianca Dahl (2002), who contrasted the Fifth Dimension program conducted in a boys and girls club with a commercial after-school educational system called Score, run as a subsidiary of Kaplan, the large for-profit company that specializes in test preparation. The programs were very similar at one level of description: both took place after school, mixed play with learning, and included young adult mentors. But the children's reactions to the two programs differed to a startling degree. The field notes from Score sessions were replete with accounts of children crying from frustration, the need for disciplinary action, and manifestations of anxiety. At Score, children had to raise their hands to interact with an undergraduate mentor. Although play and education were co-present, peer interaction and affiliation were explicitly discouraged. Moreover, play and education were mixed in strikingly different ways in the two programs. In the Fifth Dimension, play and learning were interwoven in myriad ways; the Score program used a Skinnerian-style reward system that allowed children to leave their computers and shoot basketballs only when they had achieved a certain level of proficiency at the educational challenge being presented on the computer.[3]

In the Score program, children competed vigorously with each other, and parents, who paid steep tuition costs for the program, were often present to ensure that their child was getting the academic benefits they were paying for. Parental expectations were a common source of children's anxiety, and mentors had to spend a significant amount of time calming down children who had become too upset to continue.

Such problems never occurred in a Fifth Dimension. At worst, a child might become upset because she lost a game or could not get access to the computer or undergraduate she wanted, but otherwise the entire "structure of feeling" (Williams 1976) was different. These marked differences between the two programs vividly illustrate why simple invocations of context to explain why the Fifth Dimensions functioned as they did are insufficient (for more details, see Dahl 2002). Some other explanation is needed, and for that explanation we draw upon principles developed within the family of sociocultural theories mentioned earlier.

GOING BEYOND CONTEXT IN THE DESIGN PROCESS

Common sense may have persuaded us to provide play as a major motive for children in the after-school hours, but funding sources plus our own good intentions urged upon us the need to infuse Fifth Dimension activity with learning opportunities. Hence, we needed to figure out how to combine play and educational activities to maximum effect. This was just one of many design tasks. For example, the mixture of activities we came up with for Fifth Dimensions needed to appeal to elementary-age children between five and twelve years of age, an age range that spans three conventional developmental stages: early childhood, middle childhood, and the transition to adolescence. All theories of learning and development assume that children's proclivities and their responses to play and instruction differ markedly across this age span.

We also needed to design activities that would be attractive to children of widely varying academic ability and cultural background, since our after-school settings were open not only to all of the community's children but especially to children who were struggling in school. Moreover, we had to meet our universities' expectations that participation in Fifth Dimension programs would provide high-quality education for the undergraduate participants; playing games with children after school is usually not the first exercise that occurs to a college administrator trying to design a serious laboratory course. Adding to the complexities emanating from such university requirements was the involvement of several different kinds of departments; for instance, we were compelled to address adequately the special interests of both teacher education students and communication studies majors.

A series of conceptual tools provided by different contributors to the overall sociocultural, activity-based framework proved to be useful in accomplishing this complex task of coordinating the needs of widely varying ages, abilities, cultural backgrounds, and motives for participation.

MIXING LEADING ACTIVITIES

So far we have focused on play and learning as two sources of motivation around which Fifth Dimension activities were organized. To go further in designing play and learning activities for children who vary in age and other demographic characteristics, we found it useful to draw upon the concept of "leading activities," as developed by Lev Vygotsky and his students (for an extended summary and examples, see Griffin and Cole 1984). In the Russian cultural-historical tradition, stages of development are interpreted in terms of the kinds of activity that dominate the lives of children at a given age. Each age has a different leading activity, characterized by a distinctive source of motivation.

From birth to early childhood, attachment to others is the leading activity. Play is the leading activity of early childhood, learning of middle childhood, peer interaction of the transition to adolescence, and work of the transition to adulthood (El'konin 1977). Crucial to this way of thinking about development is the recognition that, as children get older, their prior activities and associated motives do not disappear. The desire to be accepted and loved by members of one's social group does not disappear among teenagers (or college students!), any more than the desire to play disappears once children enter school. Rather, prior leading activities become part of the foundation of everyday activities upon which the new form of activity is built (Cole and Subbotsky 1993). The design implication of this insight was that we needed to create programs that would provide access to *all* of the leading activities of childhood, forming a rich collection of motives from which children could choose according to their personal preferences and stage of development.

For example, undergraduates were not assigned to work with particular children and typically worked with a variety of children. Their field notes attest, however, to the many close attachments that formed between particular undergraduates and children who sought each other out and expressed their pleasure at being together and their sadness at parting. We also needed to be sensitive to the fact that preferred forms of play and play's relation to other motives change with gender and age. In principle, we might have been able to design and run a Fifth Dimension in which every room of the maze contained age-graded games, and in fact we sought to do so as much as possible. As noted already, however, a range of standard factors were routinely in flux during a typical Fifth Dimension session, including high levels of participant heterogeneity; the working condition of computer software and hardware; the uncanny mobility of board game pieces; the ages, ability levels, and experiences of the children present; and the ratio of undergraduates to children. Such variation was the norm, not the exception. If we were to come up with the right conditions for maximizing learning and development, we needed to combine insights into leading activities with the actual social organization of participants' interactions. Here, another theoretical principle became essential.

THE ROLE OF INTERGENERATIONAL PARTICIPATION IN THE SOCIAL CREATION OF INDIVIDUAL DEVELOPMENT

We have already mentioned that the participation of undergraduates was a critical resource for staffing Fifth Dimensions at minimal cost to the community host institution as well as a source of motivation for the children. Here too, theory guided us in organizing the roles of undergraduates to regulate the quality of their interactions with children carrying out the many tasks of a typical Fifth Dimension session. To optimize learning and development in these interactions, we found concepts such as Lev Vygotsky's "zone of proximal development," Barbara Rogoff's "guided participation," and Jean Lave and Étienne Wenger's "legitimate peripheral participation" to be critical resources.

Presupposed in all of these formulations is the proposition that participation in certain kinds of social arrangements is essential to development. Vygotsky (1978, 57) formulated the idea of the social origins of individual psychological development—what he called the "general law of social development"—as follows: "Every function in the child's cultural development appears twice: first, on the social level, and later, on the individual level; first, between people (interpsychological), and then inside the child (intrapsychological)."[4]

The implications of this idea for the design of after-school activities are clear. There must be a functioning social level that includes both novices and more experienced members and a social setting that provides everyone with goals relevant to their joint participation. Otherwise, novices have no opportunity to emulate and appropriate more mature social-level functions. Since the more adept participants are pursuing goals that overlap substantially with those of less adept participants (for example, trying to catch the thief in "Carmen San Diego"), inclusion of the novices provides them with the opportunity both to learn from and to contribute to (or at least not detract from) the goal-directed actions of the adept. It is this characteristic of behavior in social institutions that Lave and Wenger (1991) formulated as the process of "legitimate peripheral participation."

This characterization of the Fifth Dimension also fits well with Rogoff's (1994, 213) concept of a community of learners in which "both mature members of the community and less mature members are conceived as active; no role has all the responsibility for knowing or directing, and no role is by definition passive." She adds that members fluidly move between the roles of teacher and learner, more experienced and less experienced peer, as all reciprocally "learn through engagement with others (in a system of ongoing guidance and support) in the everyday mature activities in their community" (216–17).

For Vygotsky, the arrangement of the social interactions involving more and less capable participants was of paramount importance as a means both of assessing the gap between participants' inter- and intrapsychological planes (in his case, teachers and their pupils) and of organizing ways to take advantage of this gap. It is in this context that he formulated the notion of a "zone of proximal development" as "the distance between the actual developmental level as determined by independent problem solving and the level of potential development as determined through problem solving under adult guidance or in collaboration with more capable peers" (Vygotsky 1978, 86).

This idea has several important implications for the design of Fifth Dimensions. First, expertise should be made available from many sources throughout the entire system of activity. With respect to the undergraduates, the implications are somewhat more ambiguous. On the one hand, the idea of them as "more capable peers" is useful because it explicitly blocks the notion that they should adopt the role of teacher. On the other hand, their greater capability with respect to various aspects of the task at hand obliges them to capitalize on their knowledge on behalf of the children. Creating the right conditions for them to play such a role entails several factors. First, though labels vary from one site to another, the role of the undergraduates is designated by terms that minimize their perceived authority: "Wizard's Assistant," "Amiga" or "Amigo," and "Intern" are representative. Second, the undergraduates are told that they are present to *play* with the children as model Fifth Dimension participants and not to be tutors—the term that staff at the community sites and university administrators are likely to use initially to describe the undergraduates' role. Third, undergraduates are instructed not to adopt the role of authority figure with respect to the children's social behavior. If conflicts or contests of will arise among children or between the undergraduate and a child, the undergraduate is expected to defer to the site coordinator and to intervene directly only when safety is at stake.

Other design features of the Fifth Dimension help to maintain undergraduates' role as peers. For one thing, at the beginning of an academic semester or quarter, the undergraduates are in fact less capable than the children who have been longtime participants in playing the games and who know how to "play the Fifth Dimension." In their early field notes, undergraduates often attest to their chagrin at their own ignorance and their desire to become more adept as quickly as possible. In addition, we provide undergraduates with a rule of thumb to answer the perennial question of how much help they should give the children: "Give as little help as you can, but enough so that both you and the child are having a good time." This heuristic has proven useful in helping undergraduates create zones of proximal development (or "zopeds").

As a consequence of such measures, data indicate that daily Fifth Dimension interactions are affectively positive and that zopeds are routinely created, even as the participant playing the role of more capable peer in dyads, triads, or larger groups is constantly changing. This characterization fits with Rogoff's idea of fluid reversals of student and teacher roles in communities of learners; such reversals seem to arise naturally in the sort of interinstitutional arrangements that make Fifth Dimensions possible in the first place.[5]

The fluid dynamics of interactions in Fifth Dimension programs also bring to mind the work of situated learning theorists, who emphasize that each context and activity in which a concept is encountered recasts understanding of it in a new and more densely textured form (Barab and Duffy 2000; Brown, Collins, and Duguid 1989; Greeno 1998; Lave and Wenger 1991).

THE CENTRALITY OF MEDIATIONAL MEANS FOR ORGANIZING ACTIVITY

Although understanding the overall context and ideas about the social organization required to maximize learning and development is critical to the design of Fifth Dimensions, the needed organizational properties could not be attained if we did not have a systematic way to introduce the deliberately constructed *mediational means* (tools or artifacts) that participants use to regulate their interactions as they pursue their personal goals

(Kozulin 1998; Wertsch 1997). Here we describe a number of the more widely used mediational means. Each site also developed its own tools to suit local conditions.

Computers

Of course, the most obvious mediational means were computers and computer networks. Computers served as media through which children engaged in a variety of games ranging from the purely recreational to the more or less deliberately educational; computer networks enabled children at different sites to interact with each other and with their mythical figureheads, and they were also essential to researcher collaboration.[6]

The particular computers used at a site depended a great deal on what was available, and availability differed wildly from one site to another. A site on the Appalachian State University campus had advanced DOS machines at the same time that other sites located in schools around Appalachian State had less powerful machines. La Clase Mágica, which is located in a mission in a working-class community, had a hodgepodge of computers of various types, depending on what its university partner and local donors could provide. Some sites had Internet access and some did not.

The extreme variability in hardware naturally led to great variability in software as well. The more powerful the computer, the glitzier the software it could run. This source of variability, however, was overshadowed by another: unless we developed the software ourselves, we were at the mercy of commercial entertainment—"edutainment"—and of educational software makers as sources of raw curriculum materials. We already knew that we had to mix play and education with possibilities for attachment and peer interaction in our computer-centered activities, but we could not depend on off-the-shelf software to provide us with what we needed. Hence, one of our primary tools could not function properly without a set of auxiliary means of its own.

Task Cards

The tool we created to regulate the relation between play and education, as well as the difficulty of engaging the software, was the task card. (At some sites, task cards were referred to as "adventure guides" or given other labels thought to make them more inviting.) In principle, every time a child played a Fifth Dimension game, his or her engagement was mediated by a task card that specified what the child had to accomplish to get credit for "beginner," "good," or "excellent" performance of the activity in question. Gaining credit for a prespecified number of "goods" and "excellents" was the criterion for promotion to the role of assistant, a role given labels such as "Young Wizard," "Maga," or "Golem." In addition to shifting control of the assessment of high-level performance away from the software designer and toward the Fifth Dimension designers, the task cards accomplished several other goals:

- Task cards provided information to undergraduates that allowed them to assist the children even if they had not encountered the particular game before and to specify a proximal goal for each child.

- Task cards connected simultaneously to play and learning and generated possible divisions of labor. If the game was designed purely for entertainment ("Pac Man," for example), the task card included more educational elements—such as formulating a written strategy or teaching a strategy to another person. By the same token, if the game was designed purely for education, the task card introduced a more playful element, such as earning the right to play a game of the child's choice if he or she achieved the level of "good."

- Task cards helped the adults who had created and maintained the programs meet a major goal: getting the children to read, write, and reflect.

- Because they functioned variously as guides, as constraints, and as obligations, task card requirements were constantly negotiated between undergraduates, children, and, at times, the Wizard.

The Maze

Another mediational means in the ideal type is the maze, a symbolic space embodied as a wall chart or physical labyrinth containing all the games and other tasks that are an official part of the Fifth Dimension. The presence of a maze with multiple rooms accomplishes several key functions:

- A maze provides an overall representation of the entire ensemble of games and challenges that the children can engage in.

- A maze provides a tool for distributing the activities in a flexible manner so that even if a computer breaks down or a desired game is occupied, the undergraduates and staff engaged with the children can find ready substitutes.

- A maze shows the children that they can and in fact must make choices among a set of alternatives; whatever their particular goals, the maze makes manifest the fact that it is *their* goals that are being pursued.

The Mythical Figurehead

In describing the ideal Fifth Dimension in chapter 1, we referred to a mythical figurehead variously known as "the Wizard," "Maga," "Golem," or "Proteo" and said to be the patron of the Fifth Dimension. The mythical figurehead fulfills several functions.

- The figurehead ensures an element of play as children engage in what otherwise might appear to be strictly a learning task, such as reading instructions for an educational game; by subordinating themselves to the figurehead, the adults can collude with the children in the pretense of the figurehead's existence and thereby play *with* them.

- The figurehead reorders power relations between adults and children in the Fifth Dimension. When conflicts arise, adults need not confront children directly, since it is the figurehead, not a participant, who has the power to adjudicate disputes. In such cases, adults as well as children must write to the figurehead, who makes proposals for how matters will proceed.

- Because it communicates only in writing, the figurehead provides many different occasions for children to engage in reading, writing, and wordplay and to use communication skills more generally.

- The figurehead provides occasions for community-building rituals, such as a Golem's birthday party or a celebration when a child "graduates" to become a young assistant to the figurehead.

Other Mediational Means

In addition to these more or less universal mediational means, each site invents tools of its own. One site may use a "hints book" in which children and undergraduates describe helpful strategies for dealing with different games. This tool has encouraged Fifth Dimension communities that use it to accumulate information, so that when the going gets tough, the smart Fifth Dimension participant knows where to look for the answers. Another site created merit badges, and another has bilingual task cards that are used by children who cannot read well but speak English and by undergraduates who read just fine but do not understand Spanish to negotiate meaningful goals and strategies as they work and play together.

THE CENTRALITY OF COMMUNICATIVE PRACTICES

Implicit in much of the foregoing is our belief that the development of communication skills in many media is of positive intellectual benefit to children. There are many theoretical justifications for emphasizing communication skills. For example, Vygotsky is perhaps best known for placing communication—the mediation of activity through language and other "psychological tools"—at the center of his theory of language, thought, and development. In arguing that "the thought is completed in the word," he focused attention on the intellectual importance of communication and the need for learners to engage in active, goal-oriented behavior. Such communicative demands also embody Jean Piaget's (1970) notion of reflective abstraction and Annette Karmiloff-Smith's (1992) idea of the importance of redescription in cognitive development.

Vygotksy is equally well known for the emphasis he placed on internalization, the process through which external experience, shaped by its sociocultural structure and dynamics, is transformed into individual experience. The emphasis on mastering tasks by teaching others what you have learned embodies both of these directions of intellectual influence through communication: the need to convert tacit, intuitive, figurative knowledge into concepts understandable by another and the need to interpret the instructions of another who may not be a particularly adept communicator.

Therefore, in designing Fifth Dimension activities, we paid close attention to arranging interactions in which adult and child participants had to pause to comment on their problem-solving efforts in oral or written reflections in addition to engaging in an ongoing dialogue as they worked together on the problem.

THE IMPORTANCE OF GOAL FORMATION

From prior work conducted in classrooms (Newman, Griffin, and Cole 1989), as well as from literature on the formation of school settings (Sarason 1982, 1997), project members shared another principle: the importance of ensuring that participants are engaged in such a way that they have many opportunities to form goals for their own actions. This principle affected both the design of activities within our various community settings and the issue of sustaining the systems over time.

We emphasized individual children's ability to form their own goals in part because research has demonstrated that when children's learning is tightly controlled by prespecified goals and procedures, the resulting learning does not transfer widely to other problems to which it might be relevant (Newman, Griffin, and Cole 1989). Therefore, we maximized goal formation in the Fifth Dimension by arranging for children to choose the games they wanted to play and the level of expertise they wished to achieve. Sometimes goals were fixed within the games themselves so as to ensure that the children had such options. When needed, we added goals that were achievable by using a task card to reach a higher level of expertise. We also added the ready-made goal of achieving the status of Wizard's Assistant, which carried rewards such as the right to choose a new game for inclusion in the Fifth Dimension maze. However, there was no fixed order for achieving such goals, and children were given other choices as well, such as choice of games, choice of partners, choice of other goals (often not those intended by the designers, such as seeing how many ways you could destroy a city in "Sim City"), and, of course, the choice not to participate.

At the level of institutional cooperation, the need to involve participants in forming goals was met differently by different researchers, depending on the time they had available for planning and the specifics of their institutional arrangements. Each adaptation of the prototype model, however, was intended to be a cooperative effort between the people affiliated with universities and the people affiliated with community institutions. Such collaborations require what Olga Vásquez (1994) refers to as "dynamic relations of exchange." Whether the point of view considered is that of a child, an undergraduate, a parent, a Fifth Dimension staff member, a university administrator, or a research associate, we have found that each participant must be sufficiently motivated to commit time and resources to the Fifth Dimension endeavor. Everyone involved must experience their participation and their efforts as preferable to any alternatives. For this to happen, a solid understanding of the authentic motives, constraints, and resources of the varied participants is key. Consequently, it became important for participants to begin by establishing common goals for a Fifth Dimension site within a particular program.

At the highest level this was easy: all of the community institutions were focused on after-school activities and saw the object of the project as providing enriched educational experiences for children. But when it came to deciding on the subgoals necessary to the joint undertaking, joint goal formation was often difficult to achieve, although everyone recognized it as a primary condition for the continued existence of the Fifth Dimension–UC Links program. As we see in later chapters, an initial failure to identify a sufficiently rich reservoir of common goals bodes ill for the longevity of a program. But even when there are common goals and goodwill, significant problems can arise owing to pressing local institutional needs, turnover in personnel (which often means loss of memory of the goal formation process), and differing time schedules for vital functions. Problems such as these led to the demise of some Fifth Dimension systems.

THE VOLUNTARY PARTICIPATION OF CHILDREN

Writing in the early 1930s, Alexander Luria (1932) made a compelling case that the optimal conditions for gaining access to the thoughts of other people arise when they are engaged in joint, voluntary activities that are highly coordinated, so that discoordinations are selective and highly diagnostic. When children are forced to engage in activities they dislike, their behavior is likely to be disruptive, creating impossible conditions for accurate psychological diagnosis of their learning difficulties and poor conditions for promoting their development.

Our focus on after-school activities not only had the virtue of providing enrichment and reinforcement of educational experience but did so under conditions that maximized the possibility for psychological diagnosis and promotion of the children's welfare. Similarly, undergraduate and graduate student participants usually elected to participate in the Fifth Dimension classes or to develop independent research projects. Thus, the nature of their role, though less open than the role of the children, also allowed for both diagnosis of their learning barriers and the promotion of their welfare.

PRIVILEGING DIVERSITY

The principle of privileging diversity is strongly implied by the Fifth Dimension principles already discussed, but it needs to be explicitly stated. From the theoretical perspective guiding this work, every Fifth Dimension activity system can be expected to differ from every other one in key respects, even when they are located in similar institutional settings in a single socioeconomic and ethnic-social ecology. However, the activity systems we constructed were not all set within identical, or even similar, institutional settings on either the university or community side, nor did they all operate with the same socioeconomic and ethnic groups. Hence, local adaptation was assumed to be a necessary condition for all Fifth Dimension systems.

On the one hand, as previously noted, researchers and implementers were encouraged to adapt systems to their local goals and to the institutional contexts, activity priorities, and resources of their local university and community institutions. Different organizational arrangements, divisions of labor in university-community partnerships, and ways of privileging local issues thus evolved from site to site. For example, a focus on bicultural-biliteracy issues was central at some sites but not others. A focus on technology issues was more central in some cases than in others.

On the other hand, researchers and implementers were encouraged to adapt systems to the social-cultural-economic ecology of the local community. In particular, they were asked to design site content and activities that engaged the cultural and linguistic practices—or "funds of knowledge" (Moll et al. 1992, 1999)—of participating children and families. The imperative for this kind of adaptation derived not only from the goal of creating accessible, appealing, and sustainable local systems but also from our other theoretical principles, which point consistently to participants' cultural and linguistic funds of knowledge as essential resources for promoting learning and development.

Privileging diversity and honoring adaptation thus encouraged local partnerships to combine their own key principles with the six described here. The openness to diversity of the Fifth Dimension design allowed participants to address both global and local issues. At the same time, when participants at different sites were encouraged to exchange ideas that worked, they came to appreciate the local creativity of each system, which then became a resource for local sustainability. The design implications of diversity, adaptation, and borrowing become visible in chapter 3, which provides thumbnail histories of the original sites funded by the Mellon Foundation, and in chapter 8, which discusses post-Mellon expansion of the Fifth Dimension.

Finally, this emphasis on diversity underlined the fact that responsibility for the conduct of local activities was local. There was no "central command" that directed activities at all the sites; power at the level of researcher interaction was also distributed.

CULTURE

Taken one at a time, the various principles generated a rich tool kit for meeting the goals of the Fifth Dimension. But of course, the principles were never taken one at a time in practice. They were all taken into account in the planning and implementation of the activities, and the success of any particular implementation depended crucially on how the various artifacts and practices generated by these principles were synthesized into a meaningful, whole activity. The concept that best captures the holistic nature of the activities in real time is *culture*.

In its most general use, "culture" usually refers to the social inheritance transmitted by each generation of a group to its progeny. In the work of our Distributed Literacy Consortium, we have used this conventional conception of culture as well as a more restricted concept, "idioculture," which seems especially suited to discussion of the unique forms of social inheritance that occur over generations of children and undergraduates interacting within a Fifth Dimension.

At the more general level, several of our consortium members have designed their local Fifth Dimensions with the culture of the local population in mind. This is true, for example, of Olga Vásquez's development of La Clase Mágica, where rooms in the maze are named for people and places of special significance to the local Mexicanos who use her program and the language on the task cards includes varying mixtures of English and Spanish to promote the goal of bilingual biculturalism.

Whatever the cultural characteristics of a Fifth Dimension's surrounding population, culture also operates locally at a far more intimate level that may be shaped by, but is by no means determined by, the sociocultural context of the community. The conditions for the development of local cultural formations were specified many years ago by Edward Rose and William Felton (1955). They found that whenever people come together in a group to engage in some form of joint activity, they quickly begin to invent new vocabulary and ways of doing things (routines), shared values, and shared goals (see also Harton and Bourgeois 2004). Gary Alan Fine (1987, 124) has referred to this process as "cultural formation," where culture is now understood to include "the meaningful traditions and artifacts of a group; ideas, behaviors, verbalization, and material objects." Fine calls the cultural form that emerges in a small group an "idioculture," which he defines as

a system of knowledge, beliefs, behaviors, and customs shared by members of an interacting group to which members can refer and that serve as the basis of further interaction. Members recognize that they share experiences, and these experiences can be referred to with the expectation they will be understood by other members, thus being used to construct a reality for the participants. (Fine 1987, 125)

This description closely fits the conditions that arise in every new Fifth Dimension. The culture that grows at each Fifth Dimension is unique, characterized by its own customs, goals, values, lexicon, and conditions of existence. At the same time, the tool kit of principles for the construction of Fifth Dimensions ensures that certain common features are discernible wherever a Fifth Dimension takes root.

SUMMARY

Several theoretical principles guide the development of a Fifth Dimension system:

- Motivate participation and situate learning in everyday cultural activities—especially, for children, play—that revolve around computers.

- Promote intergenerational collaboration in which the roles of teacher and learner are flexibly shared by participants who are diverse not only in age and educational experience but in gender, culture, language, and socioeconomic status.

- Encourage participants to formulate personal goals through recurrent choices, including whether or not to participate, what activities to do, and what level of expertise to attempt.

- Promote a wide range of communicative practices and artifacts—including culturally valued "psychological tools"—as mediating means for satisfying diverse motives and achieving personal goals.

- Purposively expand activities to create numerous occasions for reflection on problem-solving efforts through dialogue and writing.

- Honor local contexts and human diversity in site development.

Chapter 3

Portraits of After-School Systems in Flux

The previous two chapters described some of the early history of efforts to develop after-school educational enrichment activities and summarized the central theoretical ideas that guided our efforts at program design, implementation, and evaluation. Our goal in this chapter is to describe the projects that generated the data we use to evaluate our successes and failures. Although these portraits, of necessity, are brief, we hope that they will provide the reader with sufficient "local" information to evaluate critically the results presented in subsequent chapters. In each case, we describe the research focus of local Fifth Dimension implementers, the distinctive features of the sites, and some of the key challenges and opportunities that emerged in the course of implementing particular adaptations of the initial model. Two essential themes emerge from these portraits: the diversity of possible research foci, settings, and participating populations for Fifth Dimension adaptations, and, consequently, the multiple strategies required for successful adaptation, evaluation, and sustainability.

A Fifth Dimension project cannot be successfully designed and implemented if it does not resonate at some level with the goals and concerns of the community institution that houses the activity (a school, a church, a youth club) and those of the nearby institution of higher education that provides motivated faculty and students. By constructing a number of such projects, the members of the Distributed Literacy Consortium, representing many locally organized projects and a wide range of academic disciplinary backgrounds, were best situated to evaluate both the adequacy of their design principles and the factors that could explain their practical successes and failures.

Whereas many implementers of educational programs assume that "doing it right" means "doing it the same," we hope to demonstrate the crucial role of local adaptation in successful implementations of the Fifth Dimension. This principle applies not only to each local site but also to features of the university partners. Colleges and universities have their own priorities and dynamics, and they do not easily bend to accommodate such partnership arrangements. Additionally, the university participants bring different academic backgrounds and disciplinary expertise to a project, so each local project, we assume, should reflect these varied influences.

In the following sketches, we briefly describe the birth, development, and status of each implementation at the time when funding from the Mellon Foundation ceased. In chapter 8, we return to these accounts to describe later events, including new implementations and the current status of these Fifth Dimensions.

As we will see, each Fifth Dimension design and implementation encounters its own challenges and draws upon a variety of resources. With such a diversity of local implementations, we must ask whether some of them have become altogether different activities or continue to be legitimate members of the family of Fifth Dimensions. Moreover, can we draw general principles from a sample of ten implementations? We return to that question in chapter 9.

THE SITES

The projects included in the Distributed Literacy Consortium all derived from a pilot Fifth Dimension that was initiated in the early 1980s as part of a project focused on struggling readers (Griffin and Cole 1984; LCHC 1982). They also followed a period of several years during which the prototype described in chapter 1 was developed and initial research to assess the potential developmental effectiveness of such activities was carried out (Nicolopoulou and Cole 1993).

Between 1987 and 1993, the number of Fifth Dimension sites increased. Initially this growth was confined to the University of California at San Diego (UCSD) vicinity. Then, in the late 1980s the Fifth Dimension became a tool for long-distance interaction between children and researchers in a project aimed at international collaboration with a research group in Moscow, Russia. In 1988 Gillian Dowley McNamee, based in Chicago, and Catherine King, in Louisiana, joined with the group at UCSD in this effort. By 1991, when Olga Vásquez initiated her own site at UCSD, six sites were collaborating, contributing data on their local activities, and seeking common funds. Although a good deal had been learned about the conditions necessary for creating effective Fifth Dimension systems, many questions remained unanswered. We sought systematic evidence about what kinds of institutions of higher learning, communities, and community organizations were most likely to support such programs. Many questions also remained about how best to evaluate the effects of these programs. Of pressing interest to funders were questions about the importance of emerging computer and networking utilities as media for the acquisition of literacy. And of course, the issue of the conditions under which such programs could be sustained became increasingly acute as the longevity of various programs increased.

Consequently, a major goal in creating the Distributed Literacy Consortium was to ensure the inclusion of several obvious sources of variation: different kinds of institutions of higher learning with different priorities, different kinds of communities defined in terms of ethnicity and social class, and different kinds of community organizations. It is our hope that the descriptions in this chapter of various Fifth Dimension programs will clarify the role of these variations with respect to the broader implications of this work.

The Partnership Between the University of California at San Diego and the Boys and Girls Club

As the oldest Fifth Dimension–UC Links program, the partnership between the Laboratory of Comparative Human Cognition (LCHC) at UCSD and the local boys and girls club (BGC) served as the prototype upon which subsequent members of the consortium built their local systems. The prototype was described briefly in chapter 1; here we focus on the activities that grew out of the initial system constructed from the idealized model.

Research Focus   As indicated earlier, research using the Fifth Dimension had several goals in its early years. These included determining whether new communication technologies could provide useful tools and genuine motives for children to engage in reading, writing, and serious problem-solving and whether such technologies could also connect researchers at different universities to each other, universities to their communities, and children in different communities to each other. Within-site literacy activities included reading task cards, game instructions, and wizard letters; writing up strategies and hints for playing Fifth Dimension games; and writing to the wizard entity for help and to report progress. Between-site activities included written exchanges with children at other sites such as Chicago, Moscow, and New Orleans. In addition, the researchers wanted to work out a means of in situ evaluation that would warrant the money and time spent on the activities, even if randomized control groups could not be organized. Finally, they were focused on the sustainability of these university-community collaborations (and hence the sustainability of a "successful educational innovation").

Features of the Site   The BGC is located in a relatively affluent suburb of San Diego, next to the local middle school and across the street from one of the town's two elementary schools. According to census data, most of the population is Anglo, with a sizable minority of Latino (mostly Mexicano) children and a sprinkling of Asians and African Americans. Among the school-age population, the proportion of Latino children is greater than among the adult population, and many of these children came to the club. The club charged a nominal fee for participation that varied over time, and children whose families could not afford this fee were provided with scholarships.

At the start of the Distributed Literacy Consortium, the BGC was a lively, boisterous setting with rock music blaring, teenagers hanging out, and pool games usually in progress. Children typically played basketball and run-around games such as tag, or they swam, ate snacks, and mixed with friends. In this early Fifth Dimension, a vibrant elementary- and middle school–age atmosphere of play and peer interaction competed for the children's attention and interests (Cole 1996, 307ff). Daily attendance at the club fluctuated between thirty and forty children, while attendance at the Fifth Dimension, which ran Monday through Thursday, varied from a low of eight children to a high of twenty. Five to eight undergraduates ordinarily participated on a twice-a-week basis.

During the mid-1990s, the club had an open-door policy: children could come and go as they pleased. This policy applied within the club as well as between the club and the town. At the club, children could move at will between sports, arts and crafts, and supervised homework, and they had access to a game room and a computer room that housed the Fifth Dimension for three nine-week periods corresponding to the three ten-week quarters of UCSD's quarter system.

For the first two years of the site's operation, LCHC paid for most Fifth Dimension activities at the site by employing a site coordinator (a trained LCHC staff member), purchasing computers to supplement the computers donated by members of the community, purchasing software, writing task cards, and generally ensuring that the site approximated as closely as possible the prototype described in chapter 1. The BGC, for its part, supported the Fifth Dimension by providing space and the administrative support associated with running the club. Then, in the fall of 1996, by prior agreement, the BGC hired and paid for a staff person to run the Fifth Dimension (after being trained by LCHC staff).

Discipline was very relaxed at the BGC, and Fifth Dimension activities were generally quieter and more disciplined than activities in other parts of the club, with the possible exception of the homework room. A culture of collaborative learning, mixing competition and support, play and learning, was characteristic of the Fifth Dimension from the beginning

(Nicolopoulou and Cole 1993). By mutual agreement, the UCSD students, faculty, and staff who attended the Fifth Dimension did not discipline the children beyond pointing out that the activity was completely voluntary and calling on paid BGC staff if there were discipline problems that seemed likely to endanger any of the children or the equipment. Discipline problems of this nature were minimal.

Challenges   The major challenges encountered over time at the BGC site remained essentially the same, although their particular form changed as activities matured. For example, computer technology changed rapidly, requiring constant work at updating games and writing task cards. When computers broke down, there was no standardized way of repairing them quickly and no BGC budget for the repairs, although local computer repair people would occasionally donate their time. Money for new equipment was an ongoing issue, albeit not as serious as the problem of maintaining the existing equipment.

Because children could come and go as they wished, keeping an accurate record of how many and which children participated in the Fifth Dimension on a given day was a challenge. For the same reason, efforts to organize anything approaching standardized testing were consistently ineffective. Sometimes the children were occupied off-site—for example, playing in a Little League game or having a piano lesson. Sometimes only a few children came to the club because of a teacher conference day at the school. Many children moved in the course of a given year, so that the participants were always a mixture of newcomers and old-timers. And since participation in the Fifth Dimension was voluntary, even if a child was present at the club when we wanted to assess learning, she or he might decline to participate.

Another challenge was the chronic staffing problem at the club. High turnover, which is a problem in many organizations like the BGC, affected the operation of the Fifth Dimension. Although the club eventually provided a salary for a site coordinator for the time that the activity was in session, it did not provide for paid preparation time as part of its initial agreement. Both the pay per hour and the number of hours of pay per week were insufficient to support a permanent staff person.[1] At times, former UCSD participants in the practicum course served as computer coordinators at the club for a few months or a year after graduating, but more often the club recruited someone who had obtained training in the Fifth Dimension on the job, with LCHC staff providing role models and support.

Opportunities   Despite these difficulties, children's attendance at the Fifth Dimension averaged 40 percent of all the children who attended the club on a given day. At the end of any ten-week period, a survey of the record sheets of games the children had played revealed what any casual observer had already noted: the room was generally busy with children and undergraduates interacting around computer and noncomputer games. Conflicts were rare, and those that did occur were mild. Opportunities to study computer-mediated learning among children and undergraduates were ubiquitous.

There were also opportunities to study changes in the organizations that housed the activity. The BGC regularly advertised the presence of the Fifth Dimension in its literature and over the years increased the number of hours and the salary for a site coordinator, who also served as the computer room staff member when the Fifth Dimension was not in session. The friendly and relatively stable relationship between UCSD and the BGC allowed for the documentation of changes in the form of activities as new customs arose and BGC policies changed. For example, children from the Fifth Dimension were sometimes recognized publicly on awards nights at the club, and at the end of each quarter a sort of going-away party was held as a ritual way of thanking the undergraduates and easing the pain of separation for both the undergraduates and the children, who often had formed strong bonds of affection.

On the university side of the partnership, the changing organizational arrangements for the practicum course provided opportunities to study issues of sustainability that few had anticipated at the beginning. For example, the initial strategy for conducting the course was to allow temporary faculty interested in the Fifth Dimension to be instructors of the practicum course so that Michael Cole could meet his other teaching obligations without working time and a half. Such a strategy seemed viable because temporary faculty are relatively inexpensive and could be drawn from a large pool of qualified visitors and candidates living in the UCSD area. To this end, a great deal of energy was put into creating a how-to manual for the Fifth Dimension instructor.

Despite repeated attempts to implement this strategy, however, it eventually was abandoned because the rapid changes in conditions at the community site could not be understood, let alone mastered, by faculty working on a quarter-by-quarter basis, and changes within departments cut into the availability of qualified temporary people. The system that replaced it depended on young scholars on temporary research appointments who both taught the course and did research at the Fifth Dimension. This model was still in place in the summer of 2005.

The Partnership Between the University of California at San Diego and La Clase Mágica: A Bilingual and Bicultural Adaptation of the Fifth Dimension

For all of its success in incorporating multiple forms of diversity, one of the conspicuous failures of the BGC Fifth Dimension was the relative absence of participating Latino youngsters (relative to their numbers in the school-age population).[2] It was not until Olga Vásquez came to UCSD as a postdoctoral fellow in 1989 that this failure began to be addressed (for a full account, see Vásquez 2003).

Research Focus   A central focus of Olga Vásquez's interest in the Fifth Dimension was the opportunity it provided to create an ideal learning environment for immigrant children from Latin America, especially Mexico. Vásquez sought in every way to build on resources within the community, including its language and long cultural heritage. She also set out to demonstrate that local people are capable of creating and maintaining a site without relying on outside academic support, except for the initial training and provision of undergraduates. By learning through doing, she believed, local people can bring their own expertise to their own community setting. Such a system would work, she maintained, only if supported by community members, not if it was controlled by the university or any other local institution not actively a part of the community.

Features of the Site   Vásquez initiated contact with a small Roman Catholic mission that was an important community center for Mexicano families living in the area. The mission is located in a heavily Spanish-speaking, historically working-class neighborhood about half a mile from the BGC. With cooperation from the priest who performed a Spanish mass on Sundays at the mission, Vásquez made contact with the catechism director and the mission's receptionist, both of whom were high-profile members of the community.

In January 1990, these women were given elementary instruction in the use of computers for playing games and in various Fifth Dimension procedures for enriching these activities, such as task cards, a maze, and writing to a mythical figurehead. Almost immediately these community members suggested modifications to make the activities more congenial for the local Mexicano children and their parents. They suggested La Clase Mágica ("the Magic Class") (LCM) as a more appropriate name for the activity and came up with "El Maga" as the name for their cyber-entity (thus taking advantage of the gender rules of Spanish to create an entity of ambiguous gender, consistent with the overall goal of encouraging girls as well as boys to participate).

Because no space or facilities had been set aside for this new activity, LCM operated under very difficult conditions for the first two years. Initially, the computers and other artifacts were set up in front of the mission's altar, and the equipment was stored in a closet on the side of the sanctuary. Communication with El Maga was sporadic at first, but bilingual "live chats" with El Maga were a hit with the children once an Internet connection was established.

After about two years of negotiations, the project began to share space with a local Head Start facility, but even then there were periods when, owing to renovations, the site was run in the mission's large kitchen and dining room area used for special occasions. Despite these difficulties, LCM flourished: twelve to fifteen children, ranging in age from four to twelve, consistently participated in each session, and the program came to develop a character of its own.

Vásquez's commitment to a fully community-based activity extended into the very core of LCM. For example, the local site coordinators produced bilingual Spanish-English translations for task cards and indigenized other auxiliary products to make clear connections to the history and cultural practices of the participants. The rooms in the maze were named after important Mexican-origin people and places (Cesar Chavez, Xochimilco), and the "Botanical Gardens" game was supplemented by a task card identifying this as "Grandmother's garden." The tasks associated with this play world drew children's attention to their own cultural history, and its social organization highlighted diversity—not only in language and cultural origins but also in the ages of participating children and adults, in language use, and in roles and responsibilities.

Early in the development of LCM, community adults were given responsibility for running the site one day a week as a demonstration of faith in their ability to take responsibility for their site. All Fifth Dimensions are multigenerational in the sense that children, undergraduates, and older adults participate, but "multigenerational" took on special meaning at LCM. This was obvious from the beginning as the site coordinator's two-year-old daughter careened around the activities and elementary school participants who had babysitting responsibilities that could not be shirked brought along their younger siblings and cousins.

The transformations in the university courses associated with LCM were no less significant than the changes taking place at the mission. Initially, Vásquez used a course entitled "Literacy Issues in the Community" to place students at LCM. In 1993 Vásquez and Cole combined to teach an expanded practicum class that sent students both to the BGC and to LCM. This arrangement enabled students to experience both sites—an educationally beneficial opportunity that seemed to do nothing to harm the operation of either site. Eventually, owing to an expansion of resources and an expansion of Vásquez's research into the creation of other such sites, she took control of the practicum class and the resources provided it by the university, which continues to provide students for LCM.

Challenges The challenges of implementing La Clase Mágica are implicit in the stories of its origin and in the realities of the lives of working-class Latinos living in barrios within affluent Anglo suburbs. The community partners were Spanish-language-dominant and not familiar, at the outset, with computers. The activity began with virtually no facilities other than the mission space shared for a few hours per week by the community and university participants. Even after more space and common cause were found at the local Head Start center, the program was still left with a very small area in which to place enough computers and chairs for all the children and undergraduates who participated. Hooking up to the Internet from a shared phone line was inconvenient and labor-intensive, and Internet access was spotty and limited. And of course, there was no local budget mechanism to support the purchase and upkeep of computers.

It was recognized early on that there was no one "right way" to construct and maintain LCM. The cast of participants, technologies, and institutional arrangements would always be in flux. Unlike the BGC, which is part of a national organization with its own building, staff, and budget, LCM had no institutional layer between itself and the community, a condition that led to chronic financial insecurity. At the same time, freedom from institutional identity and structure became one of the special strengths of this site, rather than a negative factor in its adaptation of the prototype.

Opportunities Situating LCM directly in the local Catholic mission made a virtue of what might have been considered problematic at sites located in institutions such as boys and girls clubs and schools. With no "after-school club" culture per se in that space, local people were able to take a large role in designing the Fifth Dimension program. Vásquez found key people to manage LCM infrastructure items and transmit its culture, and they became the prime movers of events at LCM. That they received training in educational computer use was an extra, unpaid benefit.

The family structure of the local population provided many opportunities for cross-age tutoring: because older siblings and cousins were often expected to care for their younger family members, LCM usually had very small children attending daily. Moreover, many teenagers who had been to LCM as children were not only babysitting younger children but also serving as tutors.

This multigenerational structure with overlapping large families created an especially warm and inviting environment for all the participants. Adding to the comfortable atmosphere were the flexible norms of language use, which reinforced the bicultural spirit of the activities.

The Partnership Between Michigan State University and the Cristo Rey Community Center

In the fall of 1991, a Fifth Dimension project was launched by Margaret Gallego, a faculty member in the School of Education, in the multiracial community unofficially known as North Lansing. This neighborhood is flanked on one side by automobile factories and on the other by the academic community surrounding Michigan State University (MSU).

Research Focus   Gallego's research area is bilingual literacy. She sought to replicate the model of LCM, especially its emphasis on disrupting the school-based assumption that English is the only language of intellectual achievement and that Spanish or other "home" languages should be left at the door. She was interested in LCM's potential for supporting activities that encourage children to bring all of their language and cultural resources to bear in literacy activities and problem-solving. She planned to collaborate with the Julian Samora Research Institute (JSRI) at MSU, which shared her interests and had established an ongoing relationship with the Cristo Rey Community Center in North Lansing.

Features of the Site   The Cristo Rey Community Center was operated primarily through funding from United Way and other nonprofit foundations. The building housed outreach programs such as a clinic, a soup kitchen, and social events for elders. Among the educational programs it offered were adult English classes, GED preparation courses, and an after-school tutoring program for elementary-age students. This LCM shared a classroom on the second floor of the modest two-story building with an English-language program, which offered some rarely used computers for use by the LCM site.

Initially it was assumed that this site would mirror the site initiated by Vásquez, so it was named La Clase Mágica Midwest (LCMM). However, because the community center's neighborhood was home to a diverse working-class population—approximately one-third Latino with various national roots (including Puerto Rico, Costa Rica, and Mexico), one-third Asian (Chinese and Hmong), and one-third African American—it quickly became a *multi*lingual site.

Gallego, using materials already prepared at LCM in California, encouraged participants to use all their language resources in working on tasks. To capitalize on these language resources, she and her research team constructed a "translation room" in which children gained credit for translating a task card into their home language. The activities in this room served both to add to the task card collection and to promote multilingualism. The team also modified the names of many of the rooms in the maze to represent landmarks important to the North Lansing community, such as the local bakery and the park.

In its first days, the site was not well attended. The staff at the community center wanted the activity to be school-like and orderly, as did the MSU students, but the kids did not. Gallego and her team worked with the few children who did attend the site to experience the alternative culture of LCMM. These children became ambassadors for communicating how the site differed from previous educational programs offered there. It was not long before LCMM had a packed house.

Interactions throughout the sessions resembled those at other Fifth Dimension sites. Children complained when games were already in use, panicked when computer screens went blank, and engaged each other and the undergraduates, who, in turn, cajoled children into writing and finishing up tasks. There was a lot of laughter, chatter, and celebration of each other's accomplishments. Deep and intense relationships developed very quickly between the undergraduates and the children, as could be seen during the farewell sessions at the close of each semester and when students stopped by to say hello after they had completed the university course.

The Cristo Rey site operated twice a week from three to five o'clock in the afternoon. When the doors opened, the children were greeted by one of the eight to ten university students who participated at the site each semester. If their "special partner" (the student with whom a child had developed a friendship) was late in coming, the children were encouraged to help set up or to begin filling out their daily logs. Daily logs recorded each child's name, the date, the day's activity, and the university partner(s) and also included a section for participants' comments about their accomplishments. Participating children rated the perceived difficulty of the day's tasks and were asked to comment briefly on the strategies they used while playing games. (The university student usually wrote as the child dictated; the children were reluctant to participate in any type of writing activity.) Participants also listed the languages they used during their game play.

Challenges   The MSU students who participated in LCMM were enrolled in teacher education courses in reading, writing, and so forth, and they were also placed in school classrooms in connection with another class. Eager to enact their roles as teachers, they found it difficult to interact informally as the children's partners and to follow rather than lead in their interactions with the children. Their didactic approach did not sit well with the children, many of whom were considered behavior problems in their classrooms.

Although the program was clearly beneficial to the child and undergraduate populations, it did not succeed in becoming an institutional priority at either the university or the community center. Financial problems were chronic, although the use (and expense) of new computer technology was not a major factor in the site's identity or its troubles. Interestingly, the contested feature at the heart of both the success and failure of the Michigan site was its "curriculum." Neither the Cristo Rey hosts nor the faculty at the MSU School of Education viewed the activities as sufficiently educational, though it was clear that the children and the undergraduates developed academically through their participation.

Opportunities The very existence of the Cristo Rey Community Center provided a fine opportunity to widen the range of after-school institutions to come under the lens of the research team. Its constituents were multigenerational, and though it was "of" the community, it also had a prior history of connections to the university.

Once the activities gained momentum, more children came to the club than there were computers available. This shortfall provided the need and opportunity to find a way to reduce dependence on computer-based activities at a Fifth Dimension. The shortfall was made up for by a variety of board games such as Scrabble and Who's Who (a local favorite). Staff members developed task cards for these games in order to hold children's interest as they waited for a computer to become available. Once the activity reached maturity and the room was packed, an observer would see some children playing games, and some not. Some would be having snacks with friends as they eased into play, while others darted toward their favorite computer stations and fired up their games as soon as possible. This ebb and flow provided a natural rhythm in a room that at times was uncomfortably full. Gallego maintained an open-door policy, however, and never turned a child or volunteer away.

Besides engaging in activities characteristic of other sites, the children were encouraged to use several "extension activities" to apply the knowledge they gained through computer play in some new way. For instance, children were sometimes prompted to plant a seed based on the game "Botanical Gardens," to draw an underwater ocean scene based on "Shark Game," or to calculate the distance between landmarks on a local map.

This site operated for three years in North Lansing, from 1991 to 1994. Opportunities were eventually overwhelmed by challenges. Discouraged by her colleagues' lack of interest in after-school activities, Gallego left MSU and returned to San Diego, where she took part in evaluations of other Fifth Dimension sites. Ironically, even though Gallego's Fifth Dimension effort in North Lansing failed, after her departure the School of Education at MSU discovered the value of after-school activities similar in spirit to those of the Fifth Dimension. Activities directed toward after-school education have now become a part of the MSU curriculum (Gallego and Cole 2000).

The Partnership Between the Erikson Institute and Le Claire–Hearst Community Center

From 1987 through the mid-1990s, the Erikson Institute in Chicago conducted research and training projects in early literacy development. The goals of these projects were to understand the origins of literacy during the preschool years and to study the kinds of activities and assistance that facilitate reading and writing development between the ages of three and eight.

Gillian Dowley McNamee, an educational psychologist, collaborated with adults who worked directly with children at risk for school failure in schools, day care centers, and after-school programs that sought to supplement the children's educational experience. This work aimed to encourage child care workers, teachers, and parents to become conscious and proactive in arranging opportunities for children's writing and reading development and to help them understand their role in the process.

Research Focus   In 1987 McNamee began discussing possible benefits of a Fifth Dimension with a center in the community. The staff and McNamee agreed that the goal for this site would be to explore ways in which Fifth Dimension activities might help children find good reasons to write and read and the development of their literacy skills in such a setting. The researchers also explored how African American residents of the community interpreted the communication opportunities afforded by the Fifth Dimension—particularly the opportunity to interact with adults and children in far-off places—as a possible means to promoting its literacy-enhancing goals. McNamee was interested in studying how the community center staff contributed to e-mail communication and mediated children's literacy experiences in the network.

Features of the Site   When McNamee approached a social service agency serving African American families in an inner-city community in Chicago about implementing a Fifth Dimension program, the response from both staff and families was enthusiastic. The community site for the program was located in a housing project on the west side of Chicago. About 650 community families lived in city housing that they were beginning to manage themselves. Having local resident management of government-owned housing was a new experiment in the United States in the 1980s. The Chicago Fifth Dimension site was staffed by high school graduates, parents of children in the after-school program, and residents of the community. Staff was responsible for providing a range of after-school activities, one of which became the Fifth Dimension. They served twenty kindergartners and forty-five first-graders five days a week.

The Chicago site was notable for regular communication with Fifth Dimensions at other sites in the United States—including San Diego, New Orleans, North Lansing, and Boone, North Carolina—as well as a site in Moscow, Russia. Children would play games such as "Odell Lake," an ecology game built around a set of changing power relations, and then correspond with other sites about their discoveries, the strategies they found useful, and nearly any other topic they found interesting at the moment (such as their favorite word games and rap songs). At the Chicago site, telecommunications motivated both the children and the adults to engage in written correspondence with others.

Challenges There were two major challenges at the Chicago site. The first was the economic and social vulnerability of the community, its residents, and the community center itself. Staff and parents struggled to sustain family life in an environment of high crime, violence, illness, unemployment, and lack of social service resources. These daily struggles often left the children and adults searching for a firm footing at home, at school, and in the community. Staff at the community center had not attended college and found the prospects of doing so elusive given the need to work and care for their families.

The second set of difficulties derived from some of the ideals inherent in the Fifth Dimension model itself. Conflicts arose as staff and parents experienced the predominantly white, middle-class culture represented in the program materials and software. Even though the center staff and their Erikson partners worked to adapt the Fifth Dimension model to this African American urban community, the software portrayed images, challenges, and situations that were unconnected to most aspects of African American culture. In addition, though there was another site mainly populated by African American children, there were no other sites in the Fifth Dimension network run by African American adults. The Chicago staff felt isolated and unsupported in building a Fifth Dimension program identity in dialogue with and in reference to others similar to themselves.

One way that tensions around the fit between the Fifth Dimension model and the needs of the children in this community expressed themselves was through the issue of language. Residents of the community, the center staff, and the children spoke predominantly African American English, although many were also proficient at conventional English. As conversations with other Fifth Dimension sites developed, some staff and parents feared that their children's interactions with others in the larger Fifth Dimension network, where standard English predominated, would undermine their children's African American English and home culture. This effect, as one staff member described it, put their children in the position of living in a white world not of their choosing or design, and not under their control.

After five years of intense work together, the community and the university considered a number of factors in deciding to close the Chicago site. This after-school program had many pressing problems, and the Fifth Dimension was not emerging as a strong enough tool to help staff address these problems. A central tenet of the university-community partnership is local control and ownership of the program ideas and operations, but little progress had been made in moving toward this goal. Erikson Institute and community center staff agreed that they had not been able to establish the minimum economic and programmatic conditions necessary for staff to take responsibility for maintaining and continuing the Fifth Dimension. The daily challenges internal to the community, coupled with the lack of African American colleagues outside of Chicago who could inspire and support development of the Fifth Dimension in this community, left the Chicago participants without a path and with no reason to continue.

Opportunities This Fifth Dimension site was not supported by the presence of undergraduates from the Erikson Institute, in part because the Erikson curriculum was too packed with required courses to admit a new course. But in fact this "challenge" presented a research opportunity: McNamee wanted to participate in a site designed to be operated by the community center staff. Supported by a few graduate students, she provided extensive and ongoing on-site training in the use of computer technology and pedagogy to develop children's literacy and problem-solving skills. If successful, this strategy would have resulted in local control and management of this Fifth Dimension with minimal, if any, involvement from the Erikson Institute after the first two to three years. Children and adults who would not ordinarily have had access to computer technology would also have had the chance to engage in computer-based problem-solving and regular correspondence with other professionals and children around a shared set of concerns and interests in the service of their own development.

As should have become apparent, challenges and opportunities may be a useful analytic distinction but are not so easily distinguishable in real life. The staff, parents, and children valued McNamee's work, as well as their newly acquired friends at other Fifth Dimension sites and the opportunities afforded the children through work on computers, but the staff did not feel that they could sustain the growth of the Fifth Dimension at this site, particularly under real-world conditions in Chicago's inner city. When the Chicago site closed, McNamee became a Distributed Literacy Consortium specialist in evaluating changes in written language.

The Partnership Between the University of New Orleans and the Claiborne School

With help from University of New Orleans (UNO) graduate and undergraduate students in psychology and modest external funding from colleagues at LCHC, Catherine King began a Fifth Dimension site during after-school hours in a New Orleans elementary school in the fall of 1988. UNO is a large urban university located in a predominantly African American and economically depressed part of the country. One of the stated goals of the university is to use its resources to address certain problems in New Orleans and Louisiana, a number of which can be seen as intertwined: poor literacy skills, a high school dropout rate, unemployment, drug abuse, and drug-related crime. Unfortunately, the resources available to be applied to these problems are not abundant, and thus the university was attracted to the Fifth Dimension strategy of using a course to provide student labor and the local school to provide facilities.

Research Focus King's research interests included the support of children's writing, the role of correspondence to and from the Wizard, and the use of the cyber-figureheads at other sites in the consortium as inspiration for children's writing.

Features of the Site King's program drew graduate students from a UNO applied developmental program in which they not only received training in experimental research techniques but also had to apply their knowledge to problems in the community. Students worked on the project in return for research credit or in fulfillment of a practicum requirement.

The other half of King's Fifth Dimension program was carried out with the cooperation of the Orleans Parish School Board, which runs the citywide public school system; the teachers and principal of a local elementary school, the Claiborne School; and the staff of the school's after-school day care program. Claiborne was a magnet school that emphasized basic skills and put a high value on strict discipline.

This Fifth Dimension was located in two small rooms between the cafeteria and the library that were used during the school day as the resource center for gifted students. As a consequence, it boasted several computers—three Apple IIGSs, three Macintosh LCs, one Apple IIe, and one Kaypro with a printer, which was used as a word processor. (We provide this level of detail to indicate just how much the technology has changed in the course of our work.)

The student population included children from middle-class homes as well as children from government housing projects; approximately half were from the local neighborhood, and the other half came from other parts of the city. Despite the inclusive goals of the magnet school program, the student body was predominantly African American. All children who came to the UNO site were enrolled in an after-care program staffed by classroom teachers who put in long hours both before and after the regular school day.

Challenges When the UNO site was started, the university had an institutional mandate to serve the community, and the community was willing and ready to be served. The community and undergraduate populations were well served by the Fifth Dimension project, even though the "obedience to authority" social norms advocated by authorities in the local community were sometimes at odds with the "playfulness" of the Fifth Dimension.

The university's mandate to serve the community was ultimately undermined, however, by a competing institutional priority having to do with promotion and tenure. The site was terminated because the UNO Psychology Department indicated in a review of her performance that King was unlikely to be given tenure. Although her activities were appreciated in principle, the effort involved in getting the site up and running conflicted with the department's requirements for rapid and repeated publication. King knew that she could not both run the site and publish at the required rate, so in the fall of 1993 she moved to Elon College in North Carolina.

Opportunities In the regular after-care program, children were exposed to activities that differed markedly from the Fifth Dimension. They were often made to sit quietly at desks and tables; when the weather was good, some of the more energetic teachers sometimes organized a T-ball or football game for the boys. In this context, the Fifth Dimension was an attractive alternative, and it was necessary to limit the number of children allowed to participate.

Following the model provided by UCSD, undergraduates attended the after-school program as their schedules allowed. In addition to working with the children and taking field notes, the undergraduates had to become computer-literate, if they were not already, in using telecommunications between sites and in writing, distributing, and revising their work. The joint work of the entire group was discussed weekly in a research practicum seminar.

The UNO undergraduates included a large number of nontraditional students who worked while they attended school, who had families, and who had begun taking classes later in life than the traditional university student. These students brought a great deal of experience and a unique set of skills to the project. Participation in the after-school activities markedly enhanced their academic and personal development, an especially significant outcome for this largely working-class, first-generation population of college students.

The Partnership Between Elon College and the YMCA

King's next site operated in a YMCA in Burlington, North Carolina, the small town where Elon College is located. Textile mills and biomedical light industry were the main sources of employment for the parents whose children attended the after-care programs at the YMCA.

Research Focus   At Elon, a liberal arts college, King carried on with her research on children's writing. In her new position, she expected her community site development activities to fit well with the college's primary mission: teaching. When she started the Fifth Dimension program at Elon, King was still working to complete her research on writing and exploring children's uses of computer technology in literacy.

Features of the Site   The YMCA site ran two days a week from the fall of 1994 through the spring of 1995, with about twenty-five elementary-age children attending per session. In the fall, students were members of the practicum class. In the spring, some students were paid and some volunteered to help King run the site. This Fifth Dimension was modeled on King's experience with the Fifth Dimension while a graduate student at UCSD. Approximately two-thirds of the children were Anglo, and the remainder were African American. All were from working-class families. Among the twenty-six regular attendees (out of approximately one hundred children who participated off and on), boys slightly outnumbered girls.

Challenges   On the college side of this arrangement, King's research at the YMCA was viewed by her colleagues as a short-term, periodic hobby or as community service, but not as a good long-term professional investment. As a consequence, running the practicum course twice a year for this institution was impossible, and King had to invest an enormous amount of work in supporting site activities for that half of the year when no practicum course was offered.

On the community side, King reported that the Fifth Dimension was seen by the club as a babysitter: "It was not easy to get YMCA staff to see computers and games as friendly and worthwhile." As was true at the Cristo Rey Community Center in Michigan, the YMCA staff was imbued with a transmission view of education and believed that children require strict and constant discipline. To increase disciplinary control, the staff had boys and girls attend the Fifth Dimension on different days, undermining the emphasis on diversity that was part of the program's core ideology.

Without adequate backing and personnel from her college to run the program, King turned to local adults and tried to train them in the Fifth Dimension philosophy. This effort looked good on paper in that it advanced the idea that "uptake" would be aided by cultivating responsibility for running the program among local adults. However, the effort was also unsuccessful. So long as King and her students took responsibility for conducting the activities, the YMCA staff was content to have their workloads reduced. They showed no interest in making the activity their own.

Opportunities   The children, who numbered about twenty-five per session, generally worked in small groups with an undergraduate, followed task cards, worked their way through the maze, and corresponded with their local wizard. The activity was popular with the children, perhaps because their main alternative was to engage in structured homework. The Fifth Dimension was also popular because the local wizard wrote caring and silly letters to the children and carried on a busy correspondence with them. Opportunities to study literacy development and the role of new technologies abounded.

Between 1996 and 1997, the site closed. The Fifth Dimension had not become a venue in which the college and the community could explore, negotiate, and construct common ground for promoting children's learning in an after-school setting. At the YMCA, conflicting priorities in the adult population affected the kind of opportunities local children were offered. Adding financial and technological resources did not help this situation. Institutional and social norms collided, drawing the implementer into an untenable position where help from others was not forthcoming.

Appalachian State University Partnerships

Four Fifth Dimensions ran in conjunction with a specially designated teacher education course at Appalachian State University (ASU) in Boone, North Carolina. Three of these sites were located in schools with ongoing after-school programs that were limited primarily to homework supervision with some access to informal sports. The fourth ran at a computer lab on the ASU campus to which children from a nearby school were bused.

Research Focus   William Blanton conducted a number of experimental studies of the effects of participation in the Fifth Dimension at the ASU sites (see chapter 5). Because he was interested in showing the utility of combining quantitative and qualitative methodological approaches, Blanton made extensive use of ethnographic field notes; these enabled him to provide many compelling examples of the cognitive processes underlying the test results produced from the problem-solving activities at his sites. Blanton also took a keen interest in the theoretical foundations of the Fifth Dimension and the potential of computers as tools for improving academic achievement.

Features of the Site The Fifth Dimension program run by ASU had several characteristics that set it apart from others. For one thing, it ran in schools after school rather than in a community center or church. Two of the school sites used the school computer labs, and the remaining sites used regular classrooms, so the Fifth Dimension activities often took place in more than one classroom at a time. The program, which ran four days a week, two hours per session, grew quickly; by 1996, it served over 150 children, mainly second- and third-graders from predominantly Anglo-American lower- to middle-income backgrounds. Just over half of the children were girls, and attendance of eligible participants was high at slightly more than 90 percent. (As noted earlier, at many other sites children varied in the frequency with which they attended.)

An unusual characteristic of the ASU Fifth Dimension partnerships was that the College of Education had major responsibility for supporting the development of technology-based instruction in the local elementary schools. This explains why the program could run in regular classrooms—they were plentifully equipped with new and sophisticated computers that could be made available for after-school use. Importantly, the schools also had support for maintaining and upgrading their computer equipment, thus relieving the university partners of this responsibility. On the other hand, the schools provided no site coordinators. Instead, ASU graduate students in the teacher education program supervised the Fifth Dimension field experience of undergraduate "interns."

ASU has a large teacher education program, but its rural location prevents it from being able to provide early field experiences in classrooms for all of its undergraduates. Priority has to be given to field experience for methods classes and student teaching. The Fifth Dimension after-school program was ideally suited for an early field experience linked to an introduction to teaching course.

The College of Education took a great interest in the theoretical foundations of the Fifth Dimension and made the practicum course part of the required teacher education curriculum. The college also used the theoretical principles to develop its conceptual framework for teacher preparation in general. To an unusual degree, the ASU program began to "pay for itself" very early in its development.

Challenges   Several factors posed challenges to the implementation at ASU of the Fifth Dimension model. ASU students, like those at Elon College, were heavily influenced by cultural values distinct to rural North Carolina, which both shaped the regular school day and constrained the practices that could be developed in local Fifth Dimensions. For instance, students' participation style reflected their belief that children require firm guidance and strong discipline in order to develop into mature adults. In addition, standard teaching practices adhered firmly to a "transmission" model in which children were expected to adhere closely to prescribed tasks.

One reflection of these cultural values was the decision to not refer to the magical figurehead for the ASU sites as a wizard, a term that in this milieu would have raised eyebrows. The magical figurehead was instead called a golem, a term sufficiently distant from local beliefs to serve its function in the play world without raising objections. The mismatch between local norms and the typical norms of a Fifth Dimension was reflected in students' routine complaints in their field notes about the difficulty of getting children to adhere to the rules and to obey them without question. Thus, the site activities were somewhat more regimented than, for instance, at the BGC in Solana Beach, and children's participation and progress were more closely monitored by the preservice teachers and researchers who ran the sites.

Another challenge was that the introduction to the teaching course and its Fifth Dimension practicum conflicted with traditional practices shaping early field experiences, faculty assignments, time slots, and resources. The larger curriculum changes required many faculty meetings, the writing of new curricular specifications, and heated discussions about disciplinary principles and standards. Although teachers and principals were supportive, they needed to be reassured that their classrooms and labs would not be disassembled by the new after-school activities. In spite of their hesitation on this score, the system worked.

In 1999, more or less at the height of activity at the ASU sites, Blanton moved from ASU to Miami. This departure clearly posed profound challenges and put the site at risk. ASU's Fifth Dimension project was subjected to severe strains at that point in its history.

Opportunities   In 1996 Blanton's report noted that the program had grown and stabilized, that Fifth Dimensions had been started at several sites, that two more sites were on the way, and that his team was actively seeking to "replicate the model" in preparation for spreading it to other teacher education programs. In 1997 Blanton noted that new faculty were unaware that there had been a time without the Fifth Dimension at their campus. The program was being used to leverage other changes at the

College of Education. The ASU sites enjoyed years of steady growth and expansion, tempered by periodic accounts of discoordination and conflict.

The Fifth Dimension network at ASU offered a fine example of how benefits and constraints can be balanced. The strategy of opening multiple sites serving multiple populations in one region made it possible for each new site to begin with resources and credibility greater than it would have merited on its own. The larger Distributed Literacy Consortium, the electronically linked research collective, also provided a bank of experience that the ASU sites could both draw on and contribute to; unlike some other sites, such as the Erikson Institute's, ASU was able to take significant advantage of this resource. ASU Fifth Dimension sites benefited greatly from other financial and technological advantages because they were tied directly to the institutional and social goals and norms of ASU's College of Education very early on in the adaptation.

The Partnership Between the California State University at San Marcos and a Boys and Girls Club

Pat Worden and Miriam Schustack, faculty members in the Department of Psychology at California State University at San Marcos (CSUSM), began implementing a Fifth Dimension at the Escondido boys and girls club in 1991. At the time, CSUSM, located on the northern edge of San Diego County, was the newest campus in the CSU system. Its mission included an emphasis on innovative curriculum, the incorporation of computer technology at every level of instruction, and the development of programs in service learning as part of its efforts to recruit and retain students from diverse populations. Early on, Worden was recruited into an administrative position at the university, so the actual research on the Fifth Dimension fell largely to Schustack.

Research Focus Schustack's primary interests were in the potential of computers as learning tools and the development of experimental methodologies. Since true experiments were not possible at her site (for reasons that prevailed at other BGC sites as well), she focused on the implementation of quasi-experimental procedures for evaluating the effects of participation on children's acquisition of computer skills.

Features of the Site Worden and Schustack created a new course, "Field Course in Psychological Settings," as the vehicle to link their students with the local BGC, which was populated by a mixture of Latino, Filipino, and Anglo-American children. Approximately a dozen students took the course. The site, which ran twice a week, accommodated about a dozen children per session, for reasons linked to Schustack's research interests, although demand was greater. There was always a waiting list of children wanting to participate on a first-come-first-serve basis, but the particular children who attended varied over the course of the academic year.

At the end of the first year, at the request of the directors of the local BGC, the Fifth Dimension was moved to another club location with a large computer room. This club served a somewhat different population: about half were Anglo, 30 percent were Latino, and the remainder were African American and Asian American children. Through donations, the site boasted fourteen computers of various makes. At the university, the project was seen as a model for accomplishing academically sound, service-oriented education. It was an auspicious beginning.

The children at the new site had a close relationship with the Wizard and wrote back and forth frequently. Live chats were popular, and unlike children at many other sites, these children rarely argued against writing as a social practice. The BGC began to provide financial support for a site coordinator, and the institutional relationship continued to develop favorably. But attendance continued to be closely controlled to ensure that the undergraduates were able to monitor children's progress carefully, and the waiting list was correspondingly longer.

Challenges As already mentioned, Pat Worden was promoted to a senior administrative post early on in the development of the Fifth Dimension site, and the work of running the site and teaching the course was left to Schustack, an assistant professor. To ensure that quasi-experimental evaluation procedures were faithfully instituted, Schustack had to carry the heavy burden of being at the site virtually every time it ran.

At the university, efforts to have the field course positioned as an important requirement in the Psychology Department curriculum were unsuccessful because the form of research was not as experimentally oriented as the faculty wished. At the same time, efforts to have the course count as a requirement in the School of Education were also unsuccessful because the activities took place after school. As a result, course enrollments were low, a fact that would become crucial in later years.

Opportunities As noted earlier, the general plan of CSUSM seemed especially propitious for a project such as the Fifth Dimension, given the university's interest in the study of technology and learning, service learning, and diversity. These auspicious institutional preferences were manifested in the permission given to Schustack to conduct her practicum course with fewer than the normal number of students despite enrollment pressures that made such an exception costly to the university.

The community side of the system presented another major opportunity: Schustack was able to keep the ratio of undergraduates to children close to one-to-one, despite the children's frequent preference to play on the computers. Schustack was thus able to keep tight control over the activity at the site, and a ready pool of children was available to take part in a much more organized fashion than was characteristic at most Fifth Dimensions. Schustack was able to collect quasi-experimental data to satisfy her faculty and to do research that was of great value to the consortium's overall evaluation strategy. However, this virtue also had its downside.

This downside became apparent in 1995, when Schustack started the year with one graduate assistant. She began to be concerned about the lack of involvement by other faculty, which made the program dependent on her own presence; she managed, however, to have her course load reduced (owing to low numbers of participating students), and she also obtained computer support for her work at the site. In 1997 Schustack noted the generally "major improvements" in the club's support for the program, and she was relieved to have succeeded in recruiting a colleague to teach the course for her sabbatical year.

To this point, this example may seem to attest to the possibility that an untenured faculty member can find professional success in the implementation of a Fifth Dimension. In Schustack's experience, however, it was not possible in the end to override the constraints, including a lack of sustained involvement by departmental colleagues, time pressures brought about by professional success, and emerging difficulties with the community partner. When Schustack earned tenure in 1999, her almost immediate election as president of the academic senate limited her time for teaching and conducting research at the Fifth Dimension site. At this time, a new BGC director was hired who wanted to have more children using the computer room. The population of undergraduates and children involved in Schustack's site was too low to satisfy the burgeoning demands on the university and the community institutions to enroll and serve more children. Neither was there any prospect of increased enrollment in the class or greater faculty collaboration, which would have allowed Schustack to continue her research. Faced with these pressures, the CSUSM Fifth Dimension came to an end.

The Partnership Between the University of California at Santa Barbara and a Boys and Girls Club

A Fifth Dimension was started at the University of California at Santa Barbara (UCSB) in 1994 when Scott Woodbridge, an LCHC staff member, left for graduate school in education at that campus. Richard Duran, a faculty member in education already committed to community-based research, served as the principal investigator and was joined later by Betsy Brenner, an anthropologist of education who shared complementary interests, including an interest in cultural historical activity theory and human development.

Research Focus Richard Duran's research interest was in bilingual literacy and increasing the participation of minority youth in higher education. He was especially interested in ways in which immigrant youths and families can acquire critical awareness of community resources and institutions through hands-on exploration and community involvement. Betsy Brenner shared a similar interest. She had done anthropological fieldwork in Liberia and Hawaii and explored community members' hands-on knowledge of mathematics as part of daily life outside of school settings. After she got involved in the Fifth Dimension site, she also became interested in how children learn to use computers to build mechanical toys and how they develop important forms of logical and analytic thinking in the process. Following the model of La Clase Mágica, the team worked on adapting materials so as to reflect the artifacts and activities common to Fifth Dimension sites while emphasizing community exploration and bilingual literacy, with an eye toward also creating a culture of intergenerational participation and community support.

Features of the Site Club Proteo opened in the winter of 1994 in a boys and girls club in Goleta, a working-class neighborhood near the university. The site ran twice a week and served a population of sixty-two children, most of them Mexicano; boys and girls were nearly equally represented. Daily attendance varied between nine and twenty-six children, with an average participation rate of twenty children per session, along with five to eight undergraduates and one or two researchers.

The Club Proteo staff followed the LCM model in emphasizing local culture, family participation, language and culture, and community exploration as a route to literacy education. The local Wizard was named Proteo to emphasize the protean nature of the activity. Proteo wrote to and answered letters from children in English and Spanish. The maze and task cards emphasized writing about site activities and community field trips.

Several times a year families participating in Club Proteo attended special evening events, including dinners, skits, and award ceremonies, and there they received information on other community organizations with which they might collaborate. The Club Proteo program included field trips to various community organizations, including a radio station, a car dealership, and a bank. The children produced a video news broadcast and participated in a lengthy on-air radio interview that was broadcast to the wider Santa Barbara community. These field trips addressed the concern that the children's families often had marginal connections to community institutions owing to their lack of mobility or immigration status. The goals of the field trips were to help children understand better that they were part of a community where education mattered in important day-to-day functions and that being competent as an employee and participant in institutions rested on being "literate" in the practices of those institutions.

Challenges   The site opened without an official and ongoing practicum course offered by the UCSB Graduate School of Education. During its first three years, Club Proteo was staffed by independent study students, who had to be trained on-site as apprentices without the support of a regularly convened course away from the site. Woodbridge acted as the first site coordinator and Fifth Dimension pedagogy expert while training others. The following year the Graduate School of Education faculty voted to create a regular course offering under its Teacher Education Program. The course, entitled "Sociocultural Research on Teaching and Learning," was taught by Duran and later by Brenner as well. This course emphasized the theoretical and practical underpinnings of community-based educational research in multicultural and linguistically diverse settings, with added attention to critical pedagogy and cultural psychology. The course proved to be especially attractive to Spanish-English bilingual undergraduates. Disincentives for some students taking this "pass/no pass" elective course, however, were activities like writing regular field notes after field observations and conducting interviews with parents and community members, tasks that proved to be too demanding. This disincentive largely disappeared after the course began to be offered on a graded basis.

Finding its niche in the overall menu of activities at the BGC has been a perennial challenge to Club Proteo. The rules of the club permitted children to move freely in and out of Club Proteo, though they were otherwise expected to abide by Club Proteo rules and practices. To adapt to these circumstances, Club Proteo developed three participation patterns: more or less regular attendees who stayed the full length of sessions; casual drop-in children who were not regular participants; and "day care" children who were permitted only one hour of participation before moving to a mandated day care program. In addition, as funding increased, other opportunities arose for the children as the BGC instituted homework activities for them. These changes affected the regularity of children's participation in Club Proteo, however, and made it more difficult to implement complex activities requiring their concentrated attention.

Another challenge was securing the cooperation of the site coordinator to document and conduct complex learning activities. Some of the earlier non-graduate-student coordinators were resistant to altering general club practices to accommodate the more complex activities of Club Proteo, which required planning, management discipline, and data collection. This challenge was met by having graduate students serve as coordinators; they had a broader understanding of the purposes of Club Proteo and its mission to promote the education and literacy awareness of participants.

Opportunities   Duran came to this effort with a long history of involvement with the local Mexicano community and the school system. Consequently, in addition to the resources provided by the local BGC, his Fifth Dimension site was also the beneficiary of resources provided by the local school. Duran was able to conduct after-school activities at the school, and the school provided access to children who could serve as comparison groups for his research evaluating the Fifth Dimension site. Moreover, the school supported the community outreach aspect of the program by giving him access to the parents of the children from the school attending Club Proteo.

After several years of effort, UCSB was persuaded to adopt an education minor, for which the practicum course qualified; this solved the major institutional problem from the university side of the system. Brenner, who served on the committee establishing the minor, was a critical force in this development. In 1995 Duran predicted that the bilingual/bicultural spirit of Club Proteo would be difficult to sustain in the absence of a bilingual site coordinator and sufficient numbers of bilingual undergraduates to work closely with the children. Fortuitously, adoption of the undergraduate course resolved both problems, though recruitment of sufficient numbers of undergraduates remained a challenge when the course was first introduced.

On the community side, there was discussion with the club director early on about uptake and ownership. The director took up the issue of sustainability by raising the issue of what would happen when the money ran out. The BGC also helped look for school and parent support. In 1996 the BGC assumed operational and financial responsibility for the site coordinator. The director and his advisory board approved making support of the coordinator a line item in the club's annual budget at a ten-hour-per-week level. This salary was supplemented by external funding that allowed the coordinator to fulfill additional functions such as gathering and reporting attendance records on participants, helping to recruit children, and planning club activities and field trips.

In their final report, Brenner (who by this time had been awarded tenure) and Duran indicated that, while the university had made only a minor financial contribution to the project in the form of a small research grant to Brenner (in addition to the Mellon funds), the BGC had allocated the services of the BGC-wide computer and network coordinator to Club Proteo as an in-kind contribution worth $4,500.

The Partnership Between Whittier College and a Boys and Girls Club

The Fifth Dimension in Whittier, California, operates at the local boys and girls club in partnership with Whittier College, a four-year liberal arts institution about a mile from the club. A city just east of Los Angeles, Whittier has a population that is mostly Latino; Anglos constitute the second-largest group. Among schoolchildren, 80 percent are Latino. Three-quarters of the children qualify for free or reduced-cost lunch programs.

Research Focus   Don Bremme, a professor of teacher education, had two research goals: to create a cadre of transformative teachers who would work for educational and social change, and to demonstrate an educational alternative to traditional schooling in which socially and economically marginalized children could construct positive alternatives to the identities and relations to learning often encouraged by traditional schools. He also worked with the process evaluation team to collect data from other sites in the Distributed Literacy Consortium on another of his research interests: the effects of participation in the Fifth Dimension on undergraduates.

Bremme saw these goals as interdependent. He speculated that participation in the Fifth Dimension might encourage future teachers to unpack, interrogate, and reconstruct the ideas about learning and teaching they had acquired during their own traditional schooling. Simultaneously, their extended Fifth Dimension collaborations with children whose needs schools frequently failed to address would provide many opportunities to understand these children's interests and goals, funds of knowledge, and successes in deep and differentiated ways.

Features of the Site   The Whittier BGC functions primarily as a source of inexpensive after-school care for low-income Latino families. Its low membership fee is routinely waived for families who cannot afford it. Although children come from throughout the city, most live in the neighborhoods immediately surrounding the club.

The club's director of programs, who had visited the Solana Beach BGC during a regional meeting, initiated the club-college partnership. At that time, the Whittier club offered few organized activities for members.[3] Volunteers from community organizations dropped in to make presentations or run activities of short duration. Basketball and flag football teams were set up in season. On most afternoons, however, members drifted between free-play options in the gym or games room, watched TV, or simply hung out with friends. A few found their way to the club's second-floor library to play games on one of the six computers, all recently donated.

Looking for a postsecondary institutional partner at Whittier College, the director met Don Bremme, who was familiar with the Fifth Dimension through his connections with Michael Cole and the LCHC, and he immediately agreed to help develop a site. In view of the pedagogical goals mentioned earlier, Bremme linked the Fifth Dimension with a required teacher education course centered on sociocultural and cultural-historical perspectives on learning. Principles from those perspectives were used to organize the course. The curriculum routinely emerged in the issues and problems raised by class members in weekly Fifth Dimension field notes.

In this context, the program director saw the Fifth Dimension as an opportunity to accomplish several goals: building the club's educational offerings; making meaningful use of the computers; and bringing college students into the club to augment its small staff. The Whittier Fifth Dimension borrowed heavily from the principles, the model, and, initially, even the resources (including games and task cards) of the LCHC–Solana Beach Fifth Dimension site. The program ran four days a week when school was in session; initially it accommodated seventy children, but it would expand to include over two hundred in subsequent years. Attendance varied widely, with an average of eleven to twelve students per session, some attending more than half the sessions, some attending only occasionally.

Inevitably, local goals and conditions soon began shaping the idioculture of this Fifth Dimension site. For example, although initially print materials were only in English, sessions were conducted in both Spanish and English from the outset, since several first-language speakers of Spanish were always to be found among the participating undergraduates.[4] Children and college students were always partnered one to one, both to accommodate the children's language preferences and to encourage the development of close, comfortable working relationships. Since the number of children who wanted to participate each day always exceeded the number of available undergraduates and computers, procedures were soon developed for taking turns: a daily sign-up and a waiting list determined whose turn it was to participate ("those who played yesterday go to the bottom of the list today"). The result was a system that visitors often described with such phrases as "easygoing but orderly" and "lively but focused." Nearly everyone commented on the warm, close relationships between the children and undergraduates.

Challenges   The challenges to running the Fifth Dimension at Whittier initially derived from the fact that only Bremme taught a course affiliated with the Fifth Dimension or used the Fifth Dimension as a practicum site. Faculty in disciplines with practicum courses either had long-standing commitments to other field-experience sites (such as the on-campus Laboratory and Demonstration School) or found the Fifth Dimension insufficiently related to their instructional goals. In addition, although both the college and the club saw numerous benefits in maintaining the Fifth Dimension, neither had sufficient "hard money" to support the program. The site's continued presence therefore depended on a single faculty member and one foundation.

Opportunities   A January 1995 grant to Whittier College from the B. C. McCabe Foundation accelerated the Whittier site's evolution. The grant—$350,000 for three and a half years—provided scholarships and work-study support for eight Whittier College undergraduates in exchange for Fifth Dimension service. Known as McCabe Scholars, this group not only partnered with children on Fifth Dimension activities but also shared responsibilities for site coordination. They managed and kept records of program attendance, wrote e-mail to the children as the Wizard, maintained supplies, and developed new activities and task cards. Present at the Fifth Dimension four days a week, the Scholars provided continuity for both the program and the children, as well as guidance for undergraduates from the affiliated course, who attended only once a week. A faculty support line in the McCabe grant was instrumental in giving Bremme the time to supervise operations and teach undergraduates on-site every Monday through Thursday.

With the McCabe grant, the Whittier Fifth Dimension was enriched, and new programs grew around it. The McCabe Scholars translated all Fifth Dimension materials into Spanish, built a "supermaze" with additional games and task cards for those who had completed the original maze, and created new transformations and titles as goals for participants. Parties at the end of each semester honoring Fifth Dimension participants (but open to all club members) became regular program features, as did a "Hall of Heroes" to recognize Fifth Dimension citizens' special contributions. All of the undergraduates began giving individual homework help daily before the Fifth Dimension activities started, and a number of them frequently stayed after the program to assist kids with school assignments, coach club sports teams, or simply chat. Later the Scholars initiated a daily post–Fifth Dimension reading program, and McCabe funds were used to take participants on field trips. The Scholars also led club members and local school groups in McCabe-funded "Days on Campus" at Whittier College, including previsit activities that promoted college as an attainable goal and participation in college courses.

Two subsequent, three-year McCabe Foundation grants increased the number of McCabe Scholars to sixteen, provided funding for upgrading hardware and software, and increased support for other activities. Beyond these grants, other college-side assets also promoted the program's sustainability: the discretion allowed Whittier faculty in selecting and scheduling courses; the clear emphasis on teaching as the primary criterion for faculty promotion; an abiding commitment to Quaker values of social action and community service; and the college's assumption of all computer maintenance and repair costs and provision of technical assistance. On the club side, the allocation of considerable space and consistent administrative cooperation supported sustainability. The club, for example, assumed the costs of program advertising, invariably scheduled other activities around the Fifth Dimension, provided Internet connectivity and photocopying facilities, and upgraded physical facilities and amenities such as air conditioning. The McCabe Foundation's commitment to assisting boys and girls clubs, and the Whittier club in particular, deserves particular notice.

AN INTERIM SUMMARY

These descriptions of the diverse adaptations of the Fifth Dimension provide some idea of the variety of circumstances surrounding the program's design, implementation, and sustainability. In addition, these descriptions raise fundamental issues concerning the Fifth Dimension, its links to universities, and its functioning in different settings:

1. The varied reactions of different community institutions to the initial prototype design

2. The different ways in which university courses need to adapt curriculum associated with their own practicum courses

3. The implications of rapidly changing technology

4. The challenge of creating sustainable collaborations in the face of constantly changing personnel on both sides of the UC Links system

5. The special conditions that support quantitative evaluations

All of these issues arose as we explored the conditions under which Fifth Dimension programs could be successfully implemented and sustained.

Whether talking about sites that remain in operation today or ones that were short-lived, we have sought to demonstrate in this review of the settings, populations, and strategies used by program implementers that there is no "one right way" to adapt the initial model. No particular community setting or higher education setting guarantees success. In each case, we have shown that a balance of challenges and opportunities affects the interplay between populations, financial and technological resources (or lack thereof), and social and institutional norms, practices, and goals.

We return in chapter 9 to the issue of strategies for creating successful systems and sustaining them. But first we need to demonstrate that this heterogeneous set of systems is worth implementing, evaluating, and sustaining.

Chapter 4

Evaluating the Model Activity Systems:
General Methodological Considerations

E valuating the Fifth Dimension is a complex challenge. In light of the goals and design of our project, our evaluation efforts have addressed these questions:

- What are the effects of Fifth Dimension participation on children's learning, and how do those effects emerge?

- What are the effects of Fifth Dimension participation on undergraduates' learning, and how do those effects emerge?

- What factors contribute to the sustainability or demise of Fifth Dimension programs?

These questions are, of course, interrelated. In general, Fifth Dimension projects are more likely to be sustained if they are enjoyed by participating children and undergraduates and enhance their learning; reciprocally, enhanced learning for children and undergraduates ultimately depends on a program's sustainability.

Two considerations have framed our thinking about these questions: the family of theoretical ideas about the sociocultural situatedness of learning that has oriented our work (chapter 2) and the prevailing standards for social science analysis (Slavin 2003). From the perspective of the former, "moments" of individual learning (microgenesis), ontogeny, and cultural history, activity, and context are all intertwined (Vygotsky 1978; Wertsch 1985). This perspective has led us to conduct diagnostic evaluations in situ—that is, in local contexts and activities—with an eye on processes of change and ecological validity (Bronfenbrenner and Morris 1998; Cole 1996). Showing development in situ, however, does not meet the criteria of "scientifically based research" represented by the tradition of experimental and quasi-experimental designs, the random assignment of children to different "treatments," and statistical analysis of group achievement as the aggregate of measures of individual achievement (Reyna 2002). We want our evaluations to speak credibly to audiences subscribing to *both* traditions. These audiences include stakeholders in both the community and the university who influence local projects' sustainability and the career paths of our professional colleagues. Consequently, our evaluation efforts have confronted theoretical and methodological tensions with a long history in the social sciences.

We worked to resolve those tensions first by honoring our intellectual foundations. We conceptualized the Fifth Dimension as an activity system in which activity is analyzed over time at multiple, intertwined, contextual levels and each level is formed and influenced by the levels above and below it. Figure 4.1 portrays the system using the "embedded circles" representation of context introduced in chapter 2.

We then attempted to carry out evaluations at multiple levels using a mixture of quantitative/experimental and qualitative/process data. In the sections that follow, we summarize our attempts to pursue this multimethod approach applied to data on outcomes for the children (chapters 5 and 6), for the college students (chapter 7), and for institutional sustainability (chapter 8) in ways that are both scientifically respectable and practically useful to implementers. In this chapter on general methodological issues, we begin with a cautionary tale about our efforts to carry out what we considered adequate evaluation of the impact of the Fifth Dimension on children's academic development. Then we summarize the expanded efforts of the entire consortium of Fifth Dimension implementers to formulate more adequate solutions to the problems we failed to deal with effectively.

WHEN THE BEST-LAID PLANS MEET A RECALCITRANT SOCIAL ECOLOGY

When Cole and his colleagues first started to use the Fifth Dimension prototype, it was logically impossible to prove that children would benefit from spending several hours a week interacting with undergraduate students around computer-based educational activities, because the Fifth Dimension was just one of several intervention activities in a single program that focused on reading instruction (LCHC 1982). Subsequently, when they began implementing several Fifth Dimensions as self-contained after-school interventions, they had to deal with the possibility that the quality and impact of the activity might vary from one implementation to the next. For example, implementations in school-like settings might have a greater impact on academic achievement than implementation in a boys and girls club.

Figure 4.1   A Bronfenbrenner-Style Picture of Levels of Context of the Fifth Dimension and Sources of Data Available at Each Level

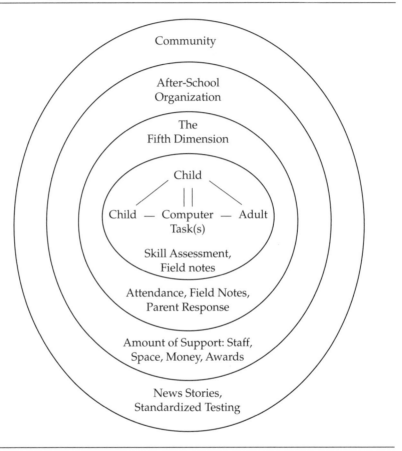

Source: Authors' compilation.

To address the issue of program evaluation, the research team proposed to carry out a full experimental study of the impact of the Fifth Dimension system in each of three institutions: a child care center, a BGC, and a library. The team's high hopes for a technically convincing evaluation appear almost shockingly naive in retrospect. In the initial grant proposal, Cole wrote:

All children participating in the program at each site will be pretested in areas of academic strengths and weaknesses and all will eventually experience the "educational treatment." But they will not all be treated at the same time. Rather, 50% of the children will participate in the specially designed activities, 50% will have the regular program of the relevant institution. At midyear, the two groups will be tested for educational gains using a mixture of pretest measures and measures specific to the treatment. Then the "no treatment" group will be allowed to participate in the program for the second half of the year. While their performance cannot be compared with a strictly comparable control group, a pseudo-control will be made up of children from the same neighborhood not participating in the program using mid-year school records. . . . Year 3 follows the same pattern as Year 2 giving us a replication of the procedures at each site.[1]

Considering only the "pure" experimental-control comparison this procedure yields us 20 experimental subjects at each site, 80 overall. Adding in the pseudo-comparison group yields 40 experimental subjects at each site. (Cole 1986, 24–25)

This presentation of the overall design plan was followed by a specification of the various measures to be administered and other information to be obtained. These tests included school-based measures of literacy and mathematics, a (then) newly designed diagnostic literacy test, report card grades, and several tests based on games and other activities that were part of the Fifth Dimension itself.

In addition to these ambitious plans to evaluate quantitatively the program effects on individual children, the team built in a means of evaluating the extent to which local staff acquired the ability to organize and run the program on their own. The two experimental periods were designed to run with the assistance of the Fifth Dimension developers until spring break, after which the local staff would be expected to take over supervision of the activity. The university course using the Fifth Dimension as a field experience would continue, and the undergraduates would still provide assistance to the children, but the Fifth Dimension project staff would withdraw to the periphery. The planners even went so far as to imagine that after the initial year of program implementation the project staff would be restricted to testing children at appropriate intervals and writing ethnographic field notes while local staff took responsibility for the conduct of the activity.

These plans were, in one respect, very forward-looking: they corresponded to the Office of Education's specifications for "proven" methods of scientifically based research (Reyna 2002). While striving to meet these evaluation goals, the planners remained alert to the debate in the educational research establishment regarding evaluation procedures based on long-standing practices in experimental psychology (for instance, random assignment of subjects to conditions and periodic testing of experimental and control groups), even in relatively controlled environments like schools. The planners were acutely aware that moving programs and evaluation outside of the school environment made the situation even more complex and contentious.

As a result of the actual conditions of *voluntary* after-school activities, the initial evaluation did not meet the criteria of either the experimental or quasi-experimental design that was promised in the grant proposal. It was not that the researchers were reluctant to follow through on their carefully conceived plans. The plans depended on three assumptions, none of which was borne out in reality. First, the plans assumed that a large pool of children wanting to participate at each site would always be available and that the limited facilities available would naturally create experimental and control groups at random in an ethical manner. Second, the plans assumed that children would participate on a regular basis. Third, they assumed that children would agree to being pretested on tasks that were not, in themselves, enjoyable. All of these assumptions proved illusory. After a year of scrambling to implement and evaluate three simultaneously running Fifth Dimension programs, Cole ruefully requested additional help from the foundation funding the project:

> Since we began the actual process of introducing the new experimental system in September [nine months earlier], I have been unable simultaneously to sustain system construction, analysis of activities within activity settings, *and* analysis of the impact of these activities on the children's academic achievement. Systems growth has been very gratifying . . . but very important evidence about the changes wrought in the children outside our activity settings is missing for this year. . . . I cannot meet my own standards for how the research should be conducted! . . . In this "year of getting started" we were supposed simultaneously to evaluate the effects of their involvement after school on the children's academic achievement. But lacking enough staff to collect these data, we need time and help to get the data collected. (Cole 1988, 1)

As reported in several subsequent publications (Cole 1996; Nicolopoulou and Cole 1993), these problems did not go away, even when we were able to obtain support for an additional staff member. We did succeed in tracking children's progress within the activity systems using as data detailed descriptions of their behavior and changes in the scores on the games they played. We were even able to compare the effects of participation in different Fifth Dimension sites on changes in children's ability to play commonly experienced educational games. But we were not successful at recruiting large numbers of children to take pretests for the purpose of evaluation. Nor did children come to the Fifth Dimension every day. Soccer practice, shortened school days, dentist appointments, and any number of alternative activities took priority from time to time, making it impossible to anticipate when a particular child would appear. And even if children did appear at the appropriate time for pretesting, they were as likely as not to refuse to take the post-test. "It's boring," or, "We already did that," the children would argue. Of course, bribery was an option, in the form of pizza or ice cream cones. But would not any improvement be suspect on these very grounds? Nor were we completely successful in getting the cooperation of the local schools in providing data for Fifth Dimension program children and the pseudo-control children, despite prior signed agreements. No ill will was intended by any of these failures. Rather, the actual social ecology of the institutions within which the project was conducted—including frequent turnover of personnel, the informality of the activity sites, and the mobility of children not only into and out of the program sites but into and out of the local schools—made a shambles of our evaluation plans.

The final report to the foundation that supported this work makes interesting reading because we were perfectly forthright about our failure to provide what we considered adequate evaluation of the program. Moreover, as reported in Nicolopoulou and Cole (1993) and Cole (1996), only one of the initial four community institutions within which we began the program wanted to continue once it became their responsibility to cover a significant part of the costs of sustaining the program. One of the four sites withdrew from participation before the program actually started. One ceased operation at midyear because it could not keep sufficient track of participating undergraduates and it feared the presence of child abusers. (This happened at a time when accusations of child abuse in day care centers were at their peak.) The remaining two institutions were perfectly content to continue so long as the university staff ran the Fifth Dimension sites. At no site did local staff take responsibility for implementing the activities.

Despite these difficulties, one institution did start to provide financial support and resources to continue the program. Not only did staff at the boys and girls club want to continue the activity and offer to pay a staff person to help run and maintain it, but the activity spread to other nearby BGCs. Enrollment in the class at the university expanded to meet both the increased desire of students to participate and the increased level of activity in the community. Moreover, when other events intervened to promote the continuation of the Fifth Dimension, we were able to keep studying the problem of how and when to evaluate such activities in professionally adequate terms (see chapter 8). With or without a technically adequate evaluation, something was working at this site to sustain and even expand the innovation.

During the late 1980s and early 1990s, the model Fifth Dimension site continued at the original BGC, the lone survivor of the initial project. (The offshoots in nearby clubs ceased operation.) As planned, the university limited its support to providing and supervising undergraduates in order to see whether a fifty-fifty division of responsibilities could sustain the activity. At the same time, new sites opened up in other locales in conjunction with efforts to use the Fifth Dimension as a tool for collaboration between American and Russian developmental psychologists: a private school in La Jolla, California, near UCSD; a community center in inner-city Chicago; an after-school program at a working-class school in suburban New Orleans (Cole 1994); and a school near the Institute of Psychology in Moscow. We continued to search, without success, for effective evaluation methods.

THE MELLON PROJECT: RETHINKING EVALUATION

The Mellon Foundation, which had mounted a program for the study of literacy and was interested in the potential of both after-school programs and technology, took an interest in the Fifth Dimension Distributed Literacy Consortium. As a result of a grant from Mellon, there was dramatic expansion in the variety of institutions and institutional partnerships supporting Fifth Dimension sites that could be studied. Another important outcome of the grant was an increase in the diversity of site structures and child populations and expanded resources to study more adequate ways to evaluate the Fifth Dimension activity system in promoting children's development, especially their basic literacy and numeracy skills.

The general character of the programs and partnerships that were put together with Mellon support is described in chapter 2. This chapter focuses on the nature of the university-community partnerships on which different forms of evaluation of program effectiveness were based. These efforts, described in chapters 5 and 6, ranged from near-canonical experimental comparisons to quasi-experimental designs of various kinds, to attempts to document changes in program participants through careful longitudinal ethnographic description at the sites and analysis of videotaped interactions.

To face the varied challenges to analysis and evaluation head-on, we formed research teams according to two principles: "site implementers" would be responsible for designing and conducting the Fifth Dimension activities at their institutions of higher education and local sites, and "evaluation teams," headed by "outsiders" and consisting of a principal investigator and several colleagues, would be responsible for evaluation, not for implementation. Each team included one or more implementers whose sites were prime centers for a specific kind of evaluation. The inclusion of this "outside" perspective constituted our hedge against the difficulties that implementers face in evaluating their own efforts.

There were three evaluation teams:

1. The "cognitive outcomes" team, headed by Richard Mayer, adopted an experimental-psychological approach to create experimental and quasi-experimental evaluations of the program's impact on the academically relevant abilities of participating children.

2. The "process evaluation" team, headed by Ray McDermott, adopted an ethnographic-anthropological perspective to document and describe the interactional work that produced children's learning and to identify in those interactions the social and cultural components that distinguished Fifth Dimension activities. Toward those ends, the process evaluation used digital video records centered on interactions around computers, participant observers' field notes, interviews with staff and others, and the field notes of participating undergraduates.

3. The "language and culture" team, headed by Luis Moll, included scholars from several disciplines. This team was initially conceived of as a "bilingual/bicultural evaluation" team because of their shared interest in the special issues of creating programs appropriate to the bilingual/bicultural populations at several of our sites. However, it soon became clear that this focus was too narrow. The presence of a large population of bilingual children did not necessarily make language use a prominent issue at a site; as discussed in chapter 3, many of the sites were sufficiently heterogeneous that there was no clear category describable by the terms "bilingual" or "bicultural." Consequently, this team, in collaboration with both the cognitive outcomes and process evaluation teams, broadened its focus and folded its evaluation activity into the activities of these two teams at sites where populations were heterogeneous and issues of variations in the choice of oral and written language were especially salient to the implementers and their community partners.

This multidimensional, multiperson, multilevel approach to evaluation, which mixed "insiders" and "outsiders" with several different kinds of disciplinary expertise, could not solve all of the problems of evaluation. But such a broad approach does represent, we believe, an intelligent response to the difficult problems of program evaluation. Moreover, we are encouraged by the fact that contemporary work on scientifically acceptable strategies for evaluating voluntary after-school programs indicates that our approach, whatever its inadequacies, did anticipate issues that would arise later, when others began to share our concern with creating successful after-school innovations. (This research is summarized in chapter 9, where we consider the lessons learned over the past decade of research, including our own.)

QUANTITATIVE STRATEGIES FOR THE COGNITIVE AND ACADEMIC EVALUATION OF CHILDREN

The effort to carry out quantitative evaluation was led by Rich Mayer, Bill Blanton, and Miriam Schustack, with cooperation from several of the participating sites. In particular, evaluation studies of cognitive outcomes were conducted at schools near Appalachian State University, the BGC in Escondido, California, the BGC near UC Santa Barbara, and La Clase Mágica near UC San Diego.

With a few exceptions, quantitative evaluation efforts were focused on the degree to which children's activities in the Fifth Dimension affected their performance on tests of academic literacy, computer knowledge, mathematical skills, and reading comprehension. To answer questions about the effectiveness of the Fifth Dimension, the quantitative evaluation group found that it was first necessary to resolve four methodological issues concerning the what, where, how, and when of the evaluation.

What to Measure

First, it was necessary to determine what to evaluate. The team wished to select dependent measures that were based on the curricular content and informal nature of the Fifth Dimension and at the same time were relevant to academic measures of literacy. Team members were well aware that the search for problem-solving transfer has a long and somewhat disappointing history in educational and cognitive psychology (Mayer and Wittrock 1996). In both laboratory studies and field studies, it is remarkably difficult to find evidence that students who learn to solve problems in one setting can transfer what they have learned to another setting (Lobato 2003). Given these past difficulties, as well as the difficulties encountered in our own early Fifth Dimension research, we accepted the assignment to evaluate the Fifth Dimension with some trepidation.

To tackle the difficulties in demonstrating problem-solving transfer in the research literature, team members invented or adapted tests to measure skills ranging from near to far transfer. *Near-transfer tests* were modeled closely on the actual activities of the children at the site. *Far-transfer tests* were taken from such sources as year-end, school-administered test scores and specially designed paper-and-pencil tasks. These tests and the results obtained from them are discussed in chapter 5. Here we focus on the different strategies suggested by the social ecology of each Fifth Dimension site for evaluating the design and data collection procedures that aim to measure cognitive change among participating children.

Where to Measure

Because they were interested in examining a range of transfer effects, team members decided to employ a range of test settings. Some of the tests were embedded within authentic Fifth Dimension activities, such as playing an educational game at the site, whereas other tests were administered in a traditional classroom setting. The goal was to determine whether skills learned in the Fifth Dimension would influence not only similar activities in the same setting but also traditional school tasks in a classroom setting.

How to Measure: The Issue of Control Groups

Determining how to create experimental and control groups in an informal field setting was perhaps the most challenging issue, and one that highlighted the independent variable. To draw causal inferences about participation, it was not enough to find that Fifth Dimension participants produced a pretest–to–post-test gain in their performance; it was also necessary to compare their performance to the performance of a comparison group that did not attend the Fifth Dimension. The Fifth Dimension sites gave rise to five methods for creating comparison groups, each suited to particular situations:

1. A group of students was invited to attend the Fifth Dimension (treatment group); for each treatment student, we identified a non-attending matched student from the same grade level, homeroom, level of English-language proficiency, and gender (comparison group).

2. A group of students was invited to participate in the Fifth Dimension (treatment group); for each treatment student, we identified one or more non-attending students who attained the same pretest score. In both methods 1 and 2, each group took a pretest and a post-test so that we could compare the pretest–to–post-test gains of the two groups.

3. Treatment and comparison students were matched based on student characteristics, as in method 1, but only a post-test was administered.

4. Treatment and comparison students were matched based on a pretest score, as in method 2, with the post-test score as the major dependent

variable. In both methods 3 and 4, we compared the post-test scores of the two groups.

5. When no non-attending comparison group was available, we compared the test performance of an experienced group of students (for example, students who had attended the Fifth Dimension at least fifteen times) and that of an inexperienced group (such as students who were tested on their first visit but who eventually attended the Fifth Dimension at least fifteen times).

When to Measure

The fourth issue—when to evaluate—was resolved in different ways at different sites. The basic criterion adopted was to test students after ten to twenty sessions in the Fifth Dimension. This fairly short treatment (compared to many other educational activities) was required by the voluntary nature of the program and the children's changing schedules. This testing focused on cognitive growth over the course of an academic year.

It is noteworthy that the quantitative evaluation research methods evolved over the course of the project through pilot testing and refinement. Several measures—including some measures of writing and recalling spoken text—were not sensitive enough to produce differences between the groups. Other measures resulted in overwhelming technical difficulties, such as the computer glitches encountered in trying to collect online data as students learned a new computer game or staff errors in administering individual tests of English-language proficiency. In addition, the team sought to replicate findings as much as possible across sites, so most measures were used at more than one site.

SITES

Each site where quantitative evaluations were undertaken presented a unique set of challenges and opportunities. In this section, we summarize those issues site by site to make clear how local social ecology, including the relationship between the investigators and the investigators' university, influences testing strategies. We begin with the sites where standard experimental designs could most easily and most closely be approximated, and then we examine less and less "pure" cases.

Circumstances at Appalachian State University enabled William Blanton and his colleagues to conduct fairly standard evaluations. In three of the four sites, children participated at their school. (The fourth site was run at ASU itself.) At these three sites, many children stayed after school for two hours and were picked up by district school buses, their parents, or car pools whether or not the Fifth Dimension was in session. Supervision was provided by after-school staff members, who monitored students doing their homework in the school cafeteria. Because the opportunity to participate in the Fifth Dimension was an attractive alternative to this homework activity, Blanton was able to recruit many more volunteers than he could accommodate. He could thus choose children at random, with the proviso that those who did not make it into the Fifth Dimension early in the year would get their turn later.

Blanton was also helped by the fact that ASU had official responsibility for helping the local schools build their technology capacities. Thus, he was well acquainted with local teachers, who helped him identify children to match to Fifth Dimension participants, and with school administrators, who provided access to test data archived by the school system.

At the University of California at Santa Barbara, Richard Mayer and Richard Duran also had extensive experience working with their local school system. Hence, they were able to administer pre- and post-tests to approximately 120 students from the school where the children attending the Fifth Dimension were a part of the student body. In addition to their own pretest scores and knowledge of student characteristics, such as age and gender, they had access to locally administered scores on language proficiency tests in Spanish and English. Such access was an important asset in this largely immigrant, Latino community.

At California State University at San Marcos, Miriam Schustack used the strategy of comparing novices and experts. At the boys and girls club where her program was conducted, there were lots of kids who wanted to participate, more than could be accommodated at any one time. To ensure that she had close control over the activities, Schustack sharply limited the number of children who could participate so that each child's progress could be carefully monitored. The children were given a pretest when they first came to the Fifth Dimension. After they had come for a prescribed number of times, they were then given a post-test. The controls put in place allowed for individual testing, with only the child and the experimenter in the room at the time.

This strategy was successful in creating a quasi-experimental design. But it also had its difficulties. Children sometimes could not be tested as soon as they became eligible, and the restriction on the number of children participating at any given time sometimes caused scuffles as children raced to gain entry or to get their names high up on the waiting list.

In addition to these three primary sites involved in cognitive evaluation, several other sites conducted other studies, but each faced some difficulties. At La Clase Mágica, Olga Vásquez faced a unique set of challenges. Because the participating children came from several schools, Vásquez and her colleagues decided to do the testing at the LCM site using tests sanctioned by the school district. Matched groups of children (attendees and non-attendees) were constructed, and testing was conducted at LCM and in the schools.

Unfortunately, not only did the settings differ, but so did the testers. Teachers did the testing at school, while trained assistants did the testing at the LCM site. Given the inconsistency in children's attendance and the difficulty of conducting individualized testing in a cramped space being used simultaneously by many other groups, the experimental and control groups could hardly be considered equivalent.

To complicate matters, the schools changed the language skills test in the second year of the project, so project staff had to use the original baseline test both at the schools and at the site. These kinds of complications did not undo the *logic* of the evaluation effort, but they certainly undermined its implementation.

A different set of challenges confronted Cole and his colleagues at their Fifth Dimension site when they sought to make quantitative evaluations of children's performance. Owing to prior problems they encountered in using pseudo-control groups created from school records (the tests used kept changing, school principals kept changing, and children moved in and out of the district), they tried to conduct evaluations using games that were a part of their Fifth Dimension. A number of basic educational games include grade norms and summary scores. Fifth Dimension staff conducted "tournaments" from time to time during the school year, awarding prizes at each grade level for children who scored well.

This effort ran into several difficulties. First, the strategy of constructing pseudo-match controls from school records was unsuccessful. Principals who had not been a party to the initial agreement balked when asked for their cooperation. Second, it went against the culture of the club to deny access to anyone who wanted to participate, so children were free to come and go as they pleased, not only on a day-to-day basis but within a day. If a swimming lesson or a basketball game was announced halfway through a Fifth Dimension session, children often dropped the Fifth Dimension activity to join the new activity. Third, the club suffered from chronic staffing problems. On one particularly memorable occasion, the post-test "tournament" was to take place during the last week of the UC San Diego quarter, but the site coordinator was called away to substitute for a staff member at a different club. Without warning, the Fifth Dimension was closed. No data could be collected. By the time the staff person returned, the UC San Diego undergraduates, having finished the academic quarter, were gone, and it was no longer possible to document properly each child's performance progress. Fourth—and this was a very important factor in documenting changes in children's performance at this and other sites—was the fact that, as happened during the initial evaluation efforts that preceded the current project, some children simply refused to take a post-test or to make any effort at performing well on it. The children eloquently explained that this sort of activity was too much like school and violated their expectation for participation in the Fifth Dimension.

THE QUANTITATIVE EVALUATION OF CHILDREN'S LEARNING

We were more successful at meeting the technical conditions of "scientifically adequate" quantitative evaluation at Fifth Dimension sites located in schools. From our account of the variation in the different forms of quantitative evaluation in our studies—from scientifically acceptable to scientifically marginal (at best)—we can see the reasons for this pattern. Schools are governmental institutions that can compel children's attendance and provide visible disincentives for failing to appear regularly or choosing not to participate in the testing regime of the programs with which they are associated. Schools operate with trained personnel who are compensated with living wages and health benefits; although schools certainly experience turnover in personnel, they have less of a problem with chronic and rapid turnover among relatively poorly trained personnel, the sort who often work for voluntary, community-based programs. Moreover, the presence of authority figures motivates children to be on their best, most school-like behavior.

All of these features work syncretically to support "scientifically valid" testing. By the same token, however, the social constraints that make such testing possible require that adults, representing governmental institutions, compel children to participate in activities that are by and large school-like in their content and social organization.[2] This kind of regime disrupts the voluntary and playful activities at the core of the Fifth Dimension, a major goal of which is to allow children to learn that learning is not inconsistent with playing. In addition, social interactions between children and undergraduates are a key component of this system. In many cases, implementing the testing would kill off the Fifth Dimension activity being studied.

QUALITATIVE STUDIES OF CHILDREN'S LEARNING

The job of the process evaluation team was to describe in detail how interactions promote learning at the Fifth Dimension sites, as well as to describe the activity-level processes that allow a learning moment to develop. The team members set about their work from an anthropological perspective, striving to view the Fifth Dimension as an unfamiliar culture to be understood and described.

Their efforts were informed by the same intellectual traditions that underlie the design of the Fifth Dimension (see chapter 2). They viewed learning as changing participation in cultural practice mediated by varying technologies. They also drew on the context-as-weaving-together metaphor described in chapter 2 to analyze how interactions at multiple levels of social organization mutually constitute each other. At a microorganizational level, they sought evidence of children's changing participation in their moment-to-moment interactions with others around computers. These data took the form of videotaped records and the field notes that undergraduates routinely wrote as requirements in Fifth Dimension–affiliated courses. At a "meso" level of organization—the level of a Fifth Dimension as a whole—they documented the social interaction that leads to learning opportunities. Participant observers' field notes, along with formal and informal interviews with staff and participants, served as main sources of data in this effort. They searched for patterns that cut across interactions at these levels, then wove them together to identify the underlying cultural and social logics that make a Fifth Dimension what it is. Their method was classic "constitutive ethnography" (Mehan 1979): an approach that viewed social structure as socially constructed from moment to moment in the everyday interactions of people and their objects.

Videotaping was instrumental for the fine-grained microlevel analysis that this approach required. Subtle but significant changes in a child's participation could unfold in as little as a few minutes in a single Fifth Dimension session as he or she assumed greater responsibility for the tasks and tools involved in playing a game. Such changes could also occur across sessions as children continued playing the same game or moved on to others entailing similar tasks and tools. Naked-eye observations could easily miss important shifts in children's participation, as well as important details of the unfolding interactions between partners that produced them. In spite of these benefits, however, the use of video technology entailed trade-offs.

Resource constraints (the budget, the availability of equipment, the experience of personnel) precluded videotaping at all sites at all times. Thus, sites for the process evaluation had to be selected in light of resource considerations. Since the process team and its video gear were located on the West Coast, data collection centered on West Coast sites. Institutional constraints entered into the picture as well. Videotaping was most easily conducted at community institutions, such as BGCs, where access was easily arranged with minimal disruption to ongoing activities and parental permission for research was granted during children's enrollment.

The process evaluation and language and culture teams could visit sites only intermittently. To set up equipment in time to videotape, team members had to arrive at the selected site early and arbitrarily choose a computer to tape. Once set in place, equipment was difficult to move, and so events of greater interest often went unrecorded. These logistics combined with the sociocultural ecology of Fifth Dimension sites to challenge our efforts to document systematically the learning trajectories of selected children. When a child chosen for videotaping that day sat down at another computer or declined to be videotaped, an important part of the record was lost. And children's attendance, being voluntary (and thus unpredictable), did not always coincide with the videotaping schedule. The videotaped record was also interrupted when games that children needed to complete were saved on computers that had become dysfunctional or had already been claimed by another child.

With experience and some minor interventions in the natural operation of sites, the researchers learned to compensate for these problems. When possible, the researchers arrived at the site early enough to talk to the site coordinator and the children present about who was going to be playing what game and where. Free passes to play a favorite game were sometimes issued as a means of enticing particular children to play specific games. In the end, these and similar strategies enabled the researchers to videotape a large number of interactions together with video scans of simultaneous developments on the computer screen. These included records of children moving from novice to expert on particular games, different children playing the same game, and data on the evolving context beyond the game.

This corpus of data was enhanced by the voluminous field notes taken by participating undergraduates at all of the sites. As Amy Olt, Michael Cole, and Scott Woodbridge (1994) have pointed out, these field notes frequently offer evidence of the dynamics of the teaching-learning processes that play an important role, it can be claimed, in bringing about cognitive change.

The process evaluation team had a major analytical conundrum to resolve: relating detailed descriptions of the interactions between children and college students in the Fifth Dimension activity system to the institutional arrangements required by the Fifth Dimension. With time, team members found that their work with program participants provided a guide to establishing that relationship. As the process evaluation team noted in its final report to the Mellon Foundation:

We found that to any example of apparent learning on tape, participants could add an account of context that would greatly expand the intelligibility and learning richness of the scene. Usually, they would embed the behavior

under analysis in a narrative biography, most often biographies of kids—
"Oh! That's so and so, and s/he is this kind of a kid"—but also biographies
of games—"Oh! That's *Dr. Brain,* which is this kind of a game"—as well as
biographies of clubs—"Oh! That's so LCM for that to happen." These biographies, emerging from the words of our informants and colleagues, shaped
our initial analytic cut on the Fifth Dimension data. Increasingly, we have
sorted our material along three biographic threads of kid, game, and site
narratives (for the use of biography as an analytic term in any account of behavior across time, see Becker 1995).

As the anthropological view yielded biographies of individual children, games, and sites that began to fill out a picture of the Fifth Dimension, the process analysis turned to look at how the context-as-weaving-
together metaphor incorporated the three biographical threads and how
the patterns embedded in each thread organized learning behavior. The
team gradually arrived at a set of themes that cut across both the levels of
individual experience and the sociocultural system. These themes linked
the interactional detail captured on videotapes and in field notes to the
Fifth Dimension activity system as a whole and represented the Fifth Dimension as a distinctive kind of social and cultural structure. Demonstrating that this structure was constituted through the everyday interactions
and practices in the Fifth Dimension, these themes were a way of describing the Fifth Dimension's contribution to children's learning and development and showing others how to reproduce the Fifth Dimension in both
principle and practice.

EVALUATION AT THE INSTITUTIONAL LEVEL

When we move from the level of assessing change in individuals to studying changes in institutions, the nature of the data changes radically. We are
now looking at a different set of appropriate indicators; in addition to continued participation by the institution, these indicators include the degree
of financial support provided by the institution, its engagement in raising
funds for the continuation of the program, its involvement in continued
staff training in running the program, and the like. Clearly, the university
and community partners differ in how they support the program, and
forms of support differ among universities and among community organizations as well.

For example, if the community partner is a school, it is likely to provide,
at a minimum, space and computer facilities (including the all-important
computer upkeep). It may or may not have teachers acting as site coordi-

nators, and it may or may not promote the Fifth Dimension activity among its students.

By contrast, if the community organization is a church or a BGC, provision of space and pay for a site coordinator can be critical issues. Even if the community organization obtains computers from any one of the many organizations that provide such equipment for after-school programs for children, maintenance of the equipment and the continued employment of a site coordinator can be daunting challenges.

Indicators of success may vary markedly between nonschool organizations. For example, at a church where the Fifth Dimension is the only after-school activity, parental support or retention of older children may be crucial indicators for evaluation. However, these evaluation criteria would be irrelevant at a BGC, which serves children of a particular age range and charges parents a fee to look after their children until they can pick them up.

Clearly, the best evaluation of the program at the institutional level depends critically on the particular goals of the collaborating institutions. What all such evaluations share in common is the simple need to assess whether the institutions still support the activity and, if so, whether assessments of the quality of the activity make it worth continuing. Since the latter assessments depend on the institutional arrangements (for example, whether those arrangements included quantitative evaluation according to predetermined criteria, such as performance on standardized tests provided by the local school, or whether evaluative efforts had to make do without control groups or with only the local staff assessment of the program), no more refined or general prescriptions for evaluation at the institutional level seem possible.

SUMMARY

Our highest ambition was to find ways to conduct diagnostic evaluations in situ—that is, in activity. To some extent this proved possible, but showing development in situ does not meet the criteria of causal social science analysis. Although in situ evaluations may be an effective tool locally, they are unlikely to be considered appropriate under contemporary views of what constitutes "real science" (Lyon 1999; Slavin 2003).

We sought to solve these problems by adopting a multi-method approach that takes advantage of the analytic potential in the broad variety of settings provided by the project. In some cases, we approached, or even met, the standard that takes the psychological experiment of individual college sophomores as the model. In other cases, we provided alternative, quasi-experimental evidence. In still others, we used a qualitative longitudinal approach that focused on interactions of a quality that, according to conclusions drawn from "proper" scientific research, should underpin the quantitative results.

In the chapters that follow, readers must reach their own conclusions about the adequacy of the evidence that the Fifth Dimension is an effective program. Some may find our strategic mixing of methods, locations, and opportunities a useful tool for thinking about their own efforts at program evaluation and analysis of psychological development. Others may argue that the work should be dismissed because we simply did not succeed in getting our local communities to adhere to scientific criteria. We hope that most readers will come to the former conclusion, but expect at least some to draw the latter.

Chapter 5

The Quantitative Effects of Fifth Dimension Participation on Children's Cognitive and Academic Skills

A Fifth Dimension site in operation creates a strong impression that good things are happening and that children are learning. Children and their undergraduate partners chatter away, problems get solved, and reading and writing abound. However, more than good impressions are needed to provide convincing evidence that the program is effective and deserving of continued support. Despite consistent claims for some time now that educational technology is a powerful tool to further learning, researchers have not found corresponding evidence that exposure to computer-based learning environments is sufficient to produce positive academic consequences (Cognition and Technology Group at Vanderbilt 1996; Cuban 1986; Mayer 1988, 1999). The evidence concerning the efficacy of after-school programs is similarly contentious (Eccles and Gootman 2002; Vandell, Pierce, and Dadisman 2005).

In undertaking to establish Fifth Dimension sites, both university and community partners have been aware of the need to determine how children's experience in a Fifth Dimension setting that emphasizes the use of computers might enhance their literacy, mathematical, and problem-solving skills. Since after-school programs are widely viewed as places that can support the goals of schooling, research teams in all of the Fifth Dimension sites have accepted the need for evaluation research to study the effects of this computer-based educational activity on children's cognition.

This chapter describes our attempts at systematic quantitative evaluation of the changes wrought by Fifth Dimension participation on the cognitive and academic skills of the child participants. Our major focus is on experimental and quasi-experimental studies that were carried out across the participating Fifth Dimension sites, but we also include some data from cases where pre- and post-test measures could be obtained but no plausible control groups could be assembled. The analyses reported here are limited to the study of effects in interactional circumstances where the children could be understood to be carrying out the tasks on their own, in contrast to the generally collaborative nature of Fifth Dimension activities. But the outcome measures in these studies do not allow us to separate out the effects of different components of the Fifth Dimension environment—for example, the impact of exposure to the games themselves versus the importance of undergraduate-child relationships as the primary causal factor involved in performance changes. Thus, although our focus is on computer-mediated learning, the outcomes documented in these studies are best attributable to the combined effects of the various aspects of the Fifth Dimension environment. We cannot claim that playing educational computer games necessarily has the same positive effects in other environments.

As discussed in chapter 4, research teams at the different Fifth Dimension sites made use of different research traditions to study the processes at work in Fifth Dimension activities, including those that allow for quantitative comparisons as well as those that emphasize qualitative specifications (Mayer et al. 1997; Schustack 1997). These different research traditions differ not only in their data collection methods but also in the rhetorical conventions they use to report findings. Descriptions of studies reported in this chapter adhere to the introduction-methods-participants-results-discussion style, a format appropriate for reporting experimental research. All of the studies described here have been published elsewhere; references to these publications are provided throughout the chapter for those readers who want fuller detail on specific studies. The goal of this chapter is not to report the specifics of each study but rather to highlight the strategies that research teams developed for conducting quantitative studies in the Fifth Dimension considered as in situ laboratories for studying cognitive development.

STUDIES WITH EXPERIMENTAL OR QUASI-EXPERIMENTAL DESIGNS

The results for quantitative studies where it proved possible to arrange for some level of experimental control can be grouped in several different ways, since each study investigated a skill or domain that is itself complex and relevant to multiple categories. The studies are grouped here by the domain or skill that was the investigative focus: computer mastery, mathematical understanding and problem-solving, and reading, writing, and grammar skills. We also describe the status of each study in terms of other dimensions of comparison, such as near versus far transfer, the amount of Fifth Dimension experience of the "treatment group" (in months or number of visits), similarity to school-based tasks, and the test-taking environment (for example, testlike versus gamelike evaluation tasks). A summary of the studies is shown in table 5.1.

The Effects of Fifth Dimension Experience on Computer Literacy

The questions guiding this set of studies were: Do children learn about computer technology from participation in the Fifth Dimension? If so, what do they learn? What facts and procedures relevant to operating computers—"computer literacy"—do children acquire? Three different approaches were used to measure computer literacy: a paper-and-pencil computer knowledge test, a test of memory for computer terminology, and a hands-on computer-use proficiency test.

The Paper-and-Pencil Computer Knowledge Test   Although children do not receive formal instruction in using computers as part of the Fifth Dimension program, computer usage is integral to their activity in the environment. The first study used a school-like test of computer literacy covering the specific kinds of computer information that children were exposed to in the environment as a measure of the computer knowledge they had gained (Schustack et al. 1994).

Children were individually given a test of forty written test items in a variety of formats (matching, fill-in, multiple-choice, true/false) that covered several areas of computer-related knowledge. The test employed photographs and diagrams and included sections on identifying computers and peripherals, mouse functions, diskette characteristics and handling, game playing, and word processing. For example, one of the multiple-choice items was:

When writing a letter to the Wizard, what do you do to save it?

a. It automatically saves when you're done.

b. Hit the Save button on the keyboard.

c. Type "save" and hit Return.

d. Pull down the "File" menu and select "Save."

The participants were twenty-six children, ages eight to eleven, at the San Marcos–Escondido site. Each participant was enrolled in the study at the time he or she first entered the Fifth Dimension. At that time, half the children were randomly assigned to the pretest. After all twenty-six had attended approximately fifteen sessions, they completed the test. Thus, half the children took the test twice, and the other half took only the post-

Table 5.1   Fifth Dimension Studies on the Cognitive and Academic Skills of Participating Children

Category	Content and Skill Evaluated	Site	Advantage from Fifth Dimension?
Computer literacy	Paper-and-pencil computer knowledge test	San Marcos–Escondido; New Orleans; Chicago	Yes, especially in writing
	Evaluation of memory for computer terminology	San Marcos–Escondido	Yes
	Hands-on computer-use proficiency merit badge	San Marcos–Escondido	Yes
Mathematical understanding and problem-solving	Understanding arithmetic word problems	Santa Barbara; North Carolina	Yes
	Puzzle tanks math strategy and problem-solving game	San Marcos–Escondido; Santa Barbara; North Carolina	Yes
	Statewide school achievement tests (math)	North Carolina	Yes
Reading, writing, and grammar skills	The following-procedures task	North Carolina	Yes
	Reading comprehension of novel game instructions	North Carolina; San Marcos–Escondido	Yes
	Statewide school achievement tests (reading)	North Carolina	Yes
	Grammar games	San Marcos–Escondido	Yes

Source: Authors' compilation.

test. Having half the children complete the pretest twice allowed for a within-children comparison. The scores of children who were given the test only after extensive experience in the Fifth Dimension were compared to the other group's pretest scores, allowing for between-children post-test comparison while controlling for possible effects of repeated administration of the same instrument.

The children who took the test twice had a mean score of 24.0 on the first administration of the test and 29.5 (out of 40) on the post-test, a gain of about 23 percent, which was statistically significant (p < .01). The improvement did not appear to be an artifact attributable to repeated administration of the same instrument, because post-test scores did not differ between children who took only the post-test and children who had also been pretested. Much of the improvement came on the portion of the test that had to do with word processing on a Macintosh—the platform on which the children did most of their letter writing. (Letter writing was a frequent activity at the San Marcos–Escondido site, with each child averaging slightly more than one letter per visit.) There was substantial and statistically significant improvement in the portion of the test that was specifically relevant to word processing: a mean of 25 percent of those items were correct at pretest compared with 79 percent correct on the post-test. On the rest of the test, improvement was less striking, with a mean of 64 percent correct at pretest compared to 73 percent correct at post-test, which was only marginally significant (p < .08). An adapted version of this test was also administered to children at the New Orleans and Chicago sites, with items modified to reflect the equipment and activities of those sites. The findings at these two sites were comparable with the findings of improved performance for those who participated in the Fifth Dimension in Escondido.

This study provides one perspective on changes in children's computer knowledge as an incidental consequence of their activity in the Fifth Dimension program. The results support our intuition that children gain basic computing knowledge from their Fifth Dimension experience. However, the study also had limitations: a paper-and-pencil test has somewhat limited validity, it is not well matched to the Fifth Dimension environment, and children were not especially eager to participate. It proved difficult to motivate children to attend to questions about computer functions that they would much rather carry out than report about in a standardized test format. Two other studies of computer knowledge were better able to utilize the activity structure of the Fifth Dimension to assess computer knowledge.

The Evaluation of Memory for Computer Terminology One of these studies embedded a traditional memory-for-terms task into a Fifth Dimension gamelike structure that children were eager to try (Schustack, Strauss, and Worden 1997). It addressed the effects of participation in the Fifth Dimension on children's knowledge of computer terminology. Previous research shows that even on tasks that do not require domain knowledge, people who are more familiar with the meanings of and relationships between technical terms show improved performance (Chi and Koeske 1983; Körkel and Schneider 1991). This experiment tested for memory of computer terminology and for Fifth Dimension noncomputer terminology as an indirect measure of domain knowledge.

The study presented children with thirty-six target words to be remembered for one second each on a computer monitor. Ten words were related to computer technology (for example, *cursor, diskette, font, undo*), ten words were related to the Fifth Dimension program (for example, *strategy, maze, journey*), ten were neutral or unrelated words (such as *parade, tomato, winter*), and six were neutral "buffer" words included at the beginning and end of the list to minimize the impact of primacy and recency effects in memory. The thirty-six target words were presented in random order for each participant. After a delay of three and a half minutes filled with an unrelated activity, a recognition task required participants to look at pairs of words (one previously presented and one new) that appeared on the computer screen and to select the one that had appeared on the study list. Each target word was paired with a nonpresented word from the same category, and the pairs were presented in random order in the recognition task.

In addition to allowing comparison between the experts and the novices, this study also used controls internal to the design. The neutral words made it possible to exclude differences in overall memory skill as an explanation for group differences—essentially, each participant served as his or her own control.

The participants were twenty-eight children, ages eight to thirteen, at the San Marcos–Escondido site. One group, termed "experts," had completed eleven to twenty-three Fifth Dimension sessions prior to testing, for an average of 15.3 sessions. The other group, termed "novices," had just signed up for the Fifth Dimension and had not yet attended any sessions.

The results proved interesting: overall correct recognition (combining all three categories of words) was almost identical for the two groups of children (67 percent correct). However, there was a highly significant interaction between the grouping variable (expert versus novice groups) and the word type. Experts showed an advantage on both computer and Fifth Dimension words and a corresponding disadvantage on the neutral words, implying that the success of these children with the domain-relevant words was due to their specific experience with those concepts rather than to any general improvement in their memory skill. The data are shown in table 5.2.

Table 5.2   Correct Recognition of Presented Words (Proportion Correct by Type)

	Computer Words	Fifth Dimension Words	Neutral Words	Overall
Novices	.61	.65	.76	.67
Experts	.70	.71	.62	.67

Source: Authors' compilation.

Children who had spent more time in the Fifth Dimension environment increased their facility with computer terminology as well as with Fifth Dimension terminology. This improvement was an indirect measure of their increased knowledge of and about these words—that is, it is evidence of transfer from the Fifth Dimension experience to more general knowledge about computers. Along with achieving significant results, we were able to implement this evaluation in a way that made it similar in tone to other Fifth Dimension activities. The memory task was presented to the children as a new game sent by the Wizard; the children seemed to enjoy it enough that many asked to play it again after they had participated.

Hands-on Computer Use: The Proficiency Merit Badge   The final study in this group of assessments measured hands-on proficiency in computer usage among children who participated in the Fifth Dimension. Although the children are not directly taught about the operation or function of computers, we hypothesized that they are indirectly learning computer technology through the usual Fifth Dimension activities, such as playing computer games and writing letters to the Wizard on the computer. This study evaluated the extent to which the Fifth Dimension helps children improve their computer skills.

This evaluation measure allowed participants as many trials as they needed to reach a preset criterion of performance. Because the design included both between-subject and within-subject comparisons, we were able to compare the performance of the same children at different points in their Fifth Dimension experience and also to compare the performance of children who had different amounts of Fifth Dimension experience when they first attempted the task. The task itself required the children to demonstrate a variety of hands-on computer proficiency skills. Structured like a scouting merit badge, the evaluation task had eight major sections, each of which had multiple subtasks:

1. Pointing out examples of specific microcomputer platforms and their components

2. Handling software media appropriately

3. Finding, launching, setting up, and successfully playing a new application requiring mouse use

4. Finding specified files in directory structures

5. Using word-processing software to write and print a letter (on the Macintosh)

6. Running a game application from a diskette, including identifying the appropriate machine to use

7. Finding specified information on a CD-based encyclopedia

8. Finding specified information on the Internet

Each of these tasks was further broken down into components with specific requirements; for example, part of the third task was to "start the game 'Brickles' on this machine; it's on the hard drive."

There were nearly one hundred components in total, each of which needed to be completed to earn the merit badge. For example, one task was to "find a Microsoft Word document called 'From the Wiz,' read the letter, shut down the computer, and turn off the electricity." To get credit for this exercise, the child had to find the file, open it, quit the application, select "Shut Down," turn off the monitor, and turn off the computer. While performing the task, the child continued working on each section until he or she had missed two consecutive questions, at which point the next section began. A child who completed all the requirements was deemed a "Computer Expert" and given a special Computer Expert ribbon to attach to his or her nametag. A list of Computer Experts who had earned the merit badge was posted on the bulletin board, and a letter was sent home to the parents describing their child's achievement. The children were very eager to earn the Computer Expert ribbon—one group of very experienced participants (who had made too many visits to meet our protocol and thus were initially excluded from participating in this study) wrote a letter of protest to the Wizard about the unfairness of not being permitted to demonstrate their mastery.

There were twenty-five children from the San Marcos–Escondido site who made at least one attempt at earning the merit badge. Not all of these children were able to perform the entire task successfully, but all completed at least one testing session. Children participating in the Fifth Dimension were eligible to do the merit badge task at several points: their first opportunity was after completing between two and four visits, and then they had another chance after twelve to fourteen visits. Children who had made more than two to four visits when the study began were tested at twelve to fourteen visits (or later). A child who had not successfully completed the task could try again repeatedly after waiting three to five additional visits between attempts.

Results showed that children whose first attempt was at two to four visits were significantly less likely to complete all the required tasks (that is, to earn the badge) on one attempt than were children who first tried after they had made more Fifth Dimension visits. In another analysis, the average number of requirements correctly completed on the first try correlated positively and significantly with the amount of Fifth Dimension experience.

The method used in this study allowed us to gather data on children's acquisition of hands-on computer skills in a manner that was consistent with the Fifth Dimension activities. The goal of becoming a Wizard's Assistant motivated the children to develop their computer skills and to have them recognized.

Computer Literacy Studies Across these three different ways of measuring computer literacy, there is solid evidence that experience in the Fifth Dimension results in specific gains in computer knowledge. Thus, part of the answer to the question of what children learn in the Fifth Dimension is that they learn facts and procedures relevant to using computers. These three studies showed that Fifth Dimension experiences had improved children's hands-on computer skills as well as their overall knowledge about computers. Although individual differences in performance were substantial, the studies also clearly showed a treatment effect.

The Effects of Fifth Dimension Experience on Mathematical Understanding and Problem-Solving

Mathematical literacy (sometimes referred to as "numeracy") is an important part of not only elementary education in general but many Fifth Dimension activities as well. Quite a few of the games, such as "Number Munchers," are mathematical in subject matter, and many others make heavy use of math in score keeping, betting, time tracking, and other quantitative aspects of game play. The studies discussed in this section have examined a variety of components of math skill, including understanding of arithmetic word problems, ability to translate formal equations into word problems and vice versa, success at mathematical problem-solving in a novel game, and overall math skill as measured by a statewide school achievement test.

Understanding Arithmetic Word Problems The first study was designed to determine whether children who had participated in the Fifth Dimension show a greater pretest–to–post-test gain in their ability to comprehend arithmetic word problems than do matched children who had not attended the Fifth Dimension (Mayer et al. 1997). A word problem comprehension test was constructed to assess children's skill in representing word problems. The test was designed to tap an academically relevant math literacy skill that shares some features of Fifth Dimension activity.

All children took a pretest at the beginning of the academic year in their regular school classroom and a post-test at the end of the year in the same classroom. The treatment children participated in at least ten sessions at the Fifth Dimension site between the pretest and the post-test, while the control group children never attended the Fifth Dimension. The tests included equivalent forms of the word problem comprehension test (WPCT) in which children had fifteen minutes to answer twelve multiple-choice questions presented in English in a three-page booklet.

The test included three types of items: word problems with instructions to select one of four equations to represent each problem; word problems with instructions to select the numbers necessary to solve each problem; and word problems with instructions to select the arithmetic operations needed to solve the problem.

A computational solution was not required for any of these problem types—it was only necessary to understand and interpret the problem. For example:

Which numbers are needed to do this problem?

Karin's home is 8 blocks from her school. School starts at 8:00. She left home at 7:42 and arrived at school at 7:54. How long did it take her to get there?

a.   8, 8:00, 7:42, 7:54

b.   8:00, 7:42, 7:54

c.   8:00, 7:54

d.   7:42, 7:54

The participants were sixteen third- and fourth-grade children who attended the Fifth Dimension program run by the University of California at Santa Barbara at least ten times (the treatment group) and sixteen non-attendees who were individually matched for grade level, English-language proficiency, schoolteacher, and gender (the comparison group). The majority of these children spoke Spanish as their primary language.

The pretest–to–post-test gain for the treatment group was significantly greater than the gain for the comparison group. This difference was also maintained on a delayed post-test administered in the fall of the following year. When the treatment group was compared to all third- and fourth-grade children at the same school matched for pretest score, the mean pretest–to–post-test gain of the treatment group was greater than the mean gain of the comparison group.

This study was replicated at an Appalachian State University site with comparable results: there were no significant differences between the mean pretest scores of the treatment group and the control group, but significant superiority of the treatment group on the post-test. The results from these two sites provide evidence that children in the Fifth Dimension learn something about formal statements and mathematical equations in the course of playing computer games and that they are able to transfer that learning to similar non-computer-related tasks.

Math Strategy and Problem-Solving in the Game "Puzzle Tanks"   The computer game "Puzzle Tanks" (Sunburst Software 1996) was introduced at three sites to measure both children's ability to transfer problem-solving strategies to new games and their mathematical problem-solving skills. At the Escondido boys and girls club, we did quantitative analyses of the children's performance at "Puzzle Tanks." In the game, children must pour juice into various-sized tanks in order to obtain a specified amount of juice, while following certain rules about filling, emptying, and measuring. The task is a version of the classic "water jar" problem studied half a century ago (see, for example, Luchins 1942). For example, in one problem players must use tanks that can hold six and five units, respectively, to get eleven units into the destination tank. The only straightforward solution involves filling one of the measuring tanks, emptying it into the destination tank, then filling the other measuring tank and adding its contents to the destination tank so that six gallons plus five gallons yields eleven gallons. The range of problems available in the game allows for the measurement of both overall success (the number of problems correctly solved) and the sophistication of the strategies employed along the way.

Some problems have multiple solutions: for example, consider the possible ways to get twelve units of juice into the destination tank using measuring tanks that can hold seven and two units, respectively. One solution is to fill the two-unit tank and then empty it into the destination tank six times. A more sophisticated strategy—in that it requires fewer moves but a greater variety of moves—is to fill the seven-unit tank, empty it into the destination tank (to get seven units), refill the seven-unit tank, use two units from that tank to fill the two-unit tank, and then empty the remaining five units from the seven-unit tank into the destination tank, which now contains the goal amount of twelve units. This game represents a problem-solving transfer test because children must apply their skills in comprehending game instructions and inventing solution strategies to a new problem situation.

There were twenty-five participating children at the Escondido site, ages eight to twelve. One group had substantial experience in the Fifth Dimension, having completed an average of 12.8 sessions prior to testing. The other group had minimal Fifth Dimension experience, having completed four or fewer sessions. Children in the two groups were of comparable age: the mean age was 10.1 for the experienced group and 10.0 for the newcomers.

The study compared the game performance of children with low versus high levels of exposure to the Fifth Dimension, controlling for age and other factors. The measurement was done in the context of children playing "Puzzle Tanks" as a new game in accordance with its task card. The task card required all participants to begin at the beginner level and to progress to higher levels as they completed problems successfully. An observer recorded each child's game activity performance move by move.

The children with greater Fifth Dimension experience were more successful at the task, as measured in several ways. The Fifth Dimension–experienced group completed more problems overall (11.8) than the inexperienced participants (9.3), a marginally significant difference. The experienced children were significantly more likely to reach championship level in the game (100 percent versus 40 percent). In comparing the quality of the solutions to the first six problems each child solved, children with experience solved the problems with significantly fewer unnecessary moves (1.3 wasted moves per problem versus 5.4 for the inexperienced children). Thus, children who had frequently attended the Fifth Dimension computer club made fewer errors and generated more sophisticated problem-solving strategies than did equivalent children who lacked this experience.

At the North Carolina site, analyses of videotapes of children playing "Puzzle Tanks" showed that student learning goes beyond mastery of problem-solving strategies (Blanton and Simmons 1998a). Children in the Fifth Dimension learn to make rapid and appropriate changes in tool use, invent new tools, and use the same tool independently and simultaneously. Children also learn to move back and forth between levels of joint activity, such as collaborating with peers and providing and receiving guidance. In a similar study conducted at the Santa Barbara site, twenty-five children who participated regularly in the Fifth Dimension performed significantly better on learning "Puzzle Tanks" as a new game than did twenty-five matched controls (Mayer, Quilici, and Moreno 1999).

These studies demonstrate that experience in the Fifth Dimension promotes the development of mathematical problem-solving skills that trans-

fer to new kinds of tasks. Even in a new game that required some procedures dissimilar to those in games they had played before, the children
with Fifth Dimension experience were more successful in mastering the
game than children lacking that exposure.

The Statewide School Achievement Tests (Math) Even though school curriculum is not directly addressed in Fifth Dimension activities, we hypothesized that there would be an effect on children's success by traditional
measures of academic performance. Such an effect would demonstrate
transfer of learning far from the walls of the Fifth Dimension. If participation in the Fifth Dimension were to yield transfer effects on standardized
measures of achievement, it would constitute convincing evidence that
the Fifth Dimension experience helps to attain the outcomes of formal education. The next study used test scores from end-of-grade math achievement tests administered by the state of North Carolina (Blanton et al.
1997). (The data from the corresponding reading test are reported in the
next block of studies dealing with reading, writing, and bilingual skills.)

Participating were fifty-two children from grades three, four, five, and
six. All children were enrolled in the same North Carolina public school.
Twenty-six of the children who had volunteered to participate in the Fifth
Dimension after-school program formed the experimental group. The
control group consisted of twenty-six children who did not attend the after-school program or participate in the Fifth Dimension. Children in the
experimental group completed between thirty and thirty-five one-hour
visits to the Fifth Dimension. Children in the control group did not participate in any organized computer activity after school, although many of
the children were engaged in a wide range of socially organized activities,
from sports to school band.

The control group and the experimental group were matched on sex
and public school classroom. The dependent measure consisted of math
post-test scores on the North Carolina End-of-Grade Tests (North Carolina
Department of Public Instruction 1994). These measures were reported as
standard scores. A pretest score was used as a covariate to control statistically for any preexisting group differences.

Results showed a significant difference between the post-test scores for
the two groups: the experimental group showed higher scores and therefore greater end-of-grade achievement in math. To assess the magnitude
of the effects, we computed a stepwise multiple regression using the math
post-test score as the dependent variable. The largest single influence on
post-test scores was the preexisting level of math skill (pretest score),
which accounted for 78 percent of the total variance in post-test scores.
However, group membership (treatment versus control) accounted for an
additional 9 percent of the variance that was significant. These results in-

dicate that involvement in the Fifth Dimension improved children's math scores on the North Carolina end-of-grade tests; this improvement can be considered evidence of far transfer.

Mathematical Understanding and Problem-Solving Studies   Taken together, these studies of mathematical understanding and problem-solving provide strong evidence that participation in the Fifth Dimension fosters children's development across a variety of mathematical skills. These tests represent a range in levels of transfer: they vary from tasks that are highly similar to Fifth Dimension activities, as with the game "Puzzle Tanks," to tasks that are very distant from those after-school activities, as in the case of school-assessed math achievement. Although the Fifth Dimension environment is not designed to provide systematic instruction in mathematics, mathematics skills are necessary to play many of the educational computer games that children learn to master. The exact source of the improvement is not clear. In addition to acquiring some content knowledge, it is possible that there is improvement in children's orientation toward academic mathematical skills, in their confidence in these skills, or in their willingness to persevere in the face of difficulties. All of these outcomes are plausibly related to the children's experiences in the Fifth Dimension activity.

The Effects of Fifth Dimension Experience on Reading, Writing, and Bilingual Skills

Learning to play Fifth Dimension games requires comprehension of linguistic material, especially in written form. Each game has a task card with a written explanation of how to set it up and play it. Moreover, many of these games cannot be played successfully without substantial amounts of reading. Thus, as they figure out and play dozens of different games, children get a great deal of practice at reading that is directed at goals, especially comprehension of instructions.

We examined children's reading comprehension and understanding of written instructions in four studies: a follow-procedures task; a reading comprehension task on novel game instructions; the North Carolina statewide school achievement tests (reading score); and a computer-based game that assessed the ability to detect and correct grammatical errors in written language (the "Grammar Games" study).

The Follow-Procedures Task   The first study examined children's ability to carry out multistep procedures: to read, comprehend, interpret, and carry out verbal instructions (Blanton and Simmons 1997). The task required children to read a list of procedures (steps) and then indicate what the outcome would be. The test consisted of two similar types of problems, with equal numbers of each type. The first test presented the child with a dot placed in one cell of an eight-by-eight grid and asked him or her to "move" within the grid. For example, one problem stated, "Start at the black dot. Go down two spaces. Go right three spaces. Where are you? Put an x in the block." This task tested whether the child was able to understand written directions, turn them into a plan of action, and then carry out that plan. The other problem type asked the child to answer questions about dates and days of the week given a traditional grid-type calendar. This task was similar to the grid problem because it required the child to understand and follow directions. This measure was a lengthened version of a procedure developed by Richard Mayer, Jennifer Dyck, and William Vilberg (1986).

Participating in the study were fifty-two third-grade children from one public school in North Carolina. The twenty-six children forming the experimental group had volunteered to participate in the Fifth Dimension portion of an after-school program. A control group comprised twenty-six children who came from the same classrooms as the experimental group but did not attend the after-school program or the Fifth Dimension. Each group had the same number of boys and girls. Children in the experimental group had made twenty to twenty-five one-hour visits to the Fifth Dimension.

The control and experimental groups were matched on sex and school classroom. Both groups received a pretest and a post-test. The main dependent variable was the score on a twenty-four-item post-test designed to measure how well children followed directions. Results showed that the post-test scores for the experimental group were significantly higher than those for the control group. These results thus indicated that the Fifth Dimension experience had enhanced the success of these children in carrying out multistep procedural directions in a task that required reading comprehension as well as the ability to translate verbal instructions into action.

Reading Comprehension of Novel Game Instructions Fifth Dimension activities place substantial demands on children to understand both the game procedures and the instructions on the task card. We hypothesized that children who participate in the Fifth Dimension learn and understand more about the procedures for playing a game than their peers with limited or no Fifth Dimension experience. We adapted a standard technique used in the measurement of reading comprehension, the Cloze completion procedure (Bormuth 1969; McKenna and Robinson 1980; Rankin and Culhane 1969; Taylor 1953, 1957), in which every nth word of a text is replaced by a blank and the participant is asked to fill in the blanks. Filling in the correct words indicates comprehension of the text—in this case, comprehending how game instructions are generally produced and how the game is played, skills that users of educational software develop with experience. If Fifth Dimension participants were more knowledgeable about how games were played and had greater experience in reading instructions, they would be more successful at the Cloze completion task on the instructions for a novel game. Two related studies were carried out, one in North Carolina and one at the Escondido site (Blanton et al. 2003).

In North Carolina, sixty-three third-, fourth-, and fifth-graders participated, divided into three groups. Twenty-one of the children in the study were regular participants in the Fifth Dimension after-school program, having attended forty or more sessions. They formed one treatment group, referred to as the "extensive participation" group. A second treatment group, referred to as the "limited participation" group, consisted of twenty-one children who had participated in the Fifth Dimension on a more limited basis (fifteen to twenty sessions). The control group consisted of twenty-one children who were not in the after-school program and had not participated in the Fifth Dimension. The children were matched by sex and classroom.

The test consisted of four paragraphs selected from the directions for "Counting on Frank," a computer game that was new to the sites. The Raygor (1977) readability estimate for the passage was the third-grade level. The technique of deleting every fifth word was used to construct the Cloze. Following an introductory paragraph that had no blanks, the text continued:

> To jump to a scene, click _____ Henry's shirt pocket. The note pad _____.
> Then, click on the "Options" tab. _____ "Options" page appears.

Entering the correct words (*on, appears,* and *the*) reflects both reading skill and knowledge of the game domain.

A task card was developed for playing "Counting on Frank" that included both the Cloze task and a goal for playing the game. Prior to playing the game, children were given the pretest Cloze. They then played "Counting on Frank" one time, followed by administration of the post-test Cloze. Their responses to the Cloze test were scored as correct only if the word provided matched the original text exactly. For this study, the independent variable was the level of time spent in the Fifth Dimension. A Cloze instrument with forty-four blanks was given as a pretest and repeated as a post-test after the game was played. Scores on this instrument provided the dependent variable. The pretest and post-test Cloze completion means for the North Carolina site are shown in table 5.3.

Table 5.3   Correct Cloze Completions (Out of Forty-Four) of North
             Carolina Participants

	Extensive Participation	Limited Participation	Control (No Participation)
Pretest	24.14	23.95	24.38
Post-test	31.05	25.67	25.86

Source: Authors' compilation.

Because there were no significant differences between the pretest scores, we could use analysis of variance on the post-test scores. Post-Cloze scores revealed that the extensive participation group was superior to each of the other two groups, which did not differ from each other. These results demonstrate that children who have spent one year or more in the Fifth Dimension learn more about procedures for playing a computer game from a brief exposure to playing that game than do their peers who have spent little or no time participating in the Fifth Dimension.

At the Escondido site, the same Cloze instrument was used. Thirty-one children were tested; of these, fourteen were new to the Fifth Dimension (they had made only one or two visits or none at all). The other group of seventeen children had made fourteen or more visits each, paralleling the North Carolina limited participation group. The results, however, were not identical to those from North Carolina. At the San Marcos–Escondido site, both groups of children (with and without Fifth Dimension experience) improved significantly between the pretest and post-test measures: the novices went from 21.29 to 24.14, and those with moderate experience went from 25.00 to 29.35. The overall improvement from pre- to post-test was the strongest effect. Group differences between children with more versus less Fifth Dimension experience were only marginally significant. We have no good explanation for this difference in results.

Statewide School Achievement Tests (Reading)   The participants described earlier in the section on the North Carolina statewide school achievement tests in math were also evaluated for their reading scores. We collected standardized reading scores on the North Carolina End-of-Grade Tests (North Carolina Department of Public Instruction 1994) for twenty-six Fifth Dimension participants (the treatment group) and twenty-six non-participating children (the control group). Results showed that, as with the statewide school achievement tests in math, preexisting differences among the children at the pretest were a significant predictor of post-test scores: the difference in pretest scores accounted for 55 percent of the variance on the reading post-test. Participation in the Fifth Dimension was also a substantial predictor, accounting for an additional 23 percent of the variance. Thus, the school achievement test scores represent a far-transfer effect from Fifth Dimension experience because the nature of the instrument as well as the environment of measurement were far removed from the play-oriented after-school setting. The finding of a significant positive effect is especially compelling because the testing was done by the school system completely independent of the Fifth Dimension program.

The "Grammar Games" Study   The purpose of the next study was to examine whether Fifth Dimension participation would show positive transfer to a written language literacy skill that was not specifically practiced in the Fifth Dimension. The study looked at children's skill at a computer game called "Grammar Games" (Davidson & Associates 1994), which requires the player to edit prose for subject-verb agreement.

Children participated in this study individually with the experimenter. The experimenter showed the child the instructions for the CD-based computer game and then told him or her how to do the task. The task itself consisted of four screens of text (which were the same for all participants) describing a trip through the rain forest. On each screen, several words were shown with boxes around them. For each of these boxed words, the child had to decide whether to change the word or leave it alone. On each screen, several of the boxed words violated the rules of subject-verb agreement in English. The child was given two passes at each screen—after the first pass, the boxes around the correct words disappeared, but the boxes remained around all the words that were still wrong.

Participating in this study were forty-four children at the Escondido site who had varying levels of Fifth Dimension experience—from no experience at all to as many as forty-three visits. They ranged in age from eight to fourteen.

Several types of analyses were done. The simplest was a t-test comparing the performance of children who had more Fifth Dimension experience with that of children who had less Fifth Dimension experience (grouped by a median split). Significantly, the more experienced children achieved higher accuracy scores. Additional analyses using multiple regression techniques showed that age was not significantly correlated with children's accuracy in performing the task, despite the wide age range of the children. The best predictor of performance was the number of sessions the child had attended at the Fifth Dimension. This powerful effect of Fifth Dimension experience appears to have overwhelmed any influence of age or school grade. The number of letters the child had written in the Fifth Dimension did not mediate this effect significantly.

These results are evidence of the Fifth Dimension's positive effects on children's literacy skills. Because the game task is different from any specific Fifth Dimension activity, there is evidence of transfer rather than practice effects. The nonsignificant effect of number of letters written supports the idea that children's literacy skills are enhanced by their participation in many Fifth Dimension activities taken together.

Reading, Writing, and Grammar Studies   These studies of reading, writing, and grammatical knowledge demonstrate that children who have had Fifth Dimension experience using a wide variety of educational computer games and software tend to develop better comprehension skills than equivalent children who have not participated in Fifth Dimension activity. These results support the premise that Fifth Dimension experience can have a positive effect on aspects of children's reading and language comprehension skills. In learning to use educational software in the Fifth Dimension and participating in intra- and intersite e-mail correspondence, children improve their skill at comprehending written language, interpreting instructions, detecting and remedying grammatical errors, and reading.

STUDIES IN WHICH ONLY PRE- AND POST-TEST COMPARISONS WERE POSSIBLE

As noted earlier, those of us assigned to conducting quantitative evaluations of the changes associated with participation in the Fifth Dimension were not always able to provide for appropriate control groups but nevertheless were able to collect simple pre- and post-testing information. Despite their shortcomings, local implementers found these data valuable even if they did not qualify for someone's meta-analysis of experimental research. Two examples illustrate the helpfulness of these quantitative comparisons in understanding the impact of participation on children despite their shortcomings from the perspective of experimental logic.

"Ace Reporter," a newsroom simulation computer game, was used at four of the sites studied by the language and culture team (San Marcos–Escondido, Whittier, and the Santa Barbara BGC and LCM) to assess changes in children's oral and written expression in circumstances related to their participation in interactions typical of the Fifth Dimension. Children engaged in a series of fact-finding activities to gain information about a news incident. They were guided through the game options by their search for answers to who, what, when, how, and why questions. When the children believed they had sufficient information, they requested an appointment with the "editor," who then quizzed the children on these questions.

A task card with beginner, good, and expert levels was constructed for the game, and children were assigned to play at one of the levels according to their age. After completing the game, each child read a text passage aloud or silently, as he or she wished. Then the child was asked to retell the passage, and the retelling was audio-recorded. Finally, prompted by questions (what, where, how, who, and when), the children wrote their own newspaper articles. Children participated in either the Spanish or English version of the game, based on their language dominance as recorded by the Language Assessment Scale.

Pretests and post-tests using the "Ace Reporter" tasks were carried out with the sixty children who were present for pretesting during the initial sessions of the school year and again in the spring during the last few site sessions. Although the children never played "Ace Reporter" during the intervening months, their performance improved markedly. Not only were they able to play the game at higher levels at the end of the year, but they provided more sophisticated oral and written renditions of the text. On the basis of information from statewide testing of children from these populations, no marked improvement in such academically relevant skills would have been expected. Consequently, community partners as well as project evaluators and implementers were pleased to note that participation in the Fifth Dimension was associated positively with literacy development.

A different lesson was learned from research on changes in the writing skills of children in New Orleans and Chicago, sites where children not only wrote a good deal in response to the task cards associated with game play but engaged in extensive correspondence with their local Wizards, often using the computer program "Print Shop" for their writing. Analyses of individual children's performance over time revealed noticeable improvement in children's composition skills, in the range of purposes for which they engaged in writing, and in their command of the mechanics of writing. To assess the extent to which these changes would be manifested on a standardized test, staff gave the children a paper-and-pencil standardized test, the Test Of Written Language (TOWL) (Hammill and Larsen 1988). In this test, children were required to demonstrate the definitions of target words by writing sentences using them, to rewrite sentences to make them more logical, and to write sentences from dictation so that their spelling and other mechanical conventions could be assessed. They were also required to write a composition from a stimulus picture. Their story was scored using the test manual for thematic maturity, complexity of words used, syntax, and spelling and mechanical conventions.

Despite the fact that children showed clear improvement in a number of attitudes, in their motivation, and in their writing skills as applied to their Fifth Dimension activities, as a group they did not show improvement on the standardized test. Gillian McNamee and her colleagues, who conducted this work, reported that while the children entered freely and energetically into writing within the context of the Fifth Dimension, they participated in the Test of Written Language very reluctantly. Research staff went out of their way to create a favorable climate for the test taking by providing ample snacks, scheduling free time before and after the testing, and allowing the children to take the test over a period of two to three days to spread the work out. The children were even allowed to take the test in small groups in which they had food and adults to encourage them if they balked at participating. But even with all of this extra effort, the children could not be cajoled, coaxed, or bribed into getting engaged in the test tasks the way they were engaged in writing in the Fifth Dimension.

These results (which mirrored those experienced at several other sites) force us to consider uncomfortable questions besides those involved in evaluating after-school activities. What does it mean when children manifest more advanced literacy skills in the idioculture of the Fifth Dimension, where they engage in writing to achieve goals they value and understand, but do not manifest these same abilities in the school-like evaluation tasks they encounter? Is this a criticism of the Fifth Dimension, or a criticism of the school?

CONCLUSIONS

Does participation in the Fifth Dimension improve students' cognitive and academic skills? Based on the evaluation studies reported in this chapter, the answer is yes. These studies demonstrate that engaging in Fifth Dimension activity helps children develop skills in many domains that are relevant to their academic success, including computer usage, mathematical understanding, language, and reading. As an aggregate of studies using a variety of methods across multiple domains of cognitive activity, the picture is consistent: children improved in their performance of reading, writing, grammar, and numeric tasks when engaged in tasks whose format and content were modeled on Fifth Dimension activities. The results are all the more compelling given that they were obtained across a large collection of measures and at several different sites.

The one negative finding appears to be an exception that proves the rule. Among the children living in the most difficult socioeconomic circumstances and participating in a program that did not fully implement the Fifth Dimension because it lacked a corps of undergraduate participants, literacy improvement seemed clear to the researchers and the staff but did not appear when the testing evoked the standardized procedures of the classroom.

In contrast with school and other types of learning situations in which children find themselves, these studies confirm that children can learn when they are invested in the goals of a task and motivated to participate in challenging activities that include an educational agenda. This project joins the ranks of the growing collection of scientifically valid evaluations of innovative educational programs aimed at improving important cognitive skills (Eccles and Gootman 2002; Vandell et al. 2005). At the same time, its results caution us to take seriously the organizational discontinuities between in-school and after-school activities and to ask which criteria of academic performance are to be privileged and why.

Since we neither compared one Fifth Dimension site with another nor systematically varied the features of any one site, these evaluation studies alone cannot pinpoint which features of the Fifth Dimension contribute most strongly to the effects we obtained. However, as we have been at pains to emphasize in earlier chapters, Fifth Dimensions are designed as idiocultures in which the ensemble of local practices, not any given tool or practice in isolation, promotes the mastery of knowledge and skills in accordance with research-based principles of learning and development. In the next chapter, we turn to descriptions of the kinds of interactions routinely encountered in Fifth Dimensions that give rise to the quantitative results we have described here.

Chapter 6

The Dynamics of Change in Children's Learning

The evaluation studies in chapter 5 provide ample evidence that participation in the Fifth Dimension has a positive impact on a range of children's academic skills, but they do not provide direct evidence about the sorts of interactions that could plausibly be linked to these desirable outcomes.[1] The purpose of this chapter is to provide such evidence, based on the research of the process evaluation team.

The process evaluation team's work answers two questions. First, was the program implemented as designed or intended in the different sites? Second, what accounts for the success of each program, as measured by the quantitative test data? The latter question is especially important to anyone interested in adopting the Fifth Dimension model and applying it to a new setting (on the role of evaluations that seek to verify the implementation of model programs, see Patton 1997, 206–7; Rossi, Freeman, and Lipsey 1999, 190–232).

Before reporting the results, we should note that the process evaluation and language and culture teams did not design their efforts to address these questions per se. Outsiders to the program who were uninvolved in its implementation, they examined the program with an anthropological eye to make sense of what was going on at the Fifth Dimension sites and what might account for the learning taking place there. Adopting an ethnographic perspective and methods, they sought to document and describe the moment-to-moment interactional work around Fifth Dimension activities, as well as the daily interactions at both the site and institutional levels interwoven with that work. Based on their analyses of those interactional patterns, they abstracted what they considered to be the defining sociocultural themes of the Fifth Dimension system. These themes, they observed, simultaneously made each Fifth Dimension a distinctive idioculture yet ensured that each encouraged learning. Their focus was on describing what a Fifth Dimension looks like in order to enable others to reproduce it in both principle and action.

The process evaluation team identified three themes from their analyses of observations, videotapes, and field notes: (1) the ways in which the relation between education and play were mediated in the interactions among participants; (2) the "entanglement" of heterogeneous players; and (3) the negotiated nature of social relations. The following sections describe those themes and present the process team's analysis of how each theme was manifested in the interactional patterns of the Fifth Dimension as an activity system and at the level of face-to-face interaction around specific tasks. Illustrative examples highlight the ways in which the Fifth Dimension's design principles come into play in children's learning.

MEDIATING PLAY AND EDUCATION

The process team noted that the Fifth Dimension was deliberately designed as a hybrid that incorporates elements of both play (computer games, recreational life) and education (school-like subject matter, quasi-formal evaluation). The Fifth Dimension is institutionally hybrid in that, as an after-school program, it occupies the space between the school day and home life. At the level of learning processes, the program's hybrid nature is manifested as the integration of play and learning. At the level of a particular game, this tension can be seen in efforts to make games both fun and skill-inducing.

The interactions in the Fifth Dimension, in other words, mediate the tension between formal and informal learning—formal in the sense that tasks are well defined and dressed up for evaluation, informal in the sense that not doing well on a task is not marked as individual failure and does not stop a child from participating. This mediational task is also, importantly, about managing the tension between knowing and not knowing. The competitive tensions that mark most classrooms can be found in the Fifth Dimension, but they are more often turned into learning moments. Instead of making an effort, as they do in school, to avoid being caught not knowing something, the children and adults participating in the Fifth Dimension seek help. We have few instances on video or in field notes of a child not engaging in a game, or not talking to an adult, for fear of failing. There is always someone to help, and the children seem to reach out for it.

Example 1: Mediating Play and Education with "Word Munchers"

The mediation of play and education can be seen vividly at the level of face-to-face interaction in the following example in which the game "Word Munchers" is being played at a boys and girls club. As in many other sessions documented in field notes and on videotape, the game itself is a resource in negotiating the balance between play and learning, incorporating as it does both school-like and play-oriented content.

"Word Munchers" challenges the player to identify a particular sound within given words displayed on a five-by-six matrix. The player must manipulate the keyboard effectively to move the muncher character up, down, left, and right to words with the target sound. In so doing, the player must also avoid a bad guy (referred to as a "troggle") who appears intermittently, moves around the board, and eliminates the player's muncher if he catches it.

The example, drawn from an undergraduate's field notes, demonstrates the qualities of Fifth Dimension interaction described here. Despite the difficulties he encounters, the child, eight-year-old Aaron, persists in participating, taking advantage of the help offered by his undergraduate partner. A division of labor emerges in which knowing and not knowing are adeptly managed, and a learning moment results. An important Fifth Dimension artifact, the task card, generates an element of tension that contributes significantly to the creation of that moment.

Adam got "Word Munchers" [from the shelf] with no problem and started to play at the first level. "Word Munchers" is divided into different categories according to vowel sounds—"e" as in tree, "ou" as in mouse. The first one was "e" as in tree. He sounded out a lot of the words correctly, but not all of them. Even when he sounded them out right, he often "munched" words that weren't in the same category. It was hard for Adam to distinguish between long and short vowel sounds, and he repeatedly stumbled over close pronunciations. An example was in the category "oo" as in book. I have to admit that the categories can be quite tricky sometimes, with only subtle differentiations between the words. For example, "hook" and "rope" both have a longish sounding "o" but they are not the same sound. This example was hard for Adam, and I think that he is just starting to get the grasp of phonics in school. Between munching the wrong words and not getting them right and his friend Charles next to him yelling at him to munch certain words, Adam was unable to finish even five levels. [It is necessary to complete five levels in the game to complete the beginner level, according to the task card.] I decided to help him out.

I told him that he had to finish five levels to complete the beginner level. By this time, Adam was frustrated and was often losing all three men on one level. "I can help you complete five levels," I told him. "I'm an expert." We switched chairs and I started to play.

Instead of just letting him watch me, though, I got him and Charlie both to verbalize the target words. This was Adam's last man and I promised him that I wouldn't let him die. I wouldn't munch on the words unless they told me to and for words they were uncertain of, I would linger on it, pronounce it a couple of times and then pronounce the category a few times. This repetition seemed to work and help Adam, especially, distinguish between long and short vowel sounds.

An example [of the difficulty in distinguishing long and short vowels] that I particularly remember was in the category "ou" as in mouse. The boys thought we had munched all the words, but we hadn't. There were a lot left, with spelling different than "ou" but with the same pronunciation. I went to the word "clown." "Clown?" I asked, and Adam said "No." "Listen again: clooowwn. And now mooouuuse. They don't have to be spelled the same to sound the same." Adam eventually accepted this idea, though reluctantly. He assumed that they had to be spelled the same, but I said the words didn't have to. They just had to sound the same. We made it to level four with me munching and the two of them giving me feedback on the words.

"Okay, now you have to finish," I told Adam. "You can make it to level five." This was the last man. I told him I'd help.

Adam did OK with prompting from both Charlie and me but he was eaten by a troggle again. Often, Adam lost control of his man and sent it careening back and forth on the maze. I warned him about troggles, but sometimes they came out of the walls and ate him. Anyway, he lost this man so I assumed it was the end of the game. He thought it was over, too, but then he realized that we had gotten a "free" man. I'm not sure how we got it, maybe because the score was so high now. Anyway, with this man Adam was able to reach level seven and complete the beginner level.

He went to Amy who told him that he needed to get the task card from me. I told him that he still needed to fill it out. He wrote down the five words—almost forgetting "a"—and then he had to distinguish between long and short vowel sounds. This was what Adam had been struggling [with] over the whole game, so I was curious to see how he'd do. There were five words. Next to them you had to identify the vowel and write next to it "long" or "short." He identified the vowels, no problem. He knew "cake" and "tree" were long, but he stumbled over a word (red) which was clearly a short "e." I helped him out by contrasting the sound to the "e" in tree. He saw the difference but after much prompting. He handed the completed task card to Amy to get his star.

Notice that the instruction going on here is different from school instruction in several ways. The undergraduate is supporting the boys in a flexible manner that is regulated by her interpretation of what they know and her knowledge of the task. Although there are three participants, the division of labor that the undergraduate negotiates allows her to pinpoint one child's biggest problem (vis-à-vis phonics): learning that in English "they don't have to be spelled the same to sound the same," a fact that is crucial, among other things, to the contrast between long and short vowel sounds.

The final segment in which the child must complete the task card provides a diagnostically relevant post-test. Aaron still has difficulties distinguishing vowel length, but we can conclude that he has received a first-rate lesson in analyzing the contrast between long and short vowels and that he has learned something about the complexities of sound-letter correspondences in English in the process. However, his understanding is still fragile and requires a good deal of further consolidation.

THE ENTANGLEMENT OF HETEROGENEOUS PLAYERS

In characterizing the Fifth Dimension as a heterogeneous system, the process team points to the high-tension but productive intertwining of diverse players, both people and institutions, that normally do not have direct relationships with one another. The Fifth Dimension is institutionally heterogeneous in bringing together community centers, schools, universities, commercial game developers, and various funding agencies; at the level of learning processes, it brings together college and university students, professors, kids, parents, other community members, and computer games; and at the level of the game, heterogeneity is manifested in the choice to use both games that can be learned quickly by newcomers and games that demand help by more knowledgeable participants.

In stressing the zone of proximal development as the key to educational development (Cole 1996; Vygotsky 1978), the heterogeneous Fifth Dimension system invites participating adults to think not so much in terms of what a teacher delivers directly to a child but in terms of what teacher and child do together that allows new ideas and new ways of proceeding to take hold, not just for the child but for the teacher's understanding of the child (and often the task) as well. In a Fifth Dimension, diverse kinds of people together build zones of proximal development and together discover their mutual relevance and growth.

Just as the Fifth Dimension relies on the enrollment of heterogeneous institutions, at the level of learning process interactions at the Fifth Dimension are based on heterogeneous social roles. The Fifth Dimension requires that the different interests of the adults and the kids be brought together through activities that fulfill the interests of each of these varied social actors. A Fifth Dimension is successful only if the children are having fun, the undergraduates are fulfilling their coursework requirements (while having fun), the community institutions are serving local families, the educational funders are satisfied that the children are learning, the software producers are making money, and the researchers are getting their work done. All of these players (with the exception, perhaps, of the software producers, who are not interactionally available) are learning new and interesting things in their interactions at the Fifth Dimension. Learning in a Fifth Dimension setting resides not so much in the progress that can be measured by a set standard so much as in a domestication of their differences sufficient for diverse players to move ahead together on joint activities.

Example 2: Heterogeneous Players and "Language Explorer"

The following example from La Clase Mágica (LCM) illustrates the ways in which heterogeneous players with multiple competencies are brought into productive relationships through the Fifth Dimension activity system. It also demonstrates how features of the Fifth Dimension's organizational structure support learning. The interaction described, as captured on videotape, unfolds across only ten minutes.[2] During that time, what begins for the child as merely an entertaining computer game is transformed into an experience in learning to read.

Several of the Fifth Dimension's theoretically informed design principles (see chapter 2) are especially prominent in the creation of this learning experience. The first is the privileging of diversity, in terms of both local goals and the local community's funds of knowledge. As described in chapter 3, the researcher's overarching goal at LCM is to promote academic success for local Mexicano children, who are frequently failed by schooling. LCM artifacts are constructed and selected in light of that goal, as exemplified in this example by the computer game the participants are playing. The game, "Language Explorer," teaches Spanish word meanings and comprehension by requiring players to match Spanish words and phrases with corresponding pictures. It is especially appropriate for the many children at the site who speak Spanish as a first language but are only just learning to read.

A second design principle salient to the learning that evolves in this example is the Fifth Dimension's intergenerational community of learners, wherein the roles of teacher and learner are reciprocally shared. The participating child, eight-year-old Sonia, is a Mexican immigrant girl whose first language is Spanish. She is learning English and just learning to read. A regular participant at LCM, Sonia has experience in working collaboratively with university students at the site, and she has played "Language Explorer" before. Sonia's partner on this occasion, Larry, is an African American graduate student whose first language is English. He is visiting the site for the first time and has very little competence in Spanish. He is also extremely nearsighted, a condition only partially corrected by his eyeglasses. Although Larry has no experience with "Language Explorer," he does have considerable experience with educational tasks of the kind presented by this game. As they play "Language Explorer," Larry's and

Sonia's respective experiences and strengths converge remarkably to create a truly collaborative learning experience.

A third design principle that emerges as significant in this example is the centrality of communicative means. For reasons outlined in chapter 2, the Fifth Dimension's design recognizes that developing diverse communication skills is intellectually beneficial for children. Following Vygotsky's precepts, this design generates recurrent occasions for the need to convert tacit, intuitive, figurative knowledge into concepts understandable by another person, as well as the need to interpret the instructions of another person. Larry and Sonia repeatedly face the need both to articulate and to clarify their points of view in the interaction, which illuminates what both are learning. Moreover, their use of both Spanish and English is absolutely critical to the learning they achieve. Such occasions for bilingual discourse are afforded by LCM's local goal and adaptation to its community context and are thus a constitutive element of its idioculture.

Finally, the opportunities for learning provided by the most prominent of the Fifth Dimension's artifacts, computers and software, are dramatically evident in this example. These artifacts, in conjunction with language, provide means through which Sonia and Larry externalize their thinking. Their actions with these artifacts make their understandings of the task mutually accessible. Because they are readily available to one another, they are open for negotiation and transformation as well as analysis.

In the transcribed dialogue, we highlight the convergence of these design principles in Sonia and Larry's interaction with "Language Explorer." In reading this dialogue, it is important to keep in mind that incorrect matches between pictures and words are indicated only after *all* of the pictures have been placed; at that point, the incorrectly placed pictures fall back down into their starting position at the bottom of the screen. If all of the pictures have been placed correctly, they stay in position and begin to wiggle "with excitement."

As the partners begin play, Sonia assumes the role of teacher. She explains and demonstrates the game to Larry, who has never played it. Sonia's understanding of what the game requires, however, is incomplete.

1 SONIA: Okay, you know how to play this?

2 LARRY: No, uh-huh. What do you do?

3 SONIA: (*Drags a picture with the cursor and swings it around the screen as she talks.*) Try to find the name, the name that says . . . hmmmm. Do we put it up here? Over here?

4 LARRY: The name that fits with the picture?

5 SONIA: (*Places the first picture in the top left space.*) Look, we've got to put it right here in the blanks, okay?

6 LARRY: Okay.

7 (*Sonia grabs a second picture and places it in a space below the first picture placed.*)

8 LARRY: What's that one? (*Points to the screen.*)

9 SONIA: Martillo. (*Grabs a third picture—showing a hammer breaking an object—and begins moving it.*) See?

10 LARRY: (*Points to the third picture as Sonia moves it.*) This is—uh?

11 SONIA: Niña. (*Places the third picture, which includes a girl below the second, completely filling the left-hand column of spaces. Grabs the fourth picture.*)

12 LARRY: What are the . . .? (*Gestures briefly toward the screen, studying it intently.*)

13 SONIA: Naranja. (*Places the fourth picture, colored orange, at the top of the next column to the right of the one just completed.*) See what I'm doing? (*Places a fifth picture below the previous one.*) And then I take them off, and then I do it again, okay?

14 LARRY: (*Studies the screen as Sonia grabs a sixth picture, which shows a bird standing on a box.*) All right. (*Gestures briefly toward the screen, then withdraws his hand as Sonia places the sixth picture.*)

15 SONIA: Pá-jaro. Pá-jaro. (*Enunciates carefully, as if teaching, while placing the sixth picture—of a bird flying above an object—below the previously placed picture to complete the second column of spaces from the left.*)

16 LARRY: Ah . . .

17 SONIA: Now let's do this. (*Grabs a seventh picture with the cursor.*)

18 LARRY: But . . . (*Leans toward the screen and points.*)

19 SONIA: You see what I'm doing? (*Moves the picture over the space at the top of the third column from the left.*)

20 LARRY: (*Glances at Sonia, then back to the screen.*) Isn't the name supposed to go with the picture?

21 SONIA: You can do it any way you want to. (*Moves the seventh picture into a space at the top of the fourth column, as if to demonstrate her point.*)

Sonia appears to recall from previous experience that the game requires the player to draw connections between words and pictures, but she seems unable to recall or formulate in words the nature of those connections. She discontinues an explanation of that connection—"Try to find the name, the name that says . . ." (line 3)—and focuses instead on the notion that the pictures need to be placed in the "blanks" (line 5). Demonstrating her perspective on the task, Sonia begins putting pictures in "blanks" without attending to the correspondence of the pictures and words. She proceeds systematically from top to bottom, filling in the first column of spaces on the left side of the screen and then the second column.

Larry recognizes immediately that the game intends the player to match each picture with the descriptor (or "name") that it illustrates. He tentatively suggests this to Sonia (line 4), as if to help her complete her discontinued thought (line 3). However, once Sonia begins choosing pictures and dragging them to fill the blanks, Larry's questions (lines 8, 10) focus on the pictures that Sonia has chosen rather than on the words under the spaces. These questions encourage Sonia to name elements in the pictures—martillo (hammer), niña (girl), pajaro (bird), (lines 9, 11, 15)—rather than attend to the words below the spaces or to word-picture relationships. Thus, for example, the picture that Sonia identifies as "martillo," which depicts a hammer shattering an object, is intended by the game to match with the word "romper" (to break).

Although the session is off to a bumpy start in these opening forty-two seconds, the interactional practices of the Fifth Dimension, in combination with the use of the computer as a tool, have already given Larry an opportunity to diagnose Sonia's operational understanding of the task. Moreover, Sonia's perspective on the game becomes clearer as the session continues.

22 SONIA: Look. (*Drags a picture to a location between two blanks; it fails to stay in that location and falls to the bottom of the screen.*)

23 LARRY: Oh, okay.

24 SONIA: See, look. Look what happens. (*Again, drags a picture to a location between two blanks; it drops to the bottom of the screen.*)

25 LARRY: So it doesn't go there.

26 SONIA: Yeah, it goes . . . yeah. So we put it right here. (*Places a picture and grabs another.*) . . . 'n' see, uh, that one goes over here. (*Places the picture, then grabs another with the cursor and moves it toward the last empty blank.*)

27 LARRY: And that fits there.

28 SONIA: Get up here. Get up here! (*She directs these remarks to the computer. She has trouble getting the final picture to the desired space, and then places it.*) There. (*All but one of the pictures falls to the bottom of the screen, indicating incorrect matches with the words under the spaces.*)

29 LARRY: Whoa.

30 SONIA: You see? *Ma-a-gic.*

31 (*Larry chuckles.*)

32 SONIA: You see? *Ma-a-gic.*

33 LARRY: Magic, yeah, it's pretty good.

Sonia's construction of the task is clearly focused on one dimension of the challenge: moving pictures to parts of the screen (the spaces) where they will "stay." In addition, she seems at this point to interpret the misplaced pictures dropping to the bottom of the screen as an example of an entertaining special effect rather than as an indication of an incorrect match between the picture and the word.

A turning point in Sonia's understanding occurs a moment later when Larry poses a question about the meaning of the Spanish words "detras de" under one of the spaces (line 36).

34 LARRY: So what does it . . . what are you supposed to do . . . I still don't . . . I mean, like you put the pictures in the places, but . . .

35 SONIA: . . . and then (*gestures toward the screen*), then, some stay, okay?

36 LARRY: Some stay, okay.

37 SONIA: You don't get my . . . you don't get me, huh? (*Moves a picture into a space.*) I'm a Spanish speaker and an English speaker. You don't even know . . .

38 LARRY: (*Breaking in on Sonia's talk and pointing to the space labeled "detras de," just below the space in which Sonia has placed the previous picture.*) "detras de" means . . . ?

39 SONIA: What? What did you say?

40 LARRY: "Detras de," that means . . . ?

41 SONIA: "Detras" (*as if correcting his pronunciation*).

42 LARRY: "Detras" (*repeating Sonia's pronunciation*).

43 SONIA: This. (*Grabs a picture and moves it toward the correct "detras de" blank.*)

44 LARRY: Behind, right?

45 SONIA: Yep, behind. (*Places the picture.*) Behind, behind. Now what . . . (*moves cursor over a blank labeled "en," which she has already filled with an incorrect picture*) . . . tell me this one.

46 LARRY: That one?

47 SONIA: Yeah, but tell me what is it.

48 LARRY: It means "on."

49 SONIA: "On."

50 LARRY: (*uncertain*) Right?

51 SONIA: Ooooohhh, I don't know. But this, but this is? (*Points to another empty space.*)

52 LARRY: This one?

53 SONIA: Uh-huh.

54 LARRY: Alrededor.

55 SONIA: La . . . que? (*She seems not to understand Larry's pronunciation.*)

56 LARRY: Al . . . rededor. This (*points to screen*) means "around"? Right?

57 SONIA: (*Has picked up another picture as Larry talks. She moves it toward the "al rededor" space.*) Yeah.

58 LARRY: Yeah.

59 SONIA: (*Moving the picture she has chosen toward the "al rededor" space and placing it.*) This is . . . there? Oh, uh, I got to take this out. (*Removes the picture she has just placed.*) Oh, good, I took it out. Like this. (*Grabs the picture that matches with the "al rededor" space.*) I'm going to put that one there. (*Moves the correct picture into the space.*)

60 LARRY: Oh, right. Okay, I get it.

Larry's question about the meaning of "detras de" (lines 36, 38) functions to reorient Sonia's actions. At this point, Sonia has in fact already placed the picture the game intends to be matched with "detras de." However, she selects from among the five as-yet-unplaced pictures one that could reasonably be interpreted as illustrating "detras de." (The chosen picture includes someone standing behind an object.) What is more, Sonia's entire sense of the object of the game now appears to be transformed. Rather than simply placing pictures in spaces that remain empty, moving top to bottom and left to right, she now asks Larry to tell her the words that are under the pictures, despite his problematic pronunciation (lines 43, 45, 49). Then she searches purposefully for pictures that seem to match those words. What was earlier an entertaining activity of moving pictures around the screen and watching the "magical" result of falling pictures has become a different task for Sonia, one that entails determining the meanings of text and the representations of those meanings in pictures. This transformation is especially evident in line 57. There Sonia exchanges one picture for a second that seems to better illustrate "al rededor." (As it happens, this is the picture the game counts as the correct match with "al rededor.")

Larry and Sonia have now worked out a participation structure in which Larry provides help by reading words aloud only insofar as it seems needed by Sonia, while she helps him with his Spanish pronunciation and meanings. As he reads they jointly make the decision about which pictures match the words.

Their conjoint effort does not lead to immediate success, but when, a few moments later, all the pictures have been placed and seven fall to the bottom of the screen, Sonia no longer interprets this effect as "magic." Instead, she begins immediately to replace the incorrectly placed pictures.

The changes in Sonia's participation with Larry and "Language Explorer" are evident as they replace the last few incorrectly placed pictures and successfully complete the matching task:

61 SONIA: Come on, tell me what that one says there. (*Points to the screen.*)

62 LARRY: That one? Is . . . this one. (*Points to the screen.*) No, that's . . . no, this one.

63 SONIA: Okay. Whatever you say. (*Moves a picture into the space.*) Is this your first time being here?

64 LARRY: Yeah, I'm new.

65 SONIA: You're new? (*Places the final picture. Three pictures drop down, indicating incorrect matches. Sonia immediately begins to place these.*) Let's try, no, we already tried, let's try this one (*grabs a picture*), because . . .

66 LARRY: Oh, "romper."

67 SONIA: (*Moves the picture into the "romper" space.*) This one, oh, that makes sense.

68 SONIA: Broke. (*Laughs.*) This one's a hard one, it's a hard one.

69 LARRY: Yeah.

70 SONIA: Now this one?

71 LARRY: "En" . . .

72 SONIA: "En!" (*Grabs the correct picture.*) "En," let's try that one. (*Moves the picture into the "en" space.*)

73 LARRY: Yeah, that one. 'Cause you're inside?

74 SONIA: Yeah. "En." (*Grabs the last picture and moves it toward the last unfilled space.*)

75 LARRY: Yeah. And "delante."

76 SONIA: (*Places the last picture correctly in the "delante" space.*)

77 BOTH: (*Simultaneously*) Cool!

In this final set of turns, Larry and Sonia are working closely together to determine the remaining small number of entries, and in the final line they are perfectly coordinated as they proclaim in unison: "Cool!" Over the course of only a few minutes during one Fifth Dimension session, Sonia has acquired some literacy skills, established a relationship of equality with an older male peer, and transformed her understanding of how to play a game. She has also inferred the helping principle of the Fifth Dimension. Larry has learned some Spanish, learned to play a bilingual game, and learned to collaborate effectively, in one context, with an eight-year-old girl.

All of this learning has happened inside of a relationship that leaves Sonia "in the driver's seat": she takes the lead in making the game moves, maintains ownership of what she is learning, and stays mindful of being Larry's teacher. Larry allows Sonia to be his guide as she introduces him to the game and, indirectly, to how kids and adults interact in this setting (although he had been coached in his role beforehand by university mentors). Larry does not confront Sonia about her incomplete understanding of the game; he never tells her that one of her picture placements is "wrong" or that she will not succeed if she continues her line of action. He is respectful of her line of thought and trusts the outcome of whatever path their work will take. He is at home with her confidence and certainty.

When Larry asks the question that ultimately shifts the course of Sonia's activity, he does so in a way that is as unintrusive as possible and does not undermine her being in charge: "'Detras' de means . . . ?" He phrases his question as a declarative sentence whose blank she can fill in with knowledge he knows she possesses. Sonia focuses on Larry's pronunciation while she reorients to the need to include the word meaning of the visual clue on the screen to complete the game successfully. Larry allows Sonia to own her learning, an experience that stands in sharp contrast to how teacher-student interactions in school are usually played out.

NEGOTIATED SOCIAL RELATIONS

The process team gleaned a third theme from the Fifth Dimension data—the theme of ambiguous or malleable power relations between the diverse players. What counts as valuable knowledge and legitimate participation is available for negotiation by every type of participant, and there is no uniformly enforced system for hierarchically ordering the differences inherent in the Fifth Dimension activities. At the institutional level, the Fifth Dimension imperfectly but partially reproduces the social agendas of formal education and the norms of the local community, as well as those of recreational mass media. At the level of learning process, this theme is manifested in the day-to-day normative practices of the Fifth Dimension, which are continuously negotiated between children and adults and between children and games. At the level of games, this form of activity allows choices between a variety of different games as well as games with a variety of players. Complexity is sought not just at the level of game skill but at the level of forging new human relations as well.

Constantly negotiated definitions of the Fifth Dimension at the institutional level are mirrored by developments in the daily round of the activities. Upon entering the activity, it is not easy to know immediately who is in charge. As noted earlier, in Fifth Dimensions an imaginary figurehead is ultimately responsible for setting responsibilities, although humans are allowed to help in the daily routine. (Some humans are thought to speak for the figurehead, although no one has ever been caught doing so.) The undergraduates are the line workers of the system and do not command much authority, so children can often be found teaching them as much as they teach the children. Fifth Dimension organizers are responsible for a little more management, but their goal is to direct the children to other modes of guidance, for example, the maze, the figurehead, or the undergraduate. In such a system, everyone's role is constantly up for definition and redefinition, and everyone is responsible for organizing learning.

Participants in the Fifth Dimension are drawing from multiple cultural codes and have diverse institutional responsibilities. Consequently, interactions in the Fifth Dimension reflect a certain indeterminate quality in its social agenda and the dominant discourse of the moment. Participants push and pull for their interests, but the norm is that most people (or at least all classes of people) manage to have a voice in the Fifth Dimension—children, undergraduates, researchers, parents, and community members. Anyone can "talk back" to anyone else, and at least for the children, participation in the Fifth Dimension maintains a voluntary feel. This allows everyone to express themselves in terms of the workings of the Fifth Dimension system, that is, in terms of the relations that the Fifth Dimension allows them. Responsibility for gaining mastery is distributed over game environments, and sharing that mastery is distributed across the various persons who inhabit the Fifth Dimension.

Example 3: Negotiated Social Relations in Roles: "Island Survivors"

The definition and redefinition of roles is particularly clear in the example that follows, drawn from field notes written by two UC San Diego undergraduates, Daisy and Julie, who participated at a boys and girls club. The roles of teacher and learner are flexibly negotiated across the sessions covered in these notes by undergraduates and participating children alike. Daisy's field notes cover eight separate interactions over a one-month period during which she worked with a particular child, Vivian. Julie's notes are from one interaction with Vivian shortly after Vivian had mastered the game she had been playing with Daisy.

In the notes we see ten-year-old Vivian develop from novice to master in playing "Island Survivors." Collaboration with another child, encouraged by the Fifth Dimension's underlying principles and emergent local culture, assists Vivian and Daisy on their path. In addition, the design and use of an important Fifth Dimension artifact, the task card, plays a critical role in that development in conjunction with the software itself.

"Island Survivors" is an ecology game that was intended to be part of the *Voyage of the Mimi* television project designed for educational purposes. The players are challenged to support an ecosystem by maintaining the life of all animal, plant, and human inhabitants of the island over a period of many months. The core concept of the game is ecological balance, which also includes the construction and interaction of food chains. Activities on the island include collecting firewood, building shelter for protection, and obtaining food by hunting, gathering, and fishing. The human inhabitants, who are stranded for a year, can also suffer setbacks from sickness. Feedback on population size is given by graphs illustrating the status of each species for each month of the survival period.

The basic cognitive challenges of the game include estimating and taking account of life cycles, food supply, weather, and health conditions. The players must be able to interpret the graphs, work within time limits, and appreciate the factors that interact in the natural ecological system. It is also important that the player be able to manipulate the keyboard effectively to move one of the survivors about the island to gather food. This aspect of the game is arcadelike: it requires different degrees of practice and dexterity. If these activities are not carefully mastered and coordinated, the human inhabitants risk starvation.

The "Island Survivors" task card requires that the children play three versions of a game that have been partially structured and saved on a disk. Each game has been constructed to confront children with a graded series of ecological challenges to ensure that they encounter interesting problems that test and expand their conceptual grasp of the underlying principles.[3]

In the initial session, Vivian has no experience with "Island Survivors." To accommodate all the children who want to play in the Fifth Dimension that day, she is paired with Anthony, who is already playing and has experience with the game. Daisy, their undergraduate partner, writes in her field notes:

I asked him if he would mind explaining this game to Vivian since she had never played before. . . . While at first he didn't say anything, as soon as Vivian sat down next to him and began watching, Anthony looked at her and began explaining everything!!! It was totally cool watching them. Anthony explained the concept of the game, that they had to survive by hunting, fishing, etc., and as he played, he carefully went over his moves. Before long, they began playing together, Vivian helping Anthony catch food. Vivian would say, "There's one" (referring to a rabbit), and Anthony would answer back, "I see it!" As soon as he would catch it, they would both say things like, "All right!"

Anthony was totally comfortable with us by now, and began taking time out to explain certain strategies he had picked up on. Because he was on the "good" level, he had mastered the tough times. He told Vivian and myself never to let our food level reach past the half way marker or else we would lose our food. [This is due to spoilage.] As they kept playing, Vivian would ask him questions like, "Are all the food levels the same in every game?", and Anthony would answer all her questions. At one point Vivian explained to me that she was worried she wouldn't do so well because she wasn't a fast typist. Before I could reassure her that being a fast typist wasn't necessary to win these games, Anthony turned to her and said, "You don't have to be fast. Only when you are fishing you have to push the keys fast, but that's easy."

Several points about Vivian's initial encounter with "Island Survivors" are noteworthy. First and most obviously, her partner, Anthony, is experienced in the norms and operating principles of the Fifth Dimension culture and readily moves into the role of "teacher." Anthony "carefully went over his moves" as he played, making his thinking available to Vivian and Daisy not only through his operations with the game but in his verbal descriptions as well. Second, although Vivian is a newcomer to the game, she is more than a passive observer. When Anthony and Vivian begin to interact, they immediately establish a division of labor that is not totally lopsided (as it is, for example, when the "expert" teaches and the "novice" observes.) Rather, Vivian makes both cognitive contributions (pointing to a rabbit) and motivational contributions ("All right!"). Their contributions are asymmetrical, to be sure. But the nature of this asymmetry bespeaks the spontaneous formation of a zone of proximal development, not unlike the collaborative structure Larry and Sonia develop in the earlier example.

Third, Vivian's learning is obviously situated in play activity. Her questions and Anthony's responses are occasioned by events that arise on the screen as they play the game. Vivian learns physical actions and acquires knowledge essential for game success in the contexts of their use rather than as "an ecology lesson" or as preparation for engaging in a different task at another time, as is the case in much of formal schooling. Nonetheless, she is learning crucial information about the artifacts on the screen and the keyboard, as well as game strategies and some initial concepts relevant to resource management in an ecosystem.

Vivian's next encounter with "Island Survivors" occurs two weeks later. Daisy's field notes reveal that Vivian is able to make use of her experiences from the previous session, but she is a long way from mastery:

We read the instructions to "Island Survivors," and then went ahead to play the game. Vivian basically knew how to play, but had an extremely difficult time using the space bar instead of the down arrow key, and using the IJKM keys to move in different directions. . . . When we went hunting, the notice came that we had caught too much food. She automatically told me that we should keep the level of food at the half-way mark and no more. After starving because of problems using the keyboard, Vivian suggested we read the hints in the hints book to see what we should do next time.[4] We read them, but basically couldn't use a lot of the suggestions since they were geared to the "good" and "expert" levels. I suggested we write a list of things we should do, or avoid, for guidance when we play again. On the list, Vivian wrote down, "Go fishing and find plants a lot, do not get too much food. It spoils. Pick one person to build the shelter, the best person to build is the Wizard."

Two days later Vivian begins her second day on the beginner level of "Island Survivors." Daisy writes:

Well, we grabbed her folder and headed to an empty computer to play "Island Survivors." We had starved to death on Tuesday, so we had to start at the beginner level again. Vivian is very goal-oriented, for she told me as we were booting the game up that she wants to race through the beginner level so that she can become an expert at this game. I said, "All right! I like the way you think! Let's tackle this game and beat it!" Vivian said, "Yeah," and began waving her arm and yelling. "GO! GO! GO!" We were definitely psyched up!

When we went fishing, Vivian began catching all the fish, but halfway through, she said, "That's all." I asked her why she was stopping and she said that she didn't want the food level to pass the halfway mark, so she was going to throw back everything else from then on. I was glad she remembered that, and felt sure we were going to pass the beginner level. One time our food level got low, so Vivian said we'd better go fishing. To her, fishing is the easiest way to catch food, and when the level would get too high, she'd just throw everything back. It got to be sort of a habit where she would go fishing, catch all that she could, then stop at the halfway point, throwing things back, then catching some, then throwing things back, then catching some. . . . It was like, hit the space bar twice, return key once, space bar twice, return key once. . . . She wouldn't even look at the screen sometimes. Finally we made it through November, and were past the beginner level. It was time to fill out her task card, and she answered the questions herself, without any help from me. When it asked her to write what you need to do to survive, she wrote, "go fishing." When it asked her for hints, she explained about keeping the food at the midmark. She was on the ball!!

Over the course of the next few days, Vivian moves on to the good level of the game. Game and task card design now come into play in expanding Vivian's practice with "Island Survivors," opening up new zones of possibility for her learning. Up to this point, Vivian has avoided the act of hunting and the need to develop the requisite skills. But now her successes make such learning necessary.

The good level is set up in such a way that the fish population has been decimated by a mischievous character. Now Vivian's strategy of fishing to survive, which was the easiest way to deal with the challenges of the beginner level, is no longer adequate. Thus, the new goals of going hunting and gathering arise naturally for her; she is forced to gather plants and animals for food. Because the animals move every few seconds when you are hunting and you have to collect a lot of plants to survive, Vivian must now confront her limited keyboard dexterity and develop the new behavioral forms needed to achieve her new goals (a developmental pattern studied extensively by Saxe 1994). As Vivian hunts, she exhibits the classical Vygotskian phenomenon of speaking to herself aloud when she encounters difficulties: she says the name of each key aloud to increase her motor control. Unfortunately, she panics and is unsuccessful in her attempts, so the humans starve.

During the next Fifth Dimension session, Vivian continues on the good level of "Island Survivors." There is evidence in the field notes that she finally begins to master the keyboard, and she completes this level. (We do not present the notes here in order to expedite our presentation.)

The first field note about Vivian attempting the expert level is of particular interest because it shows that Vivian, who now must create her own island, has acquired a conceptual understanding of how the food chain works. Daisy describes their work:

We started the next game, and this time it had us pick our own land animals and pond species for the island. Vivian didn't want to choose too quickly, so she said we should read up on all the animals first. When it came down to deciding the ones we wanted to keep, Vivian picked the turkey and rabbit. She decided that the deer were too big and were too much food, and that the turkey and rabbit were the best choices since they were edible and the right size. Then she chose leaves and blueberries because humans could eat them as well as the turkeys and rabbits. I didn't help her at all in deciding, so it was neat to see her reading the facts and deciding which animals and plants would be most beneficial to the survival of the humans. Then it was time to pick our pond species. This was a tougher decision for Vivian. She couldn't decide on what to choose because most of the species didn't seem to be good food for humans. Whereas before she chose her animals mainly on the basis that they would feed her survivors, now she had all these species that weren't meant for eating. She wanted to fish since she likes to go fishing, so she picked the bass and crayfish. She was kind of worried though, because the bass, in order to survive, eat the crayfish. She didn't want her fish population to go down because the bass were eating them up. She then picked two types of plants that the bass also ate, hoping they would eat that instead of her fish . . . pretty clever eh?

In the next session, Daisy and Vivian play "Island Survivors" again. Daisy comments that the game is "more like a ritual than playing a game. Vivian knew exactly what to do, first gather firewood, then build a shelter, and then go fishing to build up our supply of food." At this point in their interactions, Daisy and Vivian are less directed at the game and more directed at getting to know one another. Daisy writes, "For the most part, I just sat back, watched her, and enjoyed talking to her. In fact the only thing I said which related to the game after that was, 'hit return.' Because Vivian was always talking to me, she would forget to pay attention to what was happening, and the screen would never change."

The use of the word "ritual" indicates that the task has become routine and interest has shifted to interpersonal interaction involving content beyond the game. At the same time, it is evidence that Vivian has learned the patterns and implicit values of "Island Survivors" so well that she can, so to speak, run on automatic pilot.

As part of the task for achieving the expert level of the game, the player is supposed to write an entry for the "Hints and Strategies Folder." This is the same folder Vivian used as a tool when she experienced difficulty in her first attempts to play "Island Survivors." Daisy writes: "The task card told us we had to write to the hints box, and Vivian wanted to write a good one since the others in the book (for 'Island Survivors') weren't that helpful to her."

> HINTS TO ISLAND SURVIVORS, by VIVIAN. Don't get a lot of food— make sure the level is at or below the middle. Go fishing. While the fish aren't in danger it is the quickest and fastest way to catch food. Get a deer because it gives enough food (if you are desperate for food). Don't look at how much time you have left because it makes you NERVOUS! IF THE WIZARD DOESN'T CHANGE THE LENGTH OF TIME YOU NEED TO SURVIVE, WRITE A LETTER AND COMPLAIN.

Vivian's writing provides an opportunity for her to formulate and reflect on the understanding she has developed, following the principle articulated by Vygotsky that "the thought is completed in the word."

In the final field note, Julie, another undergraduate, asks Vivian to help explain "Island Survivors" to another child, Michael, with whom she is playing. Neither she nor Michael has ever played before. Julie writes:

> I elicited Vivian who was on expert level on this game to come explain the object and procedures of the game. Vivian was most helpful. She took on the role of a teacher and led us step by step through the procedures of the game. She started by having us boot the game. Michael listened diligently to what she said and followed her procedures. When the computer asked who should do different chores, Vivian had a special form. She said that the Wizard should build shelter because he is really good at it. Ann should go fishing and Joe should hunt. I asked her if the Wizard was better at building the shelter than the others and she answered, "yes, because he is the Wizard."

She said you need to find the winning combination when giving out jobs. She made it seem like some of the survivors were better at doing certain things than others.

Michael followed Vivian's instructions precisely. Vivian led us through the game step by step. First she showed us how to fish. She said that to pick up the fish to press return and to let them go press space bar. Vivian included not to catch too many fish because they will rot. She said keep your food at about half full. Michael lived by this rule throughout the rest of the game.

In hunting, Vivian commented that you must pick up the black dots. I asked her to be more explicit. How do you pick them up? She said that first you must put them in your box and then press return. She added that we must watch the graphs for the increase and decrease of certain species and keep this in account when we hunt or fish. Vivian made a wonderful teacher. She explained everything in such a manner that made learning fascinating. Both Michael and I listened attentively and questioned her on the things we did not understand.

The opportunity to teach her peers, encouraged by the Fifth Dimension's underlying theoretical principles, accomplishes several goals. First, it provides Vivian with another occasion for realizing her thoughts in words. Second, it marks a transformation in Vivian's identity that both affirms the value of her learning in relation to the Fifth Dimension community and provides motivation for further learning and development (Lave and Wenger 1991). Vivian has now come full circle from being a novice at "Island Survivors" to a publicly recognized expert. And finally, it provides us, as analysts, with firm evidence that she has mastered the conceptual and motor skills demanded by the game.

SUMMARY

The case study data reflecting the themes and the empirical data in chapter 5 point to two important findings:

1. At both the institutional level and the level of face-to-face interaction, the theoretically informed design principles of the Fifth Dimension model were routinely visible, warranting the conclusion that the model was indeed implemented.

2. The instantiation of those intellectual principles in daily Fifth Dimension processes plausibly accounts for the instances of children's learning that the process team observed and thus might explain the results obtained by the cognitive evaluation team.

In the case study data presented, it is important to note that each example could also be used to illustrate the other two themes. Adam, Sonia, and Vivian all have commitments to the play aspects of the games they are playing, and each vignette we have offered could be used to show how others in the Fifth Dimension (usually but not always adults) push a competing educational aspect and turn it into what the kids are doing while having fun. Similarly, Adam, Sonia, and Vivian all have partial knowledge of the games and of the social relations around them, so their vignettes could be used to show how they and various participants, also with partial knowledge of what is going on, negotiate to arrive at mutual cooperation on a task that requires whatever knowledge each of them can bring. Finally, Adam, Sonia, and Vivian are each potentially in an authority struggle in the sense that each wants to do things that an adult would like to redirect; in each example, child and adult carve out mutually well-defined, flexible role relationships as the roles of teacher and learner are negotiated and as both play and learning take place.

Many other examples could have been used to illustrate each of the three themes, and most examples could be used to address each theme. However, to do so would be to ask readers to work their way through the examples in something akin to real time, and that is simply impractical. This store of examples gives us some assurance that the themes we have presented really do capture the principles of the Fifth Dimension system in operation. They also give us reason to believe that the Fifth Dimension system could occupy a significant niche in the effort to promote the literacy of American children, a niche that could be filled in many neighborhoods where children have come to see learning in school as a negative experience.

In summarizing their findings, the process team came to three conclusions. First, the Fifth Dimension is a good place for all participants to get to know each other and to learn important things. Second, the Fifth Dimension fills what had been a vacuum: a cultural niche that enables productive learning. And finally, the theory of learning underlying the Fifth Dimension can be used to replicate not just Fifth Dimensions but other community-based learning systems.

Readers must, of course, decide for themselves whether the evidence from this chapter and the previous chapter warrants such conclusions. Each kind of evidence, taken by itself, is open to legitimate criticism. We believe, however, that the evidence is persuasive enough to place the burden on those who doubt the conclusions to which we have been drawn. Indeed, with these three conclusions in hand, it seems clear that we need to roll up our sleeves and build more such institutions of learning.

Chapter 7

The Effects of Fifth Dimension Participation on Undergraduates

Chapters 5 and 6 demonstrated the Fifth Dimension's success in enhancing children's educational achievement during the after-school hours. In this chapter, we discuss the effects of Fifth Dimension participation on a second group of learners: the undergraduate students who assist the children. Reports by the undergraduates themselves, program implementers, and other observers informally but consistently suggest that undergraduates benefit in many ways from their involvement in the Fifth Dimension. Here we focus on the impact of Fifth Dimension participation on undergraduates' learning as part of their university coursework.

Chapter 1 presented a general description of the university courses associated with the Fifth Dimension. These courses are located in a variety of departments—psychology, education, communication, and linguistics, among others—and the particulars of course content and pedagogy vary from site to site. All Fifth Dimension–related courses, however, engage undergraduates in a set of core activities:

1. Attending a class on campus devoted to lecture, reading, student presentations, and discussion relating to Fifth Dimension experiences

2. Participating one to two times a week at a Fifth Dimension site to work and play directly with children

3. Writing detailed field notes on experiences and observations after each visit to the Fifth Dimension site

4. Writing an end-of-course research paper based on site experience and readings

At some sites, undergraduates also interact with each other and with undergraduates at other sites through email and video conferencing.

From the outset of the project, one goal was to create not only a system that would promote children's learning but one in which university students (and other participating adults) could learn about the constraints, possibilities, and processes of children's thinking, problem-solving, learning, and development (chapter 1). In light of that goal, studies of undergraduate learning in the Fifth Dimension–university course combination were undertaken at three sites: Appalachian State University, the University of California at San Diego, and Whittier College. The learning examined and the methods employed at each site varied in response to the content and goals of the affiliated course as well as the goals of the local researchers. In general, the studies addressed this question: does participation in the Fifth Dimension promote deep understanding of the academic concepts introduced in the associated course?

Here we explain the focus of each institution's research and report the results, which suggest that Fifth Dimension participation does contribute to undergraduates' understanding of academic concepts (although we lack randomized control groups to demonstrate this conclusion in the manner of chapter 5). The chapter concludes with evidence and discussion that shed light on the processes through which these results were achieved.

STUDY 1: THE EFFECTS OF FIFTH DIMENSION PARTICIPATION ON APPALACHIAN STATE UNIVERSITY STUDENTS' PRECONCEPTIONS ABOUT TEACHING, PUPILS, AND LEARNING

At Appalachian State University (ASU), undergraduates participate in the Fifth Dimension through the initial course in the teacher education program, "Introduction to Teaching." Students routinely begin this course with ideas about teaching, learning, and other educational concepts that have been shaped by their own school experiences. A major goal of the course is for students to examine, reflect on, and reconstruct these initial perspectives in light of educational literature and field experiences.

The purpose of the ASU study was thus to determine the effects of participation in the Fifth Dimension on undergraduates' preconceptions about teaching, pupils, and learning. Participating were eighty-six undergraduates from four sections of the course who participated in the Fifth Dimension as a course practicum during the 1996–97 academic year.

Method

A special ten-item test was designed to determine undergraduates' preconceptions about teaching, learning, and pupils. For example, undergraduates were asked to respond to questions such as "What is teaching?" "What is learning?" and "What does a good learner do?" This instrument was administered at the beginning and end of the course to students who participated in the Fifth Dimension.

Pre- and post-test scores of students who participated in the Fifth Dimension sections were compared. A team of faculty and graduate students implemented the following procedures, modeled on grounded theory (Strauss and Corbin 1990), to create categories for assigning and interpreting responses:

1. Each member of the team determined potential categories and their labels independently, without knowledge of which class sections the data came from.

2. Scoring categories were compared to reach consensus on categories, and the emergent categories were labeled.

3. Team members then worked independently to assign each undergraduate response to a category.

4. Team members discussed their assignments of statements to categories and reached consensus on the category assignments.

5. Finally, they collectively reviewed categories as a final check on the consistency of category assignments.

Charts were created to display emergent categories, and researchers then worked from the charts to create larger category labels. Tables were generated to demonstrate the frequency of responses by category. The team reached complete agreement about revisions that needed to be made to the tables. Necessary revisions were made and approved by the team.

Results

Table 7.1 presents the categories for each pretest and post-test question, including the percentages of total responses by category. It should be noted that the categories changed from pretest to post-test.

Questions 1 through 3 focused on the question "What is teaching?" by asking that question as well as "What do teachers do?" and "How do teachers attain goals?" As can be seen, at the beginning of the course a ma-

Table 7.1 Pretest and Post-Test Results on Attitudes and Beliefs Survey—Study 1, ASU

Question	Pretest Categories	Percentage of Total	Post-Test Categories	Percentage of Total
1. What is teaching?	Telling	82	Creating contexts for assisted learning	92
	Helping	18	Transmission of information	8
2. What do teachers do?	Transmit knowledge	80	Develop activities for social interaction and ZPD assessment	90
	Facilitate learning	20	Set goals and outcomes	10
3. How do teachers attain goals?	Internal and external organizational control	82	ZPD assessment and interaction with students and community	93
	Caring behavior	18	State curriculum	7
4. What is learning?	Passive reception	70	A socially active person	94
	Active participation	30	Knowledge absorption	6
5. How do children learn?	Passive reception	82	By social construction of meaning	84
	Active participation	18	By observation and imitation	16
6. Interaction with other children and adults	Adult		Adult	
	Adult control	80	Respond to guidance	82
	Behavior		Behave dependently	12
	Relaxed behavior	20	Act intimidated	6
	Children		Children	
	Enjoy each other	55	Increased capacity	70
	Seek approval	25	Peer equality	30
	Peer equality	20		

Question	Response	%	Response	%
7. Describe what a good learner does during a learning activity	Passive roles	75	Maintain active participation	95
	Active Roles	25	Absorb and recite information	5
8. Describe what a poor learner does during a learning activity	Child deficit	90	Does not participate	100
	Teaching method and parent	10		
9. Attention to learning tasks	Activity dependent	70	Task dependent	93
	Short attention span	30	Handicap dependent	7
10. How do children respond to success and failure in learning?	Success:		Success:	
	Self-esteem is heightened	20	Increased participation	85
	Desire to share success with others	10	Greater achievement	15
	Increase in desire to learn	40		
	Sense of achievement	30		
	Failure:		Failure:	
	Self-esteem is lowered	20	Withdraw participation	100
	Easily discouraged	40		
	Frustrated	15		
	Tries harder	25		

Source: Authors' compilation.

jority of undergraduates (82 percent) believed that teaching is "telling," while 18 percent believed that teaching is some form of helping. Eighty percent believed that teachers transmit knowledge, and 82 percent believed that teachers attain their goals by exerting control over children. The post-test results produced categorical changes in responses. A majority (92 percent) of responses reflected the belief that teaching is about creating contexts for assisted learning, that teachers develop activities for social interaction (90 percent), and that teachers attain their goals through organized activity in the zone of proximal development with children (93 percent).

Questions 4 and 5 asked "What is learning?" At the beginning of the course, 70 percent of the undergraduates believed that learning is a passive form of knowledge absorption, while 30 percent believed that learning is active and involves the application of knowledge. Post-test responses reveal a clear change in beliefs about learning. Ninety-four percent indicated that learning is a socially constructed process. Similarly, 84 percent of the undergraduates believed that children learn through the social construction of meaning.

Questions 6 through 10 addressed conceptions about pupil characteristics. Pretest responses revealed that 80 percent of the undergraduates believed that adults should control children. Seventy-five percent viewed good learners as those who take passive roles in activity. Almost all (90 percent) attributed poor learning to child deficits. Responses about attention during learning activity revealed that most (70 percent) believed that attention depends on the activity and 30 percent believed that children have short attention spans. With regard to how children respond to success and failure, the majority believed that success increases children's desire to learn or creates a sense of achievement. Looking at the post-test results, we can see that 82 percent of the responses revealed a belief that children respond positively to adult guidance. Seventy percent believed that the outcome of children interacting with each other and with adults is an increased capacity to learn, indicating a movement away from concerns about teacher control. Ninety-five percent viewed a good learner as one who is an active participant, and the belief was unanimous that poor learners do not participate. Ninety-three percent of the responses suggest a belief that attention is task-dependent. Eighty-five percent seemed to believe that success increases participation. Finally, the group unanimously believed that students withdraw from participation as the result of failure.

The field notes written by this group about their participation in the Fifth Dimension demonstrate that developing new concepts requires struggling with preconceptions. For example, one change that occurred over the semester was the undergraduates' growing recognition that their focus should be on the children's learning and not on their own teaching performance. Undergraduates also came to understand the idea that expertise is not located solely in the teacher but is distributed in a community and that children and preservice teachers can teach each other.

In summary, a comparison of pretest and post-test data reveals a distinct transformation in most undergraduates' beliefs about teaching, learning, and children during their participation in the "Introduction to Teaching" course and the Fifth Dimension. They moved away from beliefs that teaching is mainly the transmission of knowledge, learning is passive reception, and pupils should be sequestered and controlled and came to believe instead that teaching is organizing learning activity, learning is the social construction of meaning by active participants, and children are more successful as their participation in learning activities increases.

STUDY 2: THE EFFECTS OF FIFTH DIMENSION PARTICIPATION ON USE OF THEORETICAL CONSTRUCTS AS TOOLS FOR OBSERVING, INTERPRETING, AND ANALYZING OBSERVATIONS

Undergraduate Fifth Dimension participation at the University of California at San Diego (UCSD) has been part of the "Practicum in Child Development" course since 1987. The practicum course emphasizes deep understanding of basic developmental principles, familiarity with the use of new information technologies for organizing learning, and methods for collecting and analyzing data on the processes that undergraduates help to put in play. Students spend three hours per week in class time devoted to discussion of theory and its application and three hours per week testing theory in their interactions with children at the project sites. Undergraduates are treated—and act—as "apprentice researchers"; after completing the course, some elect to continue with the projects doing independent research studies and honors theses or working as paid student researchers.

The purpose of the two-part study reported here was to document changes in undergraduates' ideas as the result of participation in the Fifth Dimension. Our prediction was that the practice of asking students to link course concepts to their practice at the Fifth Dimension site would lead to deeper understanding of the concepts' potential meaning and usefulness in practice. Consequently, we hypothesized an increase over time in the use of course concepts to mediate thinking and action. The first analysis focused on sociocultural and cultural-historical interpretations of teaching, learning, and culture based on a questionnaire. The second analysis focused on key developmental concepts in that same framework derived from student field notes.

Method for the Analysis Based on the Concept Survey

Starting in the winter quarter of 1999, surveys were administered at the beginning and end of the course each quarter to obtain undergraduates' personal definitions of teaching, learning, and culture. Over five quarters, during which time 105 students were surveyed, an average of 65 percent reported that their understanding of teaching had changed, 73 percent reported that their understanding of learning had changed, and 49 percent reported that their understanding of culture had changed. To test these self-reports of change, the open-response items requesting definitions of teaching, learning, and culture from the prepost surveys for the fall 2001 quarter were coded for consistency with definitions provided in the course readings, using a scale of zero to three for each concept. For example, in the area of teaching, a score of zero was given when the undergraduate described teaching as a one-way, teacher-centered model with the student as a passive recipient. A score of three was given when the undergraduate revealed a more complex understanding of teaching and exhibited the insight that the process of teaching is a dynamic interaction influenced by contextual factors as well as a lifelong formal and informal process. A score of one was given when the undergraduate demonstrated what was called preliminary understanding—for example, he or she defined teaching as an exchange but made no reference to context or roles. A score of two was given for demonstrations of developing understanding, such as incorporation of class concepts, including "reciprocal learning," "context," and "culture." An analogous scheme was used for the concepts of culture and learning. Two raters coded the descriptions independently. When there was disagreement, a third rating was sought; in these cases, the assigned codes represented a consensus of two independent ratings.

Results for the Analysis Based on the Concept Survey

The scores for the three concepts—teaching, learning, and culture—were aggregated so that individual scores ranged from zero to nine. Pre- and post-test scores were plotted on grids (pretest on the vertical dimension and post-test on the horizontal). As can be seen in figure 7.1, the larger distribution of scores in the post-test half (upper right) of the grid indicates that students' understanding of the concepts deepened between the beginning and end of the course. Paired t-tests of pre- and post-test scores from fifty-two undergraduates demonstrated change in the direction of

Figure 7.1   Changes in Undergraduates' Understanding of Key Course Concepts—Study 2, UCSD

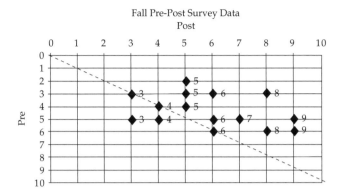

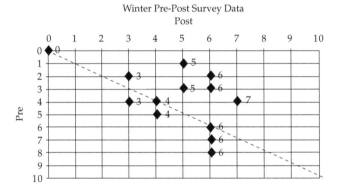

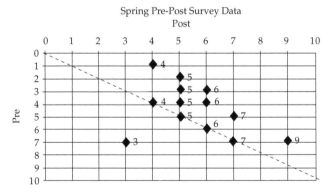

Source: Authors' compilation.

Notes: Values represent changes in the completeness and complexity of undergraduates' understandings of the concepts of teaching, learning, and culture, based on coded responses to open-response requests for definitions at the beginning and end of the chapter.

deeper conceptual knowledge of teaching, learning, and culture that was significant (p < .001).

Method for the Analysis Based on Field Notes

In addition to filling out surveys, students in the practicum course wrote field notes from each of their site visits to the Fifth Dimension according to a template that included description of the "general context," "focused observations," and "reflections" on those observations. All field notes were submitted in electronic form and then archived. At the end of the course, students produced individual and group research papers on topics of personal interest. Many of the papers discussed course topics—for example, learning how to deal with barriers to education such as gender and language differences, the challenges posed by technology, and the effectiveness of elements of the Fifth Dimension design, such as task cards and the maze. Hard copies of the research papers were archived.

In this second analysis, the database of field notes and papers for two classes (winter 2001 and spring 2001) was searched for key concepts used in the course—for example, "zone of proximal development," "community of learners," "participatory appropriation," "guided participation," and "apprenticeship" (the last three were coded as "participatory learning"). Segments of field notes and papers using these keywords were isolated in their context of use and coded as: orientational (naming the concept); instrumental (using the concept to explain interactions at the Fifth Dimension site); or reflective (questioning or expanding on the concepts as presented in the course). As in the prior analysis, two raters coded the segments independently. When there was disagreement, a third rater coded the segments; the resulting codes represented the independent rating of two raters.

Results for the Analysis Based on Field Notes

Analysis revealed that 62.5 percent of the spring 2001 group and 88 percent of the winter 2001 group used the concepts spontaneously in their field notes. Additionally, 25 percent of the 2001 spring group and 27.7 percent of the winter 2001 group shifted from an orientational use of the concepts to an instrumental or reflective use during their ten weeks of participation in the course. The concepts were used far less frequently in the papers: students tended to focus on the issues of diversity targeted during each quarter (gender in the winter and ethnolinguistic diversity in the spring). When present in the research papers, however, the concepts tended to be used instrumentally. With both the papers and the field notes, it is important to note that students used the concepts independently of any specific assignment.

THE EFFECTS OF FIFTH DIMENSION

Slightly more than one-fourth of the undergraduates demonstrated an instrumental use of the course concepts in text they wrote. A very small number of them analyzed the concepts critically, arriving at the "reflective" level. These findings were consistent with an earlier study (Cole 1996) in which undergraduates' field notes over a ten-week academic quarter were found to reveal that they first treated Fifth Dimension artifacts like the maze or task cards in an "orientational" mode, or as "things in themselves" to be understood. As the quarter progressed they began to treat these artifacts as "instrumental," or as mediators of goal-directed actions. The third category—the "reflective" mode in which the undergraduate looks critically at the artifact in use—was rarely observed in students taking the course for the first time, although it was observed in students who were participating in the course beyond the first quarter.

In summary, the results of this analysis suggest that undergraduates' understanding of course concepts developed as a result of participation in the practice of the Fifth Dimension, as indicated by the spontaneous, and sometimes changing, use of the concepts in their field notes on that practice. Similarly, the meanings of the concepts appeared to become more accessible to them over a relatively brief time (the ten weeks of an academic quarter) as conceptual tools for formulating and communicating their interpretations of their experience in practice.

STUDY 3: THE EFFECTS OF FIFTH DIMENSION PARTICIPATION ON WHITTIER STUDENTS' PRACTICES IN ASSISTING CHILDREN

At the Whittier College site, participation in the Fifth Dimension is associated with a teacher education course in educational psychology. The course content emphasizes the same perspectives on learning and development in which the Fifth Dimension's design is grounded—cultural-historical activity theory and sociocultural psychology. A principal goal of the course is for students to draw implications for teaching practice from the theoretical and research literature. Thus, the focus of Whittier's studies was to examine how students' practices change over time as they assist children in the Fifth Dimension. Whittier's research took advantage of local variations in the frequency, duration, and conditions of undergraduate participation to examine whether and how these variations affect changes in undergraduate practices.

Two groups of undergraduates participate in Whittier's Fifth Dimension site. One group, referred to as "course-only" students, participate exclusively to meet the field-experience requirement of the educational psychology course. Their responsibility consists of assisting children in the Fifth Dimension once a week throughout the twelve-week semester. In addition, they spend three class hours each week discussing their Fifth Dimension experiences and their field notes in relation to the course reading assignments. A second group of undergraduates, referred to as the "service team," also participates in the Whittier Fifth Dimension. Service team members are students or former students in the educational psychology course who have stayed involved in the Fifth Dimension by working there part-time.

Members of the service team are selected based on their interest in the program, and they receive compensation for their work through a grant from the B. C. McCabe Foundation. Like the course-only undergraduates, they assist children with Fifth Dimension activities, always on a one-to-one basis. In contrast to the course-only students, however, service team members participate in the Fifth Dimension four days a week, serve for at least a year (and often two or three years), and perform a number of management and development functions for the site in which course-only students are never involved, such as coordinating daily operations, selecting and developing new task cards, and corresponding with children on behalf of Whittier's Wizard. They also participate in a weekly hour-and-a-half team meeting to discuss the progress of the program and plan program activities.

The practices of these two groups of undergraduates were studied and compared in Whittier's research, which took an ethnographic approach and used fine-grained video analysis procedures.

Study 3a: The Exploratory Qualitative Study

The first Whittier study was conducted for exploratory purposes with two goals in mind: identifying and describing undergraduates' Fifth Dimension interactional practices with children, and determining whether there were systematic differences in the practices of undergraduate class members, service team newcomers, and service team old-timers.

Method   The primary data for the study consisted of videotapes of seventy-four Fifth Dimension sessions involving twenty-six undergraduate students.[1] Fifty of the sessions were videotaped in 1997–98 with ten students distributed in the following categories:

1. *Course-only students*: These undergraduates participated once a week only through the educational psychology course.

2. *Service team newcomers*: These students were in their first semester on the service team and were participating in the Fifth Dimension four times a week while also taking the educational psychology course.

3. *Service team old-timers*: These students, who had a year or more of Fifth Dimension service, participated four times a week and had once been enrolled in the educational psychology course.

The fifty sessions were distributed (as shown in table 7.2) to permit relevant comparisons of students' practices over time. For example, the distributions permitted comparisons between the beginning-of-semester and end-of-semester practices of students who participated for only one semester and for different amounts of time (course-only students and service team newcomers), as well as comparisons of the practices of students

Table 7.2   Distribution of Sessions Videotaped, 1997 to 1998—Study 3a, Whittier

| | Number of Sessions per Undergraduate | | | | | | |
| | Fall Semester[a] | | | Spring Semester | | | Total |
Undergraduates	Beginning	Middle	End	Beginning	Middle	End	Sessions
Class members							
Janice	3		3				6
Christie		2					2
Marta				3		3	6
Jennifer					2		2
Service team newcomers							
Susie	3		3				6
Nadia		4			2		6
Suzanne				3		2	5
Service team old-timers							
Claudia	3		3				6
Nicole		2			2		4
Sonia				3		4	7
Total sessions	9	8	9	9	6	9	50

Source: Authors' compilation.
[a] Beginning-of-semester sessions were videotaped for each student once a week during the first three weeks of the twelve-week semester. End-of-semester sessions were documented one per week during the semester's last three weeks. Midsemester sessions were routinely recorded once during the fifth or sixth weeks of the semester.

who participated with the same frequency but for different numbers of semesters (service team newcomers and old-timers).

A second set of twenty-four videotaped sessions provided supplemental data. These included single beginning-of-semester and end-of-semester sessions with sixteen students chosen at random from sixty-four sessions documented during 1995–96: ten with course-only students, four with service team newcomers, and two with service team old-timers. They also included eight sessions in which two of the 1997–98 service team old-timers (Sylvia and Claudia) appeared as newcomers in their first semester of service team participation.

Aside from designating the categories of undergraduates who would participate in the videotaped sessions and selecting undergraduates they deemed "typical" in each category, researchers made no effort to constrain the sessions or interactions. The child partners of the dyads were determined by routine site procedures—that is, by children's request or by assignment by the site coordinator. The activities of the partners were determined by the child's choices among the alternatives available for his or her position in the maze.

Analysis of the videotapes began with the fifty sessions taped during 1997–98 and proceeded in a process typical of ethnography. Two researchers repeatedly reviewed the videotapes, making field notes on their observations, and then met to discuss those notes. In so doing, they sought to identify how the observed events were related to factors such as the type of game being played and the child's age or experience with the Fifth Dimension. They were particularly interested in examining the different patterns of practice among undergraduates with different amounts of Fifth Dimension experience. The researchers repeated this process in successive iterations, reviewing the videotapes and making notes that confirmed, negated, or revised patterns they had tentatively identified during earlier viewings. When they felt confident that they had located and described the patterns of practice in the fifty 1997–98 sessions, they followed a similar procedure with the twenty-four 1995–96 videotaped sessions to check the findings derived from the initial fifty.

Results Undergraduates in their first semester of Fifth Dimension service—whether as course-only students or as service team newcomers—consistently engaged in two different patterns of interaction with the children. These varied with the type of program activity on which they and the children were working.

First, the undergraduates consistently used a traditionally didactic instructional technique when attempting to assist children when the program activity included content that was central in school curricula or presented content in task formats with which the undergraduates were already familiar. Such activities generally involved reading, writing, or otherwise operating with text (such as alphabetizing words), using arithmetic operations and numbers, or recalling or using factual information from history, geography, or science. If any of these tasks were embedded in task formats with which the undergraduates were initially unfamiliar, they began to instruct the children didactically as they themselves began to get the hang of the game.

By contrast, course-only students and service team newcomers rarely offered children assistance during program activities that involved content or tasks that lay outside the core curriculum of traditional schools or dealt with subject matter that was central in school curricula but was presented in game formats with which the undergraduates were unfamiliar. Examples of the former were strategy games, such as chess, checkers, and Othello, and art software such as "Kid Pix." The latter category included computer simulations such as "Sim City," which promotes understanding of systems and interdependency, and software such as "Tesselations," which involves working with mathematical patterns. Interviews with class members and newcomers to the service team, along with comments in class members' field notes, suggested that these and similar activities were perceived as "merely" games, without value for learning or development. This perception may explain why these undergraduates acted largely as observers during such activities. They spoke infrequently and offered little guidance, even when children's performance suggested that they could have benefited from assistance. Only when a child could not make a software program move forward at all did these undergraduates help, and then almost always by telling the child directly what to do. Otherwise, their interactions were restricted to occasional remarks on the children's game moves, such as, "Oh, nice one!" or, "Too bad!"

Since all Fifth Dimension activities involve some reading (of task cards at the very least) and writing (to Whittier's patron, the Wizard), and since the great majority of games in Whittier's maze have school-like content, didactic instruction was the predominant pattern in sessions involving course-only students and service team newcomers. Most often they led children through Fifth Dimension sessions step by step, issuing a sequence of directives and explanations regarding what to do. They sometimes gave brief "lectures" to elaborate on factual information presented in a computer game, although the information was rarely essential to the child's progress in the game. They frequently introduced initiation-response-evaluation (IRE, or classroom recitation–type) sequences typical of classroom recitation (Mehan 1979), requiring the children to respond to known-answer questions. Such queries served to "test" the children's understanding of the content presented in the games ("And what did it say the capital of Germany is?") or to push the children on to subsequent operations ("So what do you do next?"). In addition, when a child encountered text on task cards or computer screens, course-only students and service team newcomers routinely insisted that he or she read it aloud, directed the child to sound out each unfamiliar word, corrected decoding mistakes, and followed the reading with comprehension questions. During writing activities, they focused the children's attention on punctuation and spelling with questions such as, "What are you going to need at the end of that sentence?"

Although some of these undergraduate actions could be seen as providing needed assistance, the timing of them in the flow of the interaction sometimes suggested otherwise. These directives, explanations, and questions were often offered preemptively, that is, before the child had had a chance to demonstrate whether she or he really needed assistance. More often than not, service team newcomers and course-only students also kept control of the artifacts used in Fifth Dimension sessions, with the exception of the computer keyboard and mouse. They placed materials such as the task card, reference books, and maps out of the child's reach on their side of the computer and held them up for the child to read as needed. If notes were taken on game clues, the undergraduates usually wrote them down and held on to the notepad, holding it up for the child to consult at relevant moments. These and similar undergraduate actions heightened the didactic instructional quality of their interactions with their child partners.

In contrast, undergraduates with a year or more of experience on the Fifth Dimension service team seemed to interact with the children in ways that put the children's activity and actions in the lead. These undergraduates routinely provided interactional "space" in which the children could take action, attended to what the children were doing, and then responded to the children's actions in ways that helped them realize their apparent goals. They regularly offered assistance on an as-needed basis— that is, only after the child had demonstrated that he or she could not accomplish an operation alone.

Children most often controlled artifacts such as adventure cards, journey logs, and game manuals in sessions with service team old-timers, using them on their own or conjointly with their undergraduate partners. Children in these sessions usually made procedural or strategic decisions independently or in consultation with their undergraduate partners. In activities of all types, service team old-timers most often assisted children by guiding them and thinking and working collaboratively with them rather than by directly instructing them. Their hints and questions ("Look at the items we've already found and decide if there's something there we could use," or, "What's on the screen that might help you?") nearly always focused on information and procedures immediately relevant to accomplishing the operation at hand. They rarely introduced extraneous "knowledge." As the examples just given might suggest, old-timers' assistance appeared to embody ways of thinking that the children could appropriate and use later in similar situations in the game or beyond the game.

Finally, as the Fifth Dimension was designed to do, sessions involving service team old-timers frequently mixed the leading activities of childhood: learning, play, and affiliation. Play often took the form of imagining different meanings for artifacts and actions or temporarily adopting make-believe personas. Affiliation between children and their undergraduate partners was manifest in overt and affectionate physical contact as well as in conversation about personal topics such as shared family experiences and hobbies.

An illustration of how these leading activities were woven together took place at the Whittier site as Sylvia, a service team old-timer, and nine-year-old Jonas began a session playing "Where in the World Is Carmen San Diego?," a game in which players travel the world to find clues and locate a criminal. As the computer screen displayed an airplane flying to Chile, the location of the initial clues, Sylvia placed her arm conspiratorially around Jonas's shoulder, drew close to him, and whispered, "Okay, we're detectives now, and we're going to find who stole the poems of Pablo Neruda!" Jonas extended his arms like wings and replied, "Vroom! We're flying! Vroom! Y'know, I have a friend down there in Chile." "Maybe he can help us find the criminal, huh?" Sylvia responded. "Okay, now let's see where we can find our clues." As they read a clue suggesting that the criminal had traveled from Chile to Shanghai, Sylvia asked, "Do you know where Shanghai is?" When Jonas said, "No," Sylvia immediately handed him an atlas and asked, "So how are you going to find out?" She was soon guiding Jonas in looking up Shanghai in the index of the atlas. Many sessions with service team old-timers joined moments of playful pretending, affiliation, and learning in this manner, while sessions with course-only students and service team newcomers rarely did.

The practices of service team old-timers described here were consistent with those suggested by the theoretical concepts and research literature that they had studied in the educational psychology course. Those practices instantiated principles of assisted performance or guided participation as described by authors such as Barbara Rogoff (1990) and Roland Tharp and Ronald Gallimore (1988). That they did so suggests that undergraduates who participated in the Fifth Dimension four days a week for a year did indeed appropriate course concepts as tools for mediating their practice, although undergraduates with more limited experience did not.

Study 3b: The Quantitative Study

Whittier's second study was undertaken to confirm and quantify the results of the first study.

Method   Data for the second study were videotapes of thirty-eight hour-and-a-half Fifth Dimension sessions, including: twenty-one sessions with seven service team undergraduates taking the educational psychology course and in their first semester of Fifth Dimension service (one session of each at the beginning, the middle, and the end of that semester); and seventeen sessions with five of the same seven workers one year later at the same points in the semester. Videotapes of these sessions thus permitted longitudinal comparisons of undergraduate practices.

Undergraduates' attempts to help children throughout these thirty-eight sessions were coded using categories that the first study had suggested were salient, that is, those that distinguished the practices of more-experienced students from those of students with less experience. The results of the coding are shown in the following tables as percentages rather than as frequencies because the total number of interactions varied from session to session.

Results   The results shown in tables 7.3 through 7.5 confirm that these undergraduates did appropriate course concepts as tools for mediating their practice after a year of participating in the Fifth Dimension four times per week.

As table 7.3 shows, the seven service team undergraduates used largely didactic instructional practices with children during their first semester—the twelve weeks during which they were enrolled in the educational psychology course. In table 7.3, the "instructing" category includes diverse forms of direct, school-like instruction: explaining to the child what to do (often step by step); demonstrating appropriate actions and techniques (usually taking the mouse or other artifacts away from the child); giving the child facts and information related to the game context (but not necessarily needed to provide a game response); and engaging in IRE (classroom recitation–type) sequences with the child.

A year later, however, five of the same undergraduates had substantially changed their practices. They guided and assisted the children far more often than they didactically instructed them. Based on the means of guiding participation and assisting performance described by Rogoff (1990, 18–109) and Tharp and Gallimore (1988, 44–70), the "guiding" category in table 7.3 includes giving hints ("Do you see anything up here on the screen that can help you?" or, "I think we've seen what we're looking for before"), cognitive structuring ("Count the number of boxes you can complete before you decide," or, "Look for the capital letters; they're usually the names of places the crook might have gone"), and reminding the child of the procedures required to reach goals ("There's something you better fill in before you put your folder away, so you know where to start next time," or, "Did you save that?"). The "combined or unclear" category

Table 7.3   Type of Assistance Given by Undergraduates: Study 3b, Whittier (Percentage of Total Attempts in Three Sessions)

Undergraduate Experience	Instructing	Guiding	Combined or Unclear
First semester of participation	44%	24%	32%
One year later	18	59	23

Source: Authors' compilation.

includes (1) elements of instructing and guiding that are interwoven in the same interactional turn and cannot be separated and (2) types of assistance that cannot readily be categorized.

Table 7.4, which elaborates on the results shown in table 7.3, also indicates a change in practice. It demonstrates when help was offered in relation to the actions of the child. Preemptive "help" was offered in 63 percent of the instances observed among the seven undergraduates during their first semester in the Fifth Dimension. That is, they offered help before the child had had a chance to demonstrate the ability to accomplish an action without assistance. One year later, five of these seven students were offering help contingently 55 percent of the time—that is, when the child had shown, through immediate or recent performance, that he or she was unable to accomplish the required action alone. Preemptive attempts to assist had dropped significantly to 21 percent after these undergraduates had gained a year's experience. (Attempts were classified as "unclear" when it was not possible to discern the child's action or the timing of the student's offered help in relation to it.) These findings suggest that the undergraduates had learned to provide assistance only when it was needed.

Table 7.4   Timing of Undergraduates' Assistance in Relationship to Child's Action: Study 3b, Whittier (Percentage of Total Attempts Across Three Sessions)

Undergraduate Experience	Preemptive	Contingent	Unclear
First semester of participation	63%	17%	20%
One year later	21	55	24

Source: Authors' compilation.

Finally, table 7.5 demonstrates that the undergraduates learned to relinquish control of artifacts, both by turning control of artifacts over to the children and by sharing control of them with the children. These artifacts included the various print materials used in Fifth Dimension sessions, such as task cards, journey logs, free passes, and reference books, and all computer-related materials, such as floppy disks, CD-ROM disks, and peripherals such as printers, with the exception of the mouse and keyboard. Instances of use were defined as one or another party in the scene actually using the artifact—looking at it, reading it, or handling it other than idly. (See the examples described in the results section for the first study.) A stopwatch was used to time each instance of use of an artifact; instances of use under five seconds were discounted.

The results of this quantitative study clearly demonstrate that the students' practices changed. During their first semester participating in the Fifth Dimension, five of the seven students used didactic instructional strategies and often stepped in to provide assistance before it was clear that the child needed it. After a year in the Fifth Dimension, they had learned to employ different practices, and these were precisely the practices promoted by the theoretical and research literature they had studied in the educational psychology class. These results suggest that, with sufficient time, these students achieved the goal of Whittier's Fifth Dimension course combination: they appropriated course concepts as tools for mediating practice.

Since many undergraduates work at the Fifth Dimension site for only one semester or trimester, Whittier's research results might suggest that much Fifth Dimension activity takes place in a didactic atmosphere. However, Whittier's studies isolate and describe discrete undergraduate actions at particular moments in time, disregarding for analytic purposes their functions and meanings in the flow of unfolding interaction and in the context of the Fifth Dimension system. That analytic strategy serves to demonstrate graphically the "style" of undergraduates' helping efforts, but it does not yield a picture of the overall quality or atmosphere of Fifth Dimension sessions.

The quality and atmosphere of Fifth Dimension sessions are evident not in the sum of discrete undergraduate acts but rather in the ongoing activity organized by Fifth Dimension principles. As we saw in chapter 6, acts that in themselves could be labeled controlling or didactic—taking charge of artifacts, for instance, or trying to tell a child how a game should be played—function, in the context of the Fifth Dimension, as elements of collaboratively created zones of proximal development. In short, in the Fifth Dimension, as in other robust learning systems, "the structuring resources for learning come from a variety of sources, not only from pedagogical activity. . . . Mastery resides not in the master but in the organiza-

Table 7.5 Undergraduates' Use of Artifacts: Study 3b, Whittier (Percentage of Time in Use Across Three Sessions)

Undergraduate Experience	Undergraduate	Child	Shared	Variable or Unclear
First semester of participation	57%	19%	12%	12%
One year later	28	36	26	10

Source: Authors' compilation.

tion of the community of practice of which the master is a part" (Lave and Wenger 1991, 94).

SUMMARY OF THE STUDIES OF UNDERGRADUATES' FIFTH DIMENSION PARTICIPATION

The studies reported here used different indicators of learning to examine the effects of Fifth Dimension participation on undergraduates. They also explored the effects of different durations and frequencies of participation in different course contexts. The results of the ASU and UCSD studies of conceptual change demonstrate that with one semester or one quarter of participation in the Fifth Dimension and its affiliated course, undergraduate students come to define and illustrate course concepts such as teaching, learning, and culture in ways that are significantly different, richer, and theoretically better informed. Moreover, the UCSD study indicates that over the course of one quarter, with twice-weekly participation in class totaling three hours and twice-weekly site experiences, undergraduates also begin to use course concepts spontaneously and sometimes in more meaningful and instrumental ways as conceptual tools for communicating their experiences in practice. Nevertheless, the undergraduates appear to remain at the early stages of transforming the ways in which they interact with children even with conceptual guidance from their professor. Whittier's studies suggest that undergraduates do not appropriate course concepts as tools for mediating interactive practices with children in just one semester, even those who participate in the Fifth Dimension four times a week.

This set of studies calls for more systematic inquiry. For example, further research is required to understand the effects of different frequencies and durations of practicum participation on what undergraduates learn and how their learning is displayed. These studies also raise important questions about how students' prior beliefs interact with characteristics of the local site to change both their behavior and their conceptual knowledge—for example, their definitions of course concepts, their spontaneous use of those concepts to interpret their experience, and their use of those concepts in their interactions with children. Clearly these changes emerge over time. But what promotes or inhibits these changes? Are particular course pedagogies or practicum experiences more effective in promoting them?

At the Whittier College Fifth Dimension, undergraduate behavior appeared to change slowly, requiring two quarters of participation. By contrast, change at the Solana Beach Fifth Dimension was visible within a single ten-week period covering eighteen to twenty sessions. Although we have no formal analysis of the videotapes collected in Solana Beach to examine modes of interaction between the children and undergraduates, the didactic interactions that are characteristic of the Whittier undergraduates who have only limited experience at their site are virtually never encountered at Solana Beach. Does this difference arise because of variations in site idiocultures? Whittier insists on one-to-one interactions between undergraduates and children, whereas group structures are more variable at Solana Beach. Or perhaps the difference in the rate of change among undergraduates is related to the fact that Whittier students, as teachers-in-training, interpret their role at the BGC in this light, while at Solana Beach a key task is to ensure that all participants are enjoying themselves and the undergraduates are encouraged to be friends and peers with the children. Other hypotheses could be suggested, but it is clear that this is an important area for future research. Studies addressing these and similar questions can guide the fine-tuning of current Fifth Dimension courses and the development of future systems.

Regardless of the outcome of future studies, the research reported here provides evidence that participation in the Fifth Dimension does contribute to undergraduates' deeper understanding of the concepts presented in affiliated courses. In the following section, we consider how participation in the Fifth Dimension–university course combination promotes such learning.

EXPLAINING THE RESULTS

The intellectual traditions described in chapter 2 can be used to explain undergraduates' learning in Fifth Dimension–affiliated courses. Situated learning theorists (for example, Barab and Duffy 2000; Greeno 1998; Lave and Wenger 1991) emphasize that what is learned is inevitably shaped by context and activity. They point out that each context and activity in which a concept is encountered recasts understanding of it in a new and more densely textured form (Brown, Collins, and Duguid 1989). From this perspective, it is significant that Fifth Dimension courses situate undergraduates' learning in the contexts and activities of their intended use. Students in courses affiliated with the Fifth Dimension, in other words, are asked to learn and use concepts as mediating means: as tools for observing, interpreting, analyzing, and in many instances modifying phenomena that they encounter through Fifth Dimension participation. They engage in these activities consistently in multiple contexts: writing field notes, conducting and reporting the results of research projects, engaging in informed class discourse about Fifth Dimension events, and making informed decisions about how best to assist children. In traditional university courses, by contrast, undergraduates are required to learn and use the academic concepts they study only in their own academic activities—for example, taking tests. This perspective provides one theoretical explanation of the conceptual understanding displayed by undergraduates in our studies.

Cultural-historical activity theory provides another explanation. Vasilii Davydov (1988, 1990), for example, has proposed a model of learning activity that begins by identifying a substantive theoretical generalization (an abstraction) and then establishing links to its diverse, specific forms and manifestations. Through a series of "learning actions," a person forges connections between the initial abstraction and its concrete manifestations, constructing a robust theoretical concept that is usable in many contexts. Terttu Tuomi-Gröhn and Yrjö Engeström (2003) extend Davydov's work, suggesting that "boundary-crossing" between activity systems, such as between school and work activities, promotes the learning actions that result in transfer from school to work and vice versa.

> Meaningful transfer takes place through interaction between collective activity systems. For example, the school and the workplace may engage in collaborative interaction in which both activity systems learn something from each other. What is transferred is not packages of knowledge and skills that remain intact; instead, the very process of such transfer involves active interpreting, modifying, and reconstructing the skills and knowledge to be transferred.

From these viewpoints, the Fifth Dimension can be seen as providing recurrent opportunities for students to engage in learning activity that elaborates links between initial abstractions (as constructed in classrooms) and concrete instantiations of those concepts in Fifth Dimension activity; the initial concepts are thereby reconstructed into more deeply understood tools. At the same time that course concepts serve students as tools to mediate their understanding of Fifth Dimension events, Fifth Dimension organizational structures, events, and artifacts reciprocally provide students with essential resources for illustrating, concretizing, and elaborating course concepts. Crossing the boundaries of university courses and Fifth Dimension work can simultaneously generate the learning actions that, for Tuomi-Gröhn and Engeström, promote a critical examination of both systems, greater awareness of the conflicts between them, and resolutions to those conflicts. In Fifth Dimension courses, these resolutions routinely take shape—as shown in the examples provided in the remainder of the chapter—as what should be done to promote children's learning and development, rather than as the changes in ongoing systems envisioned by Engeström and others.

The following examples demonstrate the theoretical propositions just presented. They show us undergraduates in the process of elaborating abstract course concepts through concrete Fifth Dimension examples and changing their notions about what system qualities are essential for promoting learning and development as they use course concepts as tools to mediate their Fifth Dimension experiences. In the end, these examples show us undergraduates achieving the deep conceptual understanding documented by the studies reported earlier.

Concept: Zone of Proximal Development

Vygotsky's concept of a zone of proximal development is central in many of the courses affiliated with the Fifth Dimension, including Whittier's educational psychology class. In the following example, a student in that course links this abstract concept with a concrete instantiation of it as he interprets his experience in a November 14, 2002, field note.

When I think back at my sessions at the Fifth Dimension, I can think of at least one instance for every visit where I had some interaction in the zone of proximal development. This week, while I was working with Bryan Garcia, was no exception. . . . The zone of proximal development is defined by Vygotsky as "the distance between the actual development level as determined by independent problem solving and the level of potential development as determined through problem solving under adult guidance or in collaboration with more capable peers." In our case, I was the more capable peer because I was able to understand our objectives. By himself, without my assistance, Bryan was able to come close to solving the problems, but was rarely able to fully complete them on his own.

In some cases, it only took a clue or two for Bryan to make the connection and complete the task. But other times, I had to give him big hints or tell him, "I think you have to do this," in order for him to solve the contraption. For instance, he was using the different tools he had available to him, but was not using them correctly, instead just randomly placing them on the screen. I had to prompt him to read the hints that were on the screen, which told him almost exactly where to put everything. This was one case where we were working in the zone of proximal development because by himself he could not get the solution, but as I was giving hints pointing towards the correct answer, he was able to go further and get more.

Another method that I used to jump-start his thought process was to ask him questions that would push him in the right direction. I would ask him simple questions like, "What are you trying to accomplish with this contraption," or "What do you plan on doing with that block," or "What do you think you could use the flashlight for." Most of the time these questions would stimulate his thought and he would realize that he had to do something in particular with each object. After a while, my help was not needed nearly as much and he could do by himself what he was doing with my help previously. This tells me that we were working in the zone of proximal development. He was doing a decent job of thinking and solving these contraptions by himself, before I got involved, but after we worked together on some things and there was interaction between the two of us, he was able to do much more than he was before.

This undergraduate's concrete encounter with a zone of proximal development has given him an opportunity to construct a deeper understanding of this abstract concept than the passage he quotes could provide. Through work in the Fifth Dimension, he is able to elaborate what, and when, a zone of proximal development is.

Concept: Goal Formation

Many Fifth Dimension–affiliated courses also explore the importance of people forming their own goals for learning. This concept is especially salient for many undergraduates, since their own academic learning is routinely directed by goals that have been prespecified by their teachers. In the cases that follow, undergraduates encounter the significance of goal formation in the Fifth Dimension.

The first example is a field note written by a student in the Michigan State University teacher education course through which undergraduates participated in the Fifth Dimension. The field note reveals the student not only elaborating his notion of the importance of goal formation (described here in terms of students' "choices") but also identifying a contradiction in the activity system of schooling that prevents it from achieving important learning goals. Implicitly, he is proposing a way to change schools.

> After spending the last eight weeks here I have noticed that the children have learned valuable concepts that can be easily overlooked in the traditional classroom. The emphasis is not on academics and achievement (although I'm sure that they are improving in this area) but rather on social and community concepts. I have already mentioned their ability to work collaboratively and share. Also they are learning how to become responsible for their own progress. They keep track of what they have accomplished and what they need to get done. It is also their responsibility to seek resources for help. This may mean a book, a peer, or an adult. This is a concept that they miss at school. . . . There the teacher is the source of responsibility, the teacher decides what to do and evaluates the students. Another concept has to do with . . . choice in how they accomplish that goal. At school I have observed that the children have little opportunity to make choices. Knowing how to make good choices and learning to be responsible for your own actions are major skills that are implicitly taught here [the after-school club] and [are] often overlooked in traditional classrooms.

A second example addressing the importance of goal formation for learning again shows us an undergraduate connecting this abstract concept to a concrete Fifth Dimension experience and extending her understanding of it in the process. This example is derived from the interview response of a Whittier service team undergraduate. In response to an interview question about what she had been learning recently, the student commented:

> I don't think I really understood the importance of following the kids' choices until I began serving as coordinator this semester. Back in February, when participation was down, we started going around the club getting kids to play, and sometimes, you know, it was almost like twisting their arms, we encouraged them so much. But I noticed when I was walking around and helping out [as coordinator], those kids we kind of pressured weren't really getting into it and the WAs [Wizard Assistants, their college partners] were like, "C'mon, you can finish this game! You're almost done! Just one more level and you can write to the Wizard and transform." And I guess it just struck me—this whole thing depends upon kids having their own goals they want to reach, choosing to be there and making choices about what to do, and having their own reason for why they want to do it. Without that, nothing else matters. You end up like a teacher—trying to bribe them to do it.

Concept: Bilingual Code Switching

A concept given particular attention in courses affiliated with Fifth Dimension sites that serve bilingual communities is code switching. The following undergraduate field note, written by a Michigan State student, graphically and succinctly illustrates how Fifth Dimension participation gave him an opportunity to raise this concept from the abstract to the concrete.

> For the first time I heard children speaking in Spanish. A group of boys had just finished playing a game of checkers on the carpet and they were conversing freely in Spanish. They were laughing and joking about something. They spoke English occasionally. I heard comments like "Come on" and "Right." I'm not sure, was this actually code switching? I was amazed to witness this after we had read so much about it. When the boys noticed me watching them, however, they immediately stopped and quietly spoke in English again. . . . I know we have discussed this in class before, but for the first time, it had real meaning for me.

Concept: Community of Learners

Several Fifth Dimension–affiliated courses encourage undergraduates to develop an understanding of the notion of a community of learners: a community in which learning is a collaborative endeavor and the roles of teacher and student are flexibly shared (Rogoff 1994). In the following account, interpreted by the Appalachian State University student instructor, an undergraduate named Ellie locates concrete instantiations of this abstract concept in both the Fifth Dimension and its affiliated teacher education course. She expands her notion of what the concept means and thus transforms her preconception of what it means to teach.

In one of her first field notes, from February 26, 1996, Ellie writes: "I am really starting to understand what teaching is all about just through the short time I have spent with two different children." She goes on to say that she "found herself asking her students for help" and that she learned that students really like to "figure things out by themselves or with a friend." Soon thereafter, on March 12, her experience with three young girls prompts her to write: "I think that sometimes kids would rather look to other kids for help before they ask a teacher. . . . Working in a group is more beneficial to these girls and it helps me to see how other kids that young interact with each other."

A week later, on March 20, Ellie connects her Fifth Dimension observations to her experience as a student in the university course, noting the benefits of the collaboration that she has witnessed in both contexts:

> I can see why Dr. M. [the course instructor] wants us to work in groups in our course . . . everyone learns from each other. . . . It is just amazing to see how well the girls [at the Fifth Dimension site] could read and how enthusiastic they were after reading the story. I hope that their ZPD (zone of proximal development) continues to grow and that they will leave 5D [Fifth Dimension] with the ability to do tasks without our assistance and having gained more confidence.

The transformation in Ellie's concept of teaching is revealed by her description of her interaction with two young boys, Corey and Adam. On March 13, she writes in her field note:

> These two boys interact well with one another and they are a great example of how the Activity Theory works. They ask each other for help and they communicate very well. They try to explain answers to each other rather than just giving the answers. This is how I think kids should interact in public school every day.

In her beginning-of-semester response to the ASU survey question "What is teaching?" Ellie had stated: "Teachers go over lessons and activities with children and keep going over them until everyone understands and can recite back what they have learned." However, Ellie's end-of-semester response to the same question was a clear departure from her pretest response: "Teachers try to instill knowledge into their students by constructing activities that will allow children to increase their creativity and that will allow them to grow as a learner. Teachers don't just stand in front of their classrooms and give out facts, they create activities that will allow their students to interact with their peers."

Changes in Practice

Particularly in courses associated with teacher education, the learning of course concepts is ultimately directed toward mediating the practice of future teachers. The Whittier studies reported earlier indicate that progress toward that goal can be made through sufficient Fifth Dimension participation. However, one of the challenges for future practitioners, as well as for students who assist children in the Fifth Dimension, is putting into practice the principle of "help as little as possible but as much as needed." That principle is implicit in numerous theoretical concepts taught in Fifth Dimension courses, including the concepts of the zone of proximal development and the community of learners. Nevertheless, students routinely find this principle difficult to appropriate, especially those who initially operate with "transmission" views of teaching and learning.

The following example illustrates how undergraduates can learn this principle of practice during their interactions with children. The example derives from two field notes by an undergraduate participating at the University of California at San Diego's La Clase Mágica site. The first field note was written during the undergraduate's successful first meeting with Jimmy, who did not read or speak Spanish but was nevertheless successfully playing "Graficas," a game with text exclusively in Spanish.

I had heard that [Jimmy] needed extra help when it came to reading and writing, so that's why I was surprised at how well he did on "Graficas." He said that he never learned any Spanish, so I would read him the directions on the screen in Spanish and then tell him what they meant in English. Pretty soon, he caught on and would know what a word meant in Spanish just by hearing it. He even made a few guesses of what animal was named in Spanish and got them right. Jimmy had fun with this game and wanted to keep playing it when we had completed the beginner level but it was time to close up shop.

The same student wrote the second field note two days later.

I then volunteered to work with Jimmy. He was totally into this facade of helplessness and he was distracted by anything. I wasn't going to fall into this portrayal of utter helplessness. He asked me to read what was printed on the screen and I told him he could do it, I knew he could. So I stood my ground and pointed at the first word and he began to read. I told him we could rotate and I would read the next [computer prompt] and he could read after that. This seemed to give him some reassurance.

The next example demonstrates how undergraduates can learn the "help as little as possible but as much as needed" principle through interaction with one another. It is taken from the field notes of a researcher at the Whittier College site.

Karla, a college student in her second semester of work, is playing "The Secret Island of Dr. Quandary" with nine-year-old Jonas. They are trying to find their way through a maze in the game. The maze is dark, and they are lost. [To get through, the player must have previously completed a jigsaw puzzle depicting a candle in order to use a candle as a source of light in the maze.]

Claudia, a worker with two years' experience who is serving as a coordinator, notices Karla's and Jonas's difficulty as she moves around the room. Approaching the two, Claudia comments, "Oh, it's so dark in there! What do you do at home when it's dark and you can't see?" "Get the light?" answers Jonas tentatively. "Yeah," says Claudia. She pauses, as if waiting to see what Jonas will do. Jonas says nothing and continues making moves in the dark maze, to no effect. Claudia asks, "So did you see anything you could use as a light somewhere?" "I didn't see no light switch in there," replies Jonas.

"What else can you use to make light, like if your electricity is out?" Claudia asks. Jonas looks up silently at Claudia for a few seconds, then says, "Oh! There was that candle. And there was a fire by that pot!"

"Remember that you have to try out everything," Claudia reminds Jonas as she moves away. Karla and Jonas leave the "Dr. Quandary" maze and begin searching the island again for the fire and candle.

The researcher's field notes add: "Later, I heard Karla talking to Claudia in the hall. Karla was telling Claudia how cool it was that Claudia got [Jonas] to think what he'd do 'in a real situation' if it was dark. 'That's a great strategy,' said Karla."

Both of these examples illuminate the processes through which undergraduate students' practices can change during the course of Fifth Dimension participation.

CONCLUSIONS

The undergraduates who participated in the Fifth Dimension courses experienced a learning system that provided a bridge between the postsecondary classroom and real-life settings as contexts for learning. The students were encouraged to try out in practice both the formal theoretical concepts from the classroom and the informal concepts that informed their prior understandings of teaching and learning. The studies from ASU and UCSD demonstrate that over time undergraduates move away from the notion of teaching as a linear, didactic process to the idea of teaching and learning as the outcome of social interactions between children and adults engaged in socially constituted practices. The studies from Whittier College suggest that participation in the hybrid practice of the Fifth Dimension practicum courses contributes to changes in undergraduates' participation that correlate with the length of time they are engaged in the practice and their increased proficiency in using the conceptual tools associated with the practice. All three studies suggest that these changes do not occur without a certain level of participation and certain duration of time as a participant.

This finding has implications for higher education, particularly in the areas of education and the social sciences where internships not only are brief—if they exist at all—but also are usually disassociated from courses that would provide students with opportunities to reflect on theoretical concepts and their relation to practice. Prolonged opportunities to engage in practice that reflectively use core theoretical concepts are needed if postsecondary students are to become proficient in understanding and acting on the public and professional meanings associated with that practice. Devoting a substantial amount of time to practice is required if theoretical knowledge is to be transformed into knowledgeable participation that mediates not only thinking, formulating, and communicating about professional experiences but acting on that knowledge.

learning is created/helped through theoretical concepts and practice

praxis

Chapter 8

The Diffusion of the Fifth Dimension

U p to this point, we have concentrated on describing the design and implementation of Fifth Dimension after-school programs that were all funded by the Mellon Foundation and participants in the research plan laid out in earlier chapters. In this chapter, we go beyond these early programs to describe events that we could not have predicted at the outset and that speak to the question of the viability of the Fifth Dimension as a form of after-school educational enrichment. As we have seen, some of the original Fifth Dimensions failed even when funding from the foundation was available, but it also transpired that educational enrichment programs inspired by the Fifth Dimension–UC Links model began to sprout up in a variety of new socio-ecological circumstances.

Recall from chapter 3 that expansion of the Fifth Dimension beyond the University of California at San Diego began with the funding in 1988 of projects in Illinois (Erikson Institute), Louisiana (the University of New Orleans), and Moscow (the Institute of Psychology). By 1995–96, the early projects in Louisiana and Illinois, as well as one that opened in 1990 in Michigan, had closed, but the projects at UCSD and Moscow were still running, as were new projects at the University of California at Santa Barbara and at Appalachian State University in North Carolina. These last two projects and the original UCSD project had also expanded locally through the addition of new community partners and sites. Additionally, a project had opened at the Benemérita Universidad Autónoma de Puebla (BUAP) in Puebla, Mexico. In 1995–96 the Moscow project closed, but seven other projects remained in operation—four in California, two in North Carolina, and one in Mexico.

To our surprise, Fifth Dimension activity proliferated rapidly after funding from the Mellon Foundation ended—some projects started, others closed, and still others expanded locally. The acceleration began in 1996–97: though some projects closed, the number of new projects expanded dramatically in the next two years, as we can see in figure 8.1. As new projects proliferated, new networks of projects began to link up with

Figure 8.1 Diffusion Pattern of Fifth Dimension Projects to Universities, 1996 to 2002

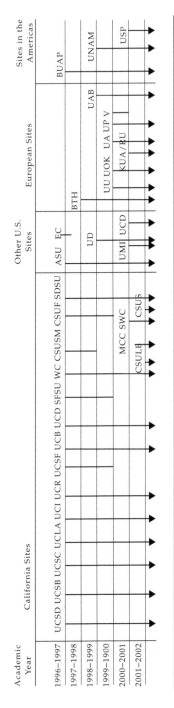

Source: Based on Nocon (2004, 271, figure 2).

California sites: UCSD, University of California, San Diego; UCSB, University of California, Santa Barbara; UCSC, University of California, Santa Cruz; UCLA, University of California, Los Angeles; UCI, University of California, Irvine; UCR, University of California, Riverside; UCSF, University of California, San Francisco; UCB, University of California, Berkeley; UCD, University of California, Davis; SFSU, San Francisco State University; WC, Whittier College; CSUSM, California State University, San Marcos; CSUF, California State University, Fresno; SDSU, San Diego State University; MCC, Mira Costa College, Oceanside; SWC, Southwestern College, San Diego; CSULB, California State University, Long Beach; CSUS, California State University, Sacramento.

Other U.S. sites: ASU, Appalachian State University, North Carolina; EC, Elon College, North Carolina; UD, University of Delaware; UMI, University of Miami, Florida; UCD, University of Colorado, Denver.

European sites: BTH, Blekinge Institute of Technology, Ronneby, Sweden; UU, Umeå University, Sweden; UOK, Oulu University, Kajaani, Finland; UA, Archangel University, Russia; UP, University of Petrovsk, Russia; KUA, University of Copenhagen, Denmark; RU, Roskilde University, Denmark; V, Vilnius University, Lithuania; UAB, Autonomous University of Barcelona, Spain.

Sites in the Americas: BUAP, Autonomous University of Puebla, Mexico; UNAM, National Autonomous University of Mexico; USP, University of São Paolo, Brazil.

what remained of the Distributed Literacy Consortium and connected it to new configurations of projects.

In this chapter, we try to make sense of this surprising expansion of the Fifth Dimension beyond its local roots (and beyond its initial funding) and the linkage of projects into networks. To do so we must first provide some history. Keeping the story as brief as possible, though as detailed as necessary, we demonstrate in this chapter that the expansion of the Fifth Dimension was facilitated by new forms of information and communication technologies (ICT) and by the openness of the Fifth Dimension design to diversity within the shared philosophical framework described in chapter 2. Not only new technologies but also shared values promoted sustained communication within the expanding Fifth Dimension networks of collaboration. Together with the university-community partnership design of Fifth Dimension sites, these factors allowed the projects and networks to take advantage of a sea change in higher education's interpretation of its mission.

PROLIFERATION AND NETWORKING

As noted, the expansion accelerated between 1996 and 1998, both nationally and internationally, with the greatest concentration in the Americas and Europe. The most rapid expansion of the Fifth Dimension occurred closest to its point of origin—California.

Expansion in California

On July 20, 1995, the Regents of the University of California eliminated affirmative action as a tool to ensure that admissions to the university system reflected the demographics of the state's population. In revising this policy, the Regents also provided for the support and development of programs to increase the eligibility rate of groups that were considered underrepresented at the university.

In response to the Regents' policy, faculty and researchers from the UCSD project, together with faculty from eight other UC campuses, developed a systemwide initiative based on the Fifth Dimension–UC Links model. Calling the initiative UC Links, they incorporated ICT into the design of a systematic K–16 model of educational enrichment built around university-community Fifth Dimension–like projects.

The proposal was funded with discretionary funds in 1996–97. The following year, all nine UC campuses (Berkeley, Davis, Irvine, Los Angeles, Riverside, San Diego, San Francisco, Santa Barbara, and Santa Cruz) and four California State University campuses (Fresno, San Francisco, San Marcos, and San Diego) ran Fifth Dimension projects. Seven of these projects were associated with a department of education, two with psychology, and one each with communication, behavioral sciences, linguistics, and La Raza studies.

UC Links was "permanently" funded by the university system in 1998, and four new Fifth Dimension–inspired UC Links sites began operating in the fall of 2001.[1] Most of the projects that operated in 2002 continued in the academic year 2004–2005, and the informal network of researchers and implementers who constitute UC Links has continued to expand.

Although the same family of sociocultural theories of learning and development informed all UC Links projects, the local sites varied even more than in the original set of sites, reflecting the increased diversity of research agendas as well as teaching goals. For example, two sites associated with UC Berkeley have explored learning among K–3 children in after-school programs at two schools identified by their districts as "needy." The projects at UC Riverside and UCLA, both taking place in schools after school, have focused on the development of literacy and academic skills in the context of teacher training. The project at UC Santa Cruz began operating in a community center but moved onto the UCSC campus when computer maintenance became an insuperable barrier. Other projects have moved into "digital storytelling" with older primary and secondary students. In spite of these differences, all of the projects share certain features: an activity structure that mixes play, education, and social interaction between children or youth and college students; a model for community-based teaching, research, and outreach; and the UC Links model for intersegmental, or cross-campus, collaboration mediated by ICT and periodic face-to-face meetings.

An illustration of this diversity in commonality is the use at several of the UC Links projects of videoconferencing to link associated courses in joint discussion, enabling students to compare their experiences in the local Fifth Dimension sites. And recently a password-protected Web space has been developed so that children can share their work online with children at other sites.

When UC Links was first conceived and funded, the "UC" referred to the University of California. However, because the Distributed Literacy Consortium included projects that were outside the UC system, the reference was changed to "University-Community." This symbolic move supports the inclusion of the new projects and networks that have formed in Europe and elsewhere in the Americas.

Expansion in Europe

In 1996 Michael Cole began discussing the possibility of adapting the Fifth Dimension model with Berthel Sutter at the Blekinge School of Technology in southern Sweden. Sutter's goal was to expand undergraduate education in a program that prepared students to be software designers. At the time, Swedish universities were being called upon by their government to take on the "third mission" of community development; this university had interpreted that call as working to expand the use of ICT in the economically depressed region in which it was located. The Fifth Dimension seemed to offer a tool for seriously addressing this mission.

The Swedish project, which opened in the School of Technology media center/library, was unusual in that different groups of researchers ran separate programs for two hours in the late afternoon for a total of two to four days per week. The space and equipment were shared, but the program content differed, as did the clienteles. The separate programs focused on ICT, English-language practice, Web page design, and construction and programming of computerized robots. This project also offered numerous short-term Fifth Dimension programs to community children each summer.

Another researcher from the Blekinge School of Technology, Monica Nilsson, started another Fifth Dimension site in an elementary school in Blekinge after visiting sites at UCSD. The goal of this site is research into the transformation and development of school structures and activities.

In 1999 researchers from the Swedish university project began collaborating with researchers from the University of Oulu, Finland, and the University of Umeå in northern Sweden, both of which had also initiated projects in 1999. In 2001 the Blekinge project began running joint activities with a new Fifth Dimension project in Denmark that had begun in 2000.

Concurrent with this expansion in northern Europe, a Spanish project associated with the Universitat Autònoma in Barcelona began in much the same way as the project in Blekinge. Spanish researchers who had developed a community-based research project in a Gypsy community in Barcelona visited several California Fifth Dimension projects and were given access to materials and reports. The Spanish team later adapted the Fifth Dimension to incorporate Gypsy cultural elements and implemented a site in the local Gypsy association hall.

The European projects share elements of the Fifth Dimension but are quite diverse. The Spanish project, like the project in Denmark, is associated with a department of psychology. While the Danish project focuses on technology skills for children in the upper elementary grades, as do some of the Swedish programs, the Spanish project runs various programs targeting literacy and academic content for children and youth. In 2004–2005 the Spanish project was operating in four Barcelona schools. The Finnish project, in contrast to the Spanish, Swedish, and Danish projects, focuses on narrative and play for preschoolers and children in the primary elementary grades.

The European projects formed networks shortly after opening. To facilitate the exchange of knowledge, regular communication, and the movement of researchers and students between the sites, researchers working with Fifth Dimension projects in Denmark, Sweden, and Norway developed the Nordic Network of Fifth Dimensions, which has generated funds for knowledge exchange. The Nordic Network, which expanded in 2000, has also been instrumental in securing grants for collaborative research and in developing two new networks of Fifth Dimension sites—one a project supported by the European Union, the other a collaboration between the European sites and American sites.

The European sites in Sweden, Denmark, and Spain received funding for a project called "Fifth Dimension: Local Learning Communities in a Global World," which began in April 2001. Its mission is to develop knowledge about learning as well as new ICT and multimedia artifacts to transform learning in schools. The target audience includes teachers, researchers in education, and people engaged in developing new ways of learning. In late 2000 researchers at the Blekinge project became aware of a funding opportunity that would support the exchange of graduate and undergraduate students between universities in Europe and the United States. With the Florida and Sweden teams taking the lead, the grant proposal was developed using international telecommunication between seven universities. The European Commission and the U.S. Department of Education's Fund for Improvement of Post-Secondary Education (FIPSE) funded the proposal in 2001. Students and researchers from both sides of the Atlantic began visiting Fifth Dimension projects abroad while developing joint transatlantic activities. The seven project teams are also developing instructional materials that will be used at all seven universities and made available to potential Fifth Dimension site developers through the Web resources www.uclinks.org and www.5d.org.

Expansion in the Americas Outside the United States

As noted earlier, the Fifth Dimension expanded into Mexico in 1995 with the opening of a project at the Benemérita Universidad Autónoma de Puebla. This project was associated with the departments of linguistics and psychology and ran after school through 2002. Different iterations of the Mexican project have since started and stopped.

In 1998 a project opened at the Universidad Nacional Autónoma de Mexico (UNAM) in Mexico City. This project is associated with the department of psychology and runs in a school during the school day. In 2001 the principal investigators from UCSB in California and BUAP in Puebla, Mexico, along with colleagues at UC Davis, UCSD, and UNAM, developed a successful proposal to study the use of high-speed Internet connections in binational learning among children, college students, and communities engaged in Fifth Dimension–inspired programs. Moving beyond the Fifth Dimension model's emphasis on educational games, these Mexican-American projects shifted the focus to more complex learning and communication activities for children and adult participants mediated by high-speed, broadband telecommunication. Designed to study the roles of globalization and personal and group agency in a technology-based international learning enterprise, the partners collaborated to build locally meaningful program activities and binationally meaningful scholarly exchange, using a culture-based approach.

A less technology-intensive but similarly meaningful scholarly exchange contributed to the extension of the Fifth Dimension to São Paolo, Brazil, in 2000. Like the projects in Berkeley, California, and Oulu, Finland, the new Brazilian project was associated with two preschool sites, both of which continue to this day.

Expansion in the United States

The project at Appalachian State University provides an interesting case of both local expansion and survival in the face of the principal investigator's departure. As a unique and enduring case, it bears further examination.

As noted in chapter 3, the ASU project sought to demonstrate the effectiveness of the Fifth Dimension as an early clinical teaching experience for teacher education candidates. The year before the Fifth Dimension was implemented at ASU, the National Council for the Accreditation of Teacher Education (NCATE) set a standard that called for teacher education candidates to engage in early field experiences. ASU's College of Education had many undergraduates who were entering teacher education, but the local school system was small; clinical sites for early field experiences were thus extremely limited. These conditions made possible the innovative strategy of implementing a Fifth Dimension project, a joint activity between the university's teacher program and local schools that met the needs of undergraduates, local schools, parents, children, and university faculty.

In its second year, the ASU Fifth Dimension expanded to four programs—three in schools and one in a teaching laboratory at the campus. All were supported by a clinical teacher preparation grant. Following the success of the Fifth Dimension, the College of Education decided to provide the administrative support, faculty time, technical assistance, hardware, software, and graduate assistants necessary to sustain Fifth Dimension programs in both the college and the public schools. In 2002 there were still four sites affiliated with the ASU project running in schools in surrounding communities. As of 2004–2005, these sites had survived the relocation of the principal investigator, William Blanton, to Miami. (Blanton quickly developed a Fifth Dimension project at the University of Miami, contributing to the Fifth Dimension's national expansion.)

Other new U.S. sites have also been started by doctoral students who, after their work with an existing project, took a job at a new institution and carried the Fifth Dimension model and philosophy with them. For example, a Fifth Dimension called La Red Mágica was developed at the University of Delaware in 1998 by Eugene Matusov, a former doctoral student who had worked with the Fifth Dimension project at UC Santa Cruz. The project at the University of Colorado at Denver, which began in 2000 as the result of communication between faculty there and Michael Cole, expanded locally when Honorine Nocon, a former doctoral student from UCSD, joined that faculty.

In a manner typical of the proliferating Fifth Dimension projects elsewhere, the new U.S. sites share the philosophy and open structure of the original projects but are diverse in their adaptations. Unlike the UCSD project, the projects in Florida, Delaware, and Colorado, like the ASU project, are associated with schools of education. All of these sites, like UCLA's, are located in low-income urban areas with large minority populations. La Red Mágica in Delaware and the Tools Club in Denver focus on technology and media development. The second site in Denver, El Aguila's Club, like La Clase Mágica at UCSD, focuses on second-language acquisition and first-language maintenance. Unlike LCM, this Denver Fifth Dimension is located in a school.

ICT AS A TOOL FOR EXPANSION AND COMING TOGETHER

A major activity of the Fifth Dimension Distributed Literacy Consortium was archiving and disseminating information to universities, colleges, and community organizations interested in exploring the development of Fifth Dimension projects in their communities. To accomplish this goal, the Mellon Foundation funded the Fifth Dimension Clearinghouse, a Web-based resource developed and housed on a server at ASU from 1998 to 2000. The move of the clearinghouse server to the University of Miami with Blanton in 2000 complicated the URL, but shortly thereafter the clearinghouse was linked to the UC Links Web site, http://www.uclinks.org. Both the clearinghouse and UC Links Web sites are also linked to http://www.5d.org, the Web resource developed by the European projects. Researchers and community partners abroad use these Web resources to share materials, research, and information about their Fifth Dimension projects. Visitors to any one of these Web sites have access to all three. This openness to learning and collaboration reflects the philosophy underlying the Fifth Dimension. The Web sites serve as resources for new projects and old; experienced Fifth Dimension hands can learn from each other while making the tools available to persons or institutions interested in developing their own projects.

We now turn to consideration of what we learned from reflecting on the diffusion of the Fifth Dimension.

MAKING SENSE

We can see from this brief history that the expansion of the Fifth Dimension after 1996 was facilitated by information and communication technology in two ways: the use of ICT between the old and new Fifth Dimension projects, and the development by many projects of new ways of using ICT. Both uses of ICT were expanded by the rapid development of telecommunication in the 1990s and the interest of private and public funding agents in supporting that development for learning. A case in point is the Fifth Dimension collaboration between UC Links and the European Union. Both networks have systematically used ICT to link geographically distributed projects. Both networks also were funded specifically to expand the use of ICT in learning activities. UC Links combined the use of the Internet and room-to-room videoconferencing to expand the undergraduate curriculum to include interaction between students working at remote Fifth Dimension sites. The shared frame but diverse local adaptations of these different sites facilitated students' critical comparisons of similarities and contrasts as well as their joint problem-solving and critical analysis of distance learning as an educational medium.

The European project was funded under the European Commission's funding framework "Information, Society, and Technology, School of Tomorrow." The EU's goal was to develop new uses for ICT that would help schools prepare students for a society ever more dependent on ICT. Using ICT in collaborative research and development involving three European countries, the EU partners also made use of local Fifth Dimension projects and sites to develop learning tools, including a Web-based game shell to which teachers can easily add their own content, a Web-based communication and construction site that permits children and teachers to construct virtual communities with others at remote sites, and the Web portal www.5d.org. As noted earlier, this last ICT learning tool is linked to uclinks.org and the Fifth Dimension Clearinghouse.

Although ICT has clearly played a significant role in the expansion of the Fifth Dimension, technological tools themselves do not explain why people and projects use them for ongoing and expanding connection and communication, or why those engaged in such communication seek to collaborate. We believe that Everett Rogers's (1995, 2002) work on the diffusion of innovations can help to explain this pattern of expanding collaboration.

According to Rogers (2002, 990), "*Diffusion* is the process through which (1) an innovation (2) is communicated through certain channels (3) over time (4) among members of a social system." Central to Rogers's approach is the idea that innovations are most likely to diffuse to potential participants who share a number of features with the initial innovators but are also somewhat different. Some degree of difference is essential for innovation and learning to occur, because too much similarity in values and experience gives people very little new information about which to communicate. Rogers (1983, 1995, 19) describes the optimal balance of similarity and difference as one in which individuals "seek network links with others who are slightly, but not too much, more technologically competent about the innovation than themselves."

In Rogers's view, the communication that helps innovations like the Fifth Dimension to proliferate does not just happen. It builds on the shared elements and common interests and values that bring people and institutions together to form social systems. In Fifth Dimension networks, people and projects are philosophically aligned with the concept that all cultures change over time and that they cannot help being in communication with each another. They share the belief that contact and communication with other cultures—within communities and across towns, states, nations, and continents—support learning and development. They also share a belief in the educational efficacy of the Fifth Dimension's Vygotskian framework, which describes learning as a social and cultural activity and views all learners in terms of their potential.

At the same time, Rogers argues, too much similarity in values can stifle communication. Sustained communication requires a balance of shared values and diversity. Otherwise, there is little to talk about. In the Fifth Dimension, a balance of shared values and diversity is incorporated into the model's design. The underlying philosophy and the structural frame of the model activity are shared, linking people who also share values and providing them with a common frame of reference for their work. At the same time, the openness of the structural frame requires that each local project and site adapt the Fifth Dimension to local needs, interests, and cultures. We believe that this common frame of reference that at the same time privileges diversity has also contributed significantly to the expansion of the Fifth Dimension.

In addition to ICT and a structure that provides a common frame of reference while privileging diversity, a review of the history of the Fifth Dimension's expansion in the last ten years also suggests that either good luck or good planning—or more likely a bit of both—has been involved. As we have seen in earlier chapters, the Fifth Dimension design assumes a partnership between a university and a community. When the Fifth Dimension work began in the early 1980s, the model's community-based research and teaching practices represented an innovation. Service to the community by universities, particularly research universities, was not part of the equation. Ten years later things had changed.

A sea change in higher education found universities and their governing bodies espousing the value of community-based learning for university students (if not community-based research) and university service to the community in the interest of community learning and development. We can see this change in the UC Regents' call in 1995 for programming that would enhance the learning of those in the community who were underrepresented at the university. We can see it in the Swedish Ministry of Education's support for a "third mission" for Swedish universities. We can see this in the requirement that education students at ASU participate in early field-based learning.

The Fifth Dimension was uniquely poised to respond to this international sea change in higher education: as a model of community-based teaching and service, it had the good fortune of being in the right places at the right times. The open structure of the Fifth Dimension model and the distributed and ICT-mediated nature of the Distributed Literacy Consortium also positioned Fifth Dimension participants in such a way that they could respond to this opportunity, both locally and globally.

The unexpected expansion of the Fifth Dimension beyond its local roots, original goals, and initial funding provides lessons about both the dissemination and the sustainability of educational innovations. These lessons include the social use of new tools and technologies; the value of common, but open, structures built on shared philosophies of learning; and the productive role of diversity in educational design. It is to these issues that we turn in chapter 9.

Chapter 9

Lessons Learned

Having provided an account of our multiyear attempt to design, implement, and sustain Fifth Dimension–UC Links after-school programs and their associated courses in colleges and universities, it is time to return to our starting point to reflect on what we have accomplished, where we have failed, and the lessons others might draw from our experience.

Our experience with the Fifth Dimension has strongly reinforced our belief that understanding issues of designing, implementing, and evaluating after-school activity programs requires constant attention not only to aspects of the activity designed for children but to the institutional arrangements that form the necessary context for the activity, as well as the historical and socio-ecological circumstances in which such efforts are carried out. Although all of these issues are simultaneously in play when we consider any example of an educational innovation, it is not possible to discuss them all at once. So for the sake of convenience, we discuss questions of design, implementation, evaluation, and socio-ecological circumstances sequentially. We end by discussing the contemporary circumstances of such efforts and their broader implications.

QUESTIONS OF DESIGN

As indicated at several points in this book, we saw in the after-school hours an opportunity to provide not only more "time on task" for standard school lessons but an entirely new kind of development-enhancing environment. Like others (Halpern 2003; Honig and McDonald 2005), we had come to believe that the unique contribution of after-school time is *not* to run homework rooms where children simply spend more time on preset tasks, just as they do when filling out their workbooks at school. Our own prior empirical research had demonstrated that failure to allow children to form goals (a dominant feature of classroom practices) decreases both transfer of knowledge and motivation to learn, especially for those children whose family backgrounds do not socialize them into the normative school culture (Newman, Griffin, and Cole 1989).

The challenge was to create forms of activity that would give children many opportunities to take initiative with respect to tasks that they found interesting while maintaining the adult goal of improving educational achievement.

Now that we have taken a look at many Fifth Dimension programs based on the theoretical principles we proposed in chapter 2, it is appropriate to revisit our results to see how useful these ideas proved to be in practice.

Taking Context into Account

A primary consideration for Fifth Dimension programs is the importance of conducting the activity on weekday afternoons between the time children leave school and the time their parents arrive home for the evening (for recent discussions of this time in children's lives, see Larson and Verma 1999; Noam 2003). From early in the twentieth century until the last few years, it has been widely assumed that children should be free to play during this period in their day, either unsupervised in their homes and neighborhoods or in adult-supervised settings (Halpern 2003). Moreover, many developmentalists have argued that such play is important to children's development (for a review, see Cole, Cole, and Lightfoot 2005). As we noted in chapter 1, side by side with this valorization of play has been concern that, left unsupervised, children get into mischief and fail to acquire the intellectual skills and social graces thought necessary for social success—in effect, that lack of supervision puts them at risk for a life of poverty and crime.

By our analysis, the social demand that children's after-school time be organized to amplify the experiences provided by the school and reduce crime created contradictions between several factors:

- Adult beliefs in the efficacy of play and children's desire to play after school

- Adult suspicions of play combined with their fears about social order

- Children's distaste for the rigid social control practices characteristic of schools combined with their desire to escape adult control

Consequently, our fundamental challenge was to design an activity that could overcome these contradictions by blending play with educational tasks in such a way that children would be drawn to it, as they are to play, while adults would view it as advancing their goals for social order and children's development—particularly their educational achievement.

Taking into Account Leading Activities

According to the Vygotskian theoretical tradition, the periods of childhood enshrined in our educational structures are most fruitfully conceived of in terms of the major forms of activity that characterize them, because such an analysis points toward the factors that are likely to motivate children's participation (Griffin and Cole 1984). Roughly speaking, the leading activity of infancy is to become affiliated with, accepted into, and attached to the social group; symbolic, pretend play becomes the leading activity in early childhood, followed by learning in middle childhood, peer interaction in adolescence, and work in adulthood.[1] An important point about leading activities and their related motives is that "old" leading activities do not disappear; they remain as motivational resources under the right conditions (Cole and Subbotsky 1993).

Since our focal population was elementary-age children, we assumed that the appropriate way to bring as many motivation-inducing, leading activities to bear was to place our focus on games (especially games that involve various rules, which Piaget identified as of special interest to this age group); to retain elements of fantasy play; and to rely on the fact that the children would be anxious to be accepted and loved by their peers and the undergraduates and that they would be interested in learning how to excel at the various gamelike activities we provided. Therefore, we expected the enormous variety of individual activities and the social norms of the Fifth Dimension to maximize the possibility that any given participant would find something engaging to do.

The simultaneous presence of several leading activities at any given time combines with the multigenerational social structure of Fifth Dimensions to support the creation of zones of proximal development (zopeds) by its very structure. First, we expected play itself to create zopeds, following Vygotsky's (1978) evocative notion that in play children are a head taller than themselves. Play was encouraged not only by the presence of many games but in the character of mythical figures and the many opportunities these quasi-fictional entities provided for the undergraduates and children to pretend together. Second, the presence of undergraduates—"more capable peers"—as coparticipants ensured that learning would lead development, both through their modeling of learning actions and through their academic knowledge.

Our experience taught us that the Fifth Dimension supported zoped-like interactions in other ways as well because the concept of a more capable peer takes on a different meaning in Fifth Dimensions. The undergraduates may be chronologically older than the children and more capable in their school-based knowledge, but they often have less experience in the local idioculture and less expertise in attaining locally valued goals, such as solving a puzzle in "Zoombinis," knowing who is likely to want to work or play with whom, constructing a bird from origami, or—as many undergraduates learned to their chagrin—playing chess! It is interesting in this regard that undergraduates often came to define a zoped as entailing a mixture of play and learning-teaching that is not to be found in Vygotsky's work but was a pervasive feature of their own experience in a Fifth Dimension.

Bridging Theoretical Starting Points

Some scholars make a sharp distinction between approaches to learning and development that focus on mediational artifacts, and others that focus on modes of participation (Matusov and Hayes 2000). However, our belief is that the mediated joint activities seen in a typical Fifth Dimension that foster the formation of zopeds simultaneously satisfy the conditions for the formation of a "community of practice." As both the language and culture and process evaluation teams reported, each Fifth Dimension community has its own rules and values and its own idioculture in which children, college students, local staff, and academics pursue activities that constitute a "play world" (a Fifth Dimension, a Clase Mágica, a Club Proteo, and so on). In this play world, expertise is widely distributed, participants are encouraged to share information about how to achieve various goals, and patterns of engagement in particular activities are fluid, changing from hour to hour, from day to day, and from month to month. Children's learning and development are recognized not only by their competence in culturally valued tasks (both in the local Fifth Dimension and in the community in which it is implemented) but also by their changing roles within the social group and correspondingly different modes of participation.

Looking at Fifth Dimension sites as local communities of practice helps both to motivate and to explain the design strategy of selecting program content that reflects the host community's history and identity as natural means for enhancing local activities. An important motive for some children was to become a Wizard's Assistant as a means of gaining access to more sophisticated activities or greater freedom in choosing what to do each day. For others who attended programs that routinely made visits to local businesses or the local university or college, the development of broader community awareness provided a rich source of new motives. Such variations were central to the modes of participation at all of the sites.

Our desire to keep the arrangements flexible so that children and adults could take up various other tasks when their first choice was unavailable required that we take some care in selecting and designing tools that would blend play and learning. For example, if an activity was gamelike in its surface features but school-like in its content and internal structure (for example, "Mathblasters," a drill and practice activity disguised as a game), we designed the auxiliary tools to make the game less school-like by titrating the demand level of the game, allowing children to play it cooperatively, and using progress achieved rather than absolute level attained as the measure of success. By contrast, we supplemented blatantly arcade-style games whose intellectual content was minimal ("Pacman" was an early favorite) with artifacts that enhanced their intellectual content, such as requiring the child to write a hint about a good strategy for avoiding the troggles or a note to El Maga about what made the game enough fun to warrant keeping it in the Fifth Dimension.

The combination of a focus on local communities of practice and mediational means provided the design strategies for making reading, writing, information seeking, and explaining routine means to the end of having a good time. Also helpful was the rule of thumb that undergraduates were encouraged to adopt: that they assist the children just enough to ensure that they and the children both had a good time. This guideline encouraged children's independence and initiative and helped to ensure that the activity remained fun so that the children would come to it of their own accord.

Privileging Diversity

It should be clear to the reader that the principle of privileging diversity applies along many dimensions of Fifth Dimension programs simultaneously. First, as illustrated by the design of several of the sites, issues of linguistic and cultural diversity played a prominent role in the selection of games, the design of artifacts such as the maze and the task cards, the involvement of adults from the broader community, and the language practices promoted. Second, we knew from our pilot work that even when all the undergraduate participants are taking the same course at the same university, the elements of the initial Fifth Dimension prototype must be modified and blended at each site to take into consideration the spatial arrangements, the host community, and the available technical resources. (Does the site have computers? Does it have access to the Internet or a reliable mechanism for computer repairs? Do undergraduates speak the language of the local community, even a little? Is the host institution one where adults expect to hand over responsibility for their children or one where adults are expected to continue to be involved?) Third, we needed to consider the age and gender mix of the children at the site. Activities attractive to first-graders could not be expected to appeal to sixth-graders, and those for boys would be different from those for girls. The presence of preschoolers might provoke negative reactions in an Anglo neighborhood but feel perfectly normal and entertaining in a Mexicano neighborhood. Ethnic and linguistic backgrounds, ages, genders, kinds of equipment, and different kinds of space all entered into the design of a blended space that would produce a form of activity recognizable as a Fifth Dimension yet unique in its particular instantiation of the prototype.

Turning diversity into a resource for learning and development required strategic use of all the other design principles. The fact that young children knew more about the activities than the undergraduates sometimes impressed on the undergraduates the tenuous and conditional nature of their academic and age superiority, leveling the playing field and helping to create mutual respect in place of age-related and ethnic stereotypes. This happened in a variety of ways. One common instance of such learning is illustrated in chapter 6: the child Sonia understands Spanish but cannot read yet, while Larry, the undergraduate, can read but does not understand Spanish. Such interactions can quickly turn a child who is considered less capable or peripheral into a fount of knowledge and a center of attention.

Designing the University Courses

The principles revisited here apply as much to the design of college or university courses as they do to the design of Fifth Dimension activities at the community site, although the specifics in each case clearly differ. The principle of context plays a role in determining where the requisite course will fit into the curriculum, who will teach it, how it will be organized, and how much support it may garner. At a research university where Fifth Dimension students are from the psychology or communication department, a convincing argument is likely to be made that these social science students need to have a serious laboratory course. In the context of a department of education, the designers might attend to the need to understand principles of teaching and learning in formal versus informal educational settings, or the role of transmission in learning, or ways to become comfortable with linguistic and cultural differences between teachers and students.

Theoretically, it is not the blending of play and learning that preoccupies the designers of university or college courses but the goal of finding the maximal way to mix the theoretical work carried out on campus with the practice of participating in children's development at the site.

Designing Interinstitutional Collaborations

When Cole and his colleagues undertook the design of the initial Fifth Dimension, they gave what seems to us now shockingly little thought to the need to design the arrangements between the community site and the university. In the overall plan, the college teacher–researcher was expected to design the local Fifth Dimension adaptation along with colleagues from the community site and to supervise the college students' work. Although a plan for training local site personnel in the rationale and procedures of the Fifth Dimension was routinely included in the design activities, this aspect of the work was assumed to more or less "take care of itself." In reality, such collaboration did not take care of itself. It was often the community people who needed to train the university researchers in what it means to conduct research in the community and for researchers to teach their administrations what it means to enter into a partnership beyond academia, in deed and not just in rhetoric.

QUESTIONS OF IMPLEMENTATION

As every designer of a product and every consumer of a designed product knows, it is one thing to design a new tool or institution and quite another to implement it. It would be totally misleading to leave the reader with the impression that a Fifth Dimension can simply be "planted" in a community organization, where it will live or die as a consequence of the fit between the original design and the environment into which it was inserted.

It is an important fact that implementation is the continuation of design activities under new conditions, requiring as it does just as much work, time, and ingenuity. It is no wonder that Web sites about the implementation of after-school sites (for example, www.afterschoolalliance.org) suggest that implementers devote a year to implementation before they start seeking funds to sustain their site. It takes at least this long to know what in fact it is that one is seeking to sustain!

An important commonality across projects is the never-ending need to deal with the dynamics of change at both the community site and the university; those dynamics inevitably lead to changes in the relation between the two loci. Although a number of measures have been taken to reduce the work of implementing a Fifth Dimension, none of those measures has ever seemed adequate to reduce the workload to the level of, say, running the arts and crafts room at the boys and girls club or conducting a lecture class for twenty-five to thirty undergraduates.

As we hope the reader has come to expect, the specifics of the extra work differed from site to site. Despite local variations in the specifics of the issues involved, all of the programs have experienced an ongoing need for interaction between the two collaborating institutions to keep them coordinated with each other. Eventually we realized that even if the cost of running the Fifth Dimension is only a fraction of what a comparable laboratory would cost at a university, and only a fraction of the cost of hiring a large number of highly motivated, supervised undergraduates to work with the children, the program does require a kind of staff person for whom none of the projects initially budgeted and whose work is otherwise absorbed by project personnel. The job requirements for such a staff person ideally include knowledge about the theoretical principles of Fifth Dimension design; the ability to complete low-level maintenance work on various Fifth Dimension tools, including computers, task cards, and software; the willingness to visit the college course and the site on a regular basis; and the time to read samples of student field notes and chat with students and child participants. We learned that in Scandinavian organizational research such a person is called "a spider," an especially appropriate term for a person who travels around a network, carrying the news from one place to another and repairing torn "threads" (Nocon 2004).

We have more to say later in the chapter about the real time costs of implementation when we discuss the challenges to sustainability.

QUESTIONS OF EVALUATION

In chapters 4 through 6, we presented the rationale and results of our evaluation research in terms of two basic approaches. One sought to document the processes occurring in the course of the activities at various sites; the other sought to measure quantitatively the outcomes of such in situ processes in terms that could be interpreted within the framework of "scientifically based" assessments. Here we summarize what each of these two approaches suggests about our success in designing and implementing Fifth Dimensions, and we add another evaluative criterion: how the community evaluates its local program, as indicated by the resources the community puts into it.

Process Evaluation

The outside researchers charged with evaluating the processes in the Fifth Dimension programs at the various sites came to the following conclusions, which we present here in somewhat abbreviated form.

First, these researchers observed that *learning, more than is the case in the many classrooms we have studied over the past two decades, is a constant possibility at Fifth Dimension clubs.* The children who participate in these programs learn how to play some games in which various lessons they are learning at school are present in an entertainment format at the same time that they learn broader lessons about life from their participation in the informal settings of the Fifth Dimension—such as how to work as well as play with others, how to handle mastery, and how to negotiate social relations. All of these lessons are much easier to learn in a Fifth Dimension than in school, where the institutional knowledge transmission agenda takes up so much time. The Fifth Dimension, partially by the design of its own learning theory and partially because it is always in a struggle to survive, is a self-conscious learning institution.

The outside researchers' second conclusion about the processes that occur in Fifth Dimension programs derives from their understanding of the cultural context of American schools. It is possible to look at American culture as the product of millions of people struggling to make knowledge acquisition and ownership into the ultimate mechanism for access to the rewards of society. Figuring out what knowledge counts is a major political battle, and the answers must be carefully framed in relation to standardization, equity, and fairness (Varenne and McDermott 1998). In this system, there are constant skirmishes for legitimacy between education and entertainment, between people with access to different kinds of knowledge and people with access to different levels of authority. This is the cultural context for school as a battleground, and tension, if not open conflict, is certainly the experience many children have with most educational institutions. In their evaluation, the outside researchers noted that *the Fifth Dimension provides relief for children from many of the tensions inherent in our educational institutions.*

It is not possible for children to fail the Fifth Dimension in the sense in which it is possible to fail in school. It is possible to have an unproductive Fifth Dimension experience, and it is essential for all participants to realize that they are responsible for making the activities productive. To accomplish this goal the designers and implementers of Fifth Dimensions must ensure that interesting tasks (both educational and entertaining) are available, that many kinds of people are ready to lend many kinds of knowledge, and that there are ways to legitimate how to do the best job possible (a negotiated social order). These themes, which marked participation in the Fifth Dimensions we studied, are the hallmarks of the sort of environment in which a good learning theory can be built upon in new institutional contexts.

Product (Performance) Evaluation

The process evaluation team's conclusion that the interactions between children and undergraduates are infused with academic tasks that classroom ethnographers find valuable is, of course, gratifying. But this qualitative process analysis does not speak to the need for a variety of quantitative approaches to evaluation, including experimental and quasi-experimental methods and simple pre- and post-test comparisons using tests and tasks valued by the educational community. Both the local and academic communities want such information because resources, including knowledge of "what works," are often in short supply. In addition, researchers who do not conduct such quantitative evaluations are excluding themselves from the growing discussion on educational design, and the design of after-school programming in particular. This kind of evidence cannot stand alone, as the National Research Council (NRC) Committee on Community-Level Programs for Youth has made clear (Eccles and Gootman 2002). However, in combination with the evidence presented in chapter 5, such product-level data do corroborate and make interpretable the conclusions of the process evaluation team.

In the discussion of evaluation in chapter 4, we sought to make it clear that we did not think it would be easy to find the conditions that would allow us to collect quantitative evidence of the efficacy of the Fifth Dimension in many settings. We were not disappointed in this dour expectation, but we are encouraged by the fact that in some conditions it was possible to undertake matched comparison control studies and that other conditions allowed us to carry out cleverly designed quasi-experimental evaluations.

What conditions make it possible to conduct standardized experimental studies of Fifth Dimension–UC Links after-school programs? Several answers present themselves. One answer appears to be scarcity of opportunity coupled with high demand, as suggested in the grant proposal that initiated this research. Significantly, the NRC report on community programs for youth noted that it was in neighborhoods with few facilities for after-school programs that scientifically acceptable experimental studies were most likely to be found (Eccles and Gootman 2002).[2]

The site whose conditions best matched these dual criteria was at Appalachian State University, where children were recruited from the after-school custodial care provided because adults in this rural area could not be home in the middle of the afternoon to greet them. Doing supervised homework in settings with high child-adult ratios was the alternative to participation in the Fifth Dimension, so a great many more children wanted to participate in the Fifth Dimension than could be accommodated. Consequently, it was possible to test far more children than could participate at one time and establish experimental control comparisons. We can also view Miriam Schustack's success in conducting quasi-experimental studies in this light: by strictly limiting access to her Fifth Dimension and using a sign-up sheet to keep the number of children participating equal to the number of undergraduates present, she created conditions that allowed her both to keep close count of each child's participation and to obtain cooperation in her pre- and post-testing.

But the conditions that permitted experimental and quasi-experimental studies were not limited to conditions that combined desirability with scarcity. The experience of Richard Mayer and Richard Duran at UCSB is instructive in this regard (see chapter 4). Because their long involvement in the local school system had made their program's value and their commitment visible to the community, they received enough community help that they were able to create comparison groups for their quantitative studies.

Another condition that is likely to support standard experimental evaluations is conducting activities in schools after school. We take it to be no accident that sites located in local schools—where children were supervised during the after-school hours until buses came to pick them up as dinnertime approached—supplied our own easiest cases for evaluation. A sizable proportion of the 21st Century Community Learning Centers are conducted in schools, and teachers are an important part of the workforce for implementing these programs. The challenge in these cases is balancing a continuation of the school day by other fiscal means while also following the Fifth Dimension principle of balancing play, peer interaction, and school-style learning (Polman 2004). Parental or community involvement is, almost by definition, excluded from consideration at such venues. ASU minimized the former set of problems by having trained college students, already imbued with the principles of the Fifth Dimension, serve as site coordinators. ASU's relationship to the schools as supporters of technological innovation combined with the structural features of schooling and its disciplinary regime provide the built infrastructure that enabled standardized testing, but it also endangered theoretically appropriate implementation.

Evaluation in the Most Difficult of Circumstances

In a great many cases, despite a number of creative efforts, even quasi-experimental approaches were foiled. For example, time and again the language and culture team ran up against the same kinds of problems that Cole had encountered in his early research on the Fifth Dimension (see chapter 3). Not only did the voluntary nature of the program make selection factors an ever-present possibility, but at all the sites they studied they had to account for rapid, ubiquitous, and unpredictable changes—in routines at the site, in the child participants, in school-based testing that rendered test results impossible to interpret, and in school and site personnel. Because of staff turnover, agreements reached one year did not survive long enough to allow post-testing the next year.

Acknowledging that these dynamics reduced the potential for uniform testing, we have felt compelled to also recognize that the Fifth Dimension–UC Links program's focus on local adaptation stands in direct contradiction to the ideals of those charged with administering large-scale programs, which must be held accountable to government bodies for how they spend their money.

As Larry Cuban (2004) noted in a recent address, different stakeholders in educational reforms are wedded to different criteria for determining what constitutes a reasonable standard of evaluation. As in the national debate about the 21st Century Community Learning Centers program, the goals of policymakers and bureaucrats, who must provide evidence of how public moneys will be spent, are likely to focus on quantitative evidence of effectiveness and the fidelity of a single model using standard measuring instruments. To these players, deviation from the initial design is a sure measure of failure. To teachers and principals, however, as Cuban (2004, 9–10) points out,

> the very same modifications are viewed as healthy signs of flexibility, inventiveness, and active problem solving in reaching effectiveness. How, practitioners ask, can you determine whether an innovation is successful unless we adapt the change to the unique conditions of this classroom, this school? The practitioner-derived standard of *adaptiveness* (the flip side of the fidelity standard) becomes essential prior to applying any other criteria. The question boils down to one of power and status: whose standards count?

It should be clear that these considerations apply equally to our efforts to evaluate the Fifth Dimension–UC Links program in its various manifestations. The operations of the programs at each site are consistent with the overall principles and purpose of the system, but the programs are, in principle, not identical point for point. These variations, combined with the voluntary nature of participation, make uniform testing of subjects randomly assigned to uniform experimental treatments a rare occurrence.

Community Evaluation

In concluding this discussion of evaluation challenges, we want to examine an evaluation criterion that is largely ignored in the literature on after-school programs: the extent to which the community demonstrates its evaluation of the program through its efforts to support it. When a foundation in Whittier not only provides and renews grants to support students participating in the local Fifth Dimension, it provides powerful evidence of the value of the activity to those for whom it is intended. The same is true when former students who become teachers start up Fifth Dimensions in their new circumstances, or when La Clase Mágica parents create a nonprofit foundation to support the program, help to run it, and write grant proposals or have backyard sales to raise money for it. When a boys and girls club makes an exception to its salary policy and pays a higher salary to the person charged with overseeing the Fifth Dimension in recognition of the special demands involved and the need for continuity of programming, that community is showing its support for the program. By the same token, when the community does not value the activity, as was true at Elon College and in East Lansing, its lack of enthusiasm makes itself felt in an absence of the human and fiscal resources that the project requires.

The same criteria apply to the institutions of higher learning that form the other side of the Fifth Dimension–UC Links systems. In an era of tight budgets and skyrocketing student-faculty ratios, it requires a special kind of appreciation for a college or university to authorize a course that must be taught throughout the academic year and at ratios approximating those of a fine arts studio class.

It is standard for such institutions to proclaim their commitment to their local communities, but unusual when they back up that commitment by allowing faculty to teach smaller-than-usual classes (as Schustack, Vásquez, and Cole have been able to do at CSU San Marcos and at UCSD) or by providing supplementary funds for teaching assistants in these classes (as UCSD has been doing for many years). When it comes to the institutional provision of costly resources in difficult times—which seems to us one compelling criterion for evaluating activities such as the Fifth Dimension—the Fifth Dimension program has been successful in many, but not all, cases.

The criterion of value to the community, it should be noted, bears little or no relationship to the criterion of experimental evaluation. This is demonstrated to some extent in cases such as the strong support given to the Fifth Dimension in Whittier, where qualitative process evaluation is standard but experimental evaluation has never been undertaken. It is even clearer at the national level, where the initial evaluation of the 21st Century Community Learning Center programs was extensive, expensive, and largely negative, but funding was increased nonetheless (Mathematica Policy Research Institute 2003).[3] What does the community know, or think it knows, that standard academic evaluations are missing?

We believe, along with Larry Cuban (2004), that the criteria for measuring the success of innovations shift markedly depending on who is doing the evaluating. What local communities know is that programs that can be modified to fit local needs and run at a reasonable cost (judged by local standards) and that engage children's enthusiastic participation in activities approved of by adults are not necessarily programs that yield quantitative results based on research with standardized tests administered under conditions that compel children to perform.

THE POTENTIAL OF NEW COMPUTER AND COMMUNICATION TECHNOLOGIES

One of the goals of the Mellon Foundation in supporting our research on after-school programs was to identify critical factors that contribute to, or detract from, the efficacy of new communication technologies in promoting educational achievement. It is important to remember that when we began this research the Internet was just coming into being and the World Wide Web was still not visible on the educational horizon. Many Fifth Dimension–UC Links projects operated with a potpourri of low-end computers, including Kaypros, Apple IIes, and early IBM PCs. All of the researchers had access to each other via electronic mail, but several of the sites had no e-mail access.

From prior research, we knew that if elementary school children are given reasons they find compelling to write to children in other locations, they will do so (LCHC 1989; Levin et al. 1987). Children have produced joint newspapers, some of them bilingual, and a few relatively enduring pen pal relationships have generated fifteen to twenty exchanges over the course of a few months among nine- to ten-year-olds. But by and large, the communicative potential of computers, despite our strong belief in that potential, has not been a major factor in the implementation or success of Fifth Dimensions, although it has been a prominent factor in design planning.

An interesting exception to this generalization has been the power of mythical figureheads such as the Wizard, El Maga, and Golem to motivate children's writing and reading, either through the exchange of letters or through online chatting. Online chats have proven especially attractive to the children. In some locations it is the mystery surrounding the figurehead's identity that appears to motivate the children, and adults have come up with a variety of stratagems to foster their interest. For example, at one of the BGCs the site coordinator and the undergraduates foster speculation about the identity of the Wizard/ess. The adults have confounded the children by having a leading candidate be absent from the site when the chat begins, but appear in the middle of the chat, just as the children are certain they have figured out who is writing to them. In one of the locations frequented by Mexicano children, El Maga is treated more or less as a godmother (comadre), and the conversations are often serious and thought-provoking, in contrast with the playful nature of quests at the same site for El Maga's true identity. This more somber relationship with the figurehead is no less successful in promoting children's reading and writing skills, and probably more conducive to development-enhancing communication with a caring adult.

It is clearly not possible for us to evaluate the independent contribution of computers as media for Fifth Dimension activities because their use is so intertwined with noncomputer activities and varies so much from one site to another. Generally speaking, as already indicated, the computer technology available to the different sites trailed the leading-edge technology available at universities or in the homes of the well-educated and well-to-do. In fact, the children often had access to more sophisticated computers and educational computer games in their schools than at their local site. The sites' outmoded computers were partly the result of necessity—there was never sufficient money to provide state-of-the-art computers—and partly an outcome of the effort to create sustainable programs—sites were always highly dependent on hand-me-down equipment.

We can say with some certainty that computers are neither necessary nor sufficient to create a successful Fifth Dimension. When a site began at San Diego State University, it had several new computers, and the plan was to make computers a centerpiece of the program. But the computers soon fell into disrepair. Money for repairs was not forthcoming, so the implementers gave up on computers altogether, using a variety of off-the-shelf board games and similar activities instead. The site ran just fine. By the same token, several sites used computers as an important, if not exclusive, medium of programming and nevertheless failed.[4]

These facts do not mean that computers have no place in the overall tool kit available to us for designing, implementing, and sustaining Fifth Dimensions. Parents clearly believe that it is important for their children to become familiar with computers and to learn skills associated with them of the sort tested by Schustack's computer literacy test. Many children are attracted to the Fifth Dimension by the presence of computers, and we have no doubt that for some children this attraction makes possible the kind of deeper involvement reflected in our evaluation studies.

This involvement, however, has had its downsides. We went to great lengths to ensure that there were plenty of computer activities that research suggested would appeal to girls, and at many sites girls even outnumbered boys in Fifth Dimension participation. But most commercially available computer software presupposes one or, at most, two players, and a great many of them are "shoot-'em-up" games that appeal more to boys than girls. Even though the site could vary the mix of games and balance gender-specific content through the use of task cards, it often happened that boys dominated a particular computer because of the gender-specific appeal of the game to be played there.

The World Wide Web holds great potential for enriching after-school activities such as the Fifth Dimension, but it also poses daunting challenges. It is not just pornography, violence, and chat-room predators that adults need to worry about. Many of the educational Web sites for children are either directly geared for use during school hours or saturated with commercial advertising. In addition, the variety of content on the Web, combined with the lightning speed with which that content is updated to attract potential new users, defies the capacity of Fifth Dimension implementers to reorganize specific games into the combinations of play and education that are its hallmark.

This same story of thwarted or threatened potential applies to the new technologies that allow not only e-mail exchanges among children but exchanges of static visual images and digital video, including music and spoken narratives. We have found that the production of such materials is very enticing to children, but the exchange of these materials is greatly restricted by fears of sexual predation.

Probably the most important impact of computers as communication media on the project has been on the way the college courses are taught—for example, Web boards have been used as common spaces where students can see each other's field notes and instructors' comments and provide help to each other. Equally important has been the role of computers in the widespread and ongoing exchanges between researchers who, in communicating time-saving information, curriculum ideas, and frustrations, have thus been able to maintain a "meta-community" of practice among themselves.

THE DIFFICULTY OF PRIVILEGING DIVERSITY

Earlier we summarized the ways in which diversity is central to the design of each site, the specific idioculture of which depends crucially on how diverse participants and resources are blended to arrive at a system of activities that fits the specifications of a community of learners that children would voluntarily join after school. That summary also specified how we were able to capitalize on the diversity within sites to enhance learning—for example, by requiring the sharing (and hence communicating) of information across languages and levels of expertise, regardless of the age of the participants. We also detailed the special challenges facing sites in the poorer, generally Mexicano neighborhoods where facilities (space, telephone access, availability of trained personnel) were less adequate.

We had very much hoped that we would be able to use the diversity of participants and activities across sites as a further stimulus for children, students, and adults to interact for their mutual benefit. Through early study of children in San Diego who created a newsletter with Inuit children on the north slope of Alaska (Riel 1985) and of children in different parts of the United States who created a newspaper with children in Russia, we knew that marked differences in children's lives can be a genuine motive for them to interact—through speaking, writing, or reading. In our experience since then, however, we have learned that it takes a great deal of adult work to arrange the circumstances that make such interactions attractive to children. In face-to-face interactions, it is essential to provide genuinely engaging activities with roles for all the children; otherwise, meetings among children whose communities are often in conflict simply recapitulate that conflict. The same can be said of interactions mediated through computer networks—the feedback needs to be interesting and prompt if the children are going to want to continue communicating. Such levels of coordination were generally difficult to achieve among children at different Fifth Dimension sites. At this child-to-child level of the project, we too often failed in our attempts to capitalize on the diversity represented in the project as a whole.

Our expectations were not disappointed, however, when it came to communication between adult researchers and, at times, college students at different sites. Students interacting through their courses were often highly involved and productive in these exchanges. And there is no doubt that the regular exchange of information about successful and unsuccessful practices at diverse sites was of considerable value to the researchers.

BENEFITS FOR COMMUNITY INSTITUTION STAFF AND COLLEGE STUDENTS

The evidence is mixed regarding our goal to design the Fifth Dimension–UC Links program so that it benefited college students and the staff of the community organization as well as the children.

By and large, we believe that the impact on the staff of the various community organizations with which we worked was linked to particular socio-ecological circumstances. As a rule, where the programs were successful, the community organizations themselves underwent change, and arguably the staff involved benefited from this change through the reduction of child-adult ratios and the infusion of other resources into their centers, including increased community support. But owing to rapid staff turnover, the effects of participation in the program rarely cumulated.

One major exception was La Clase Mágica, where there had been no after-school program initially. Olga Vásquez worked directly with members of the community, who received their training even as they helped to shape the program in the process of running it during its formative years. These people became genuine experts in the implementation of La Clase Mágica and its offshoots, which they had taken a hand in creating.

An interesting variation on this kind of change occurred at Whittier College, where Latino students who had been a part of the Fifth Dimension went on to become teachers and, in their new roles, started their own Fifth Dimensions. Significantly, these next-generation programs were modeled on La Clase Mágica, which fit the needs of the local community. The new Fifth Dimensions were run in collaboration with after-school programs based in the school—a genuine hybrid that had not existed previously.

We believe that the evidence presented in chapter 7 indicates that participation in Fifth Dimension practicum courses has a powerful effect on undergraduates. Admittedly, we do not have comparison groups that would allow us to demonstrate quantitatively the changes in conceptualization, writing ability, and motivation that are routinely encountered in the practicum courses. But most of the members of this project have taught in colleges and universities for many years, and none of us has seen a course consistently have such a great impact on students.

Our collective belief is that there are two key ingredients to the effectiveness of the practicum classes. First, the high level of responsibility given to undergraduates for making the Fifth Dimension function well for the children requires that it function well for the undergraduates themselves. Second, undergraduates routinely realize that the theoretical work conducted on the college campus is not an empty exercise but a rare opportunity to gather intellectual tools to tackle the difficult task of promoting children's development. We have no other reasons for why this particular form of laboratory course has had such a major impact on students' self-image, conceptual development, and increased thoughtfulness about their future careers.

LESSONS ABOUT SUSTAINABILITY

It has been eighteen years since the first Fifth Dimension was opened with the explicit goal of creating an effective and sustainable after-school activity. We think the evidence for the effectiveness of the program has been firmly established. But what about its sustainability?

As the reader is aware from our accounts in chapter 4 of the earliest stages of the research and the material presented in table 8.1, some Fifth Dimension sites have been ongoing communities of practice for several years and the number of sites has periodically increased in several parts of the United States and in other countries. However, many other sites have disappeared, to be remembered only in these pages and the memories of those who participated in them. What factors can we confidently associate with the sustainability of what we have demonstrated to be a successful educational innovation?

What Is Sustainability?

It should be clear from the emphasis throughout this volume on the necessity of local adaptability and diversity that we interpret sustainability in relational terms. Fifth Dimensions and their community hosts, on the one hand, and colleges and universities, on the other, are quite obviously social institutions that are constantly in flux. From inception onward, a Fifth Dimension requires ongoing exchanges between these institutions and between individuals and departments within the institutions simply in order to function. Every aspect of these relations is constantly changing, along with the institutions themselves. So whatever it means, the sustainability of a Fifth Dimension must refer not only to some invariant properties of the constituent institutional processes but also to their relationships to each other. Radical change in any part of this system of relationships could result in the disappearance of a Fifth Dimension, although universities and the institutions that host the after-school activity may continue separately.

We mention this relational perspective on sustainability because it is very seductive to think of an activity such as the Fifth Dimension as an entity, a *thing* to be sustained, thereby backgrounding the relational work that its continuation entails. We ourselves often speak this way about Fifth Dimensions, and as a shorthand way of talking about sustainability it is perfectly natural ("There used to be a Fifth Dimension in Moscow, but the person who ran it left the country, so it died").

Sustainability of After-School Programs: Common Wisdom

Perhaps the most common explanation for why after-school programs fail (assuming that those who run them and those who use them agree that they are desirable programs) is that the initial funding ceased; failing to find new sources of funding, the program disappeared—after all, people need to earn a living!

Superficially, this explanation works just fine. On a national listserv where people discuss their efforts to create and sustain after-school programs, the following is a common inquiry: "We have created a very successful program, but the funding agency says that they do not support ongoing programs, only new innovations. What am I to do?"

In recognition of this chronic problem, the Afterschool Alliance (www.afterschoolalliance.org) has created a "sustainability workbook" based on the experience of its 2002 study of 21st Century Community Learning Center programs. The Alliance's "tips for sustaining an after-school program" include:

- Create a sustainability plan for your program in its initial stages.

- Create a working group to address sustainability in a consistent and ongoing manner.

- Pursue other funding sources before your initial grant expires.

- Capitalize on your program's history and achievements when pursuing funding.

- Use tried and true avenues of funding [many such are provided as examples].

- Engage your program's community partners in actively pursuing other funding for the program.

This list is accompanied by two case studies. Each illustrates the case of an extraordinary person who implemented a program with support from the 21st Century program and went on to win wide regional recognition through persistent networking, coalition formation, and political lobbying. A theme common to both cases is the visibility of a strong leader in the local community. One of these implementers notes that sitting on many community boards and committees allows him to get the word out about the program. The second implementer emphasizes collaboration and comments that "it is more than asking for money . . . it is making connections, building strong programs, generating trust, and becoming visible."

This conclusion fits well with the experiences of members of the Distributed Literacy Consortium. For example, Honorine Nocon (2004), who worked with colleagues from La Clase Mágica and the nearby BGC Fifth Dimension as well as with the developers of a new version of the Fifth Dimension at a local school and with those who formed a community coalition to support all three sites, concluded her analyses of the development of this system with this observation about what could be called "the 4Cs model":

> The study also suggests that when productive, the process of sustainability is: collaborative, communicative, creative, and continuing. It is collaborative in that participants have strong relationships and direct involvement in planning and implementing the educational innovation. They also participate actively in ongoing evaluation and refinement of the innovation. The process is communicative in that participants have voice and opportunities to make visible needs, concerns, and potential solutions to the shared problem of productive integration of the reform. The process is creative in that it remains open to change in the educational innovation and attentive to

changes in the local and structural contexts of implementation. It is a continuing process in that innovations are sustained through long-term commitment. (Nocon 2004, 729)

This characterization of local sustainability is complemented by the work of Alice Naylor and Mark Evans at Appalachian State University. Ten years after the ASU program had begun, and two years after its initiator, Bill Blanton, had moved to another university, Naylor and Evans (2003) conducted a study of the condition of the ASU Fifth Dimension through observations and interviews with participants in all parts of the program. They concluded that working cooperatively and with a strong commitment to a useful theory, maintaining adequate communication, and having committed leaders were the key ingredients that sustained the program at ASU, which, like a great many of the sites where it was initiated, considered the Fifth Dimension a fundamental part of teacher education.

Beyond the local context, where the 4Cs model (Nocon 2004) applies, perceived social needs in the larger context play an important role, relatively independent of locally operating coalitions. Thus, for example, a statewide controversy about the appropriateness of bilingual education in California created the conditions for the major expansion of the Fifth Dimension beyond the California members of the Distributed Literacy Consortium (see chapter 8). The University of California, faced with a crisis of credibility when its Board of Regents banned the use of affirmative action in admissions, felt it necessary to demonstrate its commitment to the state's non-Anglo families. The Fifth Dimension program was well known to Richard Atkinson, the chancellor on the UCSD campus, where it began; after Atkinson became president of the entire university system, he supported an all-campus faculty initiative to expand the project to all campuses of the university. Hence, when funding from the foundation that had begun the project was terminated, several of the consortium members obtained funding under the larger umbrella of the University of California, which enabled them not only to continue their activities but also to expand them significantly.

This umbrella did not cover the largest consortium member outside of California, the site at Appalachian State University, but the story of its sustainability illustrates similar processes at work. As indicated in chapter 3, the ASU program was located in its College of Education, and through the efforts of its initiator, the college incorporated the Fifth Dimension into its teacher education program as one of the paths that students could take toward fulfilling their teaching apprenticeship obligations (referred to locally as "clinical teaching sites"). The dean of the college was strongly supportive of the theoretical thrust of the Fifth Dimension, as were a key group of faculty. Money that Blanton had raised from the state to support the clinical teaching sites remained available as a permanent part of the College of Education budget, providing support for software, incidental expenses, and a key staff position, as well as stipends for graduate students who wanted to conduct their dissertation research on the Fifth Dimension and become local site coordinators. Here the larger context was the state-mandated programs for teacher training and the success of the Fifth Dimension as a vehicle for this required training.

Of course, what the larger context giveth the larger context can also take away. In the past year, largely in response to the fiscal crisis touched off by the combination of an economic downturn and the high cost of producing electricity, the budget of the University of California has been severely slashed and outreach efforts continuously threatened with elimination. These changes underline our point that sustainability is not a problem solved at a single moment in time, but a work in progress involving multiple players and levels of social aggregation. Keeping in mind these points that apply to after-school programs—and probably to promising educational reforms more generally—we turn to the special issues of sustaining the Fifth Dimension–UC Links system.

Sustaining Fifth Dimension–UC Links Programs: Special Issues

The basic strategy underpinning the Fifth Dimension–UC Links system is to accumulate resources through interinstitutional collaboration so that both institutions can accomplish valued goals that neither could afford on its own. Suggestions for this kind of collaboration between universities and community organizations are by no means new (Corrigan 2000), but little has been written about them; as a result, evaluations are sparse, and the special issues associated with maintaining such collaborations when they are judged by participants to be successful have not been explored (Mariage and Garmon 2003).[5]

At the most abstract level, education and children's welfare are, of course, the common institutional goals of the collaborative arrangements on which the Fifth Dimension–UC Links intervention is based, and there is little doubt that both universities and community organizations need help to achieve this goal. Voluminous research indicates that community organizations have difficulty implementing high-quality programs when they have poorly trained staff, high rates of staff turnover, high child-adult ratios, and poor physical facilities (Halpern 2003; Vandell, Shumow, and Posner 2005). Colleges and universities have great difficulty implementing laboratory-style courses for students in the social sciences as a routine part of their education, although the value of such courses is beyond doubt.[6] The difficulty is that laboratory-style courses not only are labor-intensive but also usually require the building and maintenance of special on-campus facilities that are prohibitively expensive or simply impossible to build for logistical reasons. At best, a campus preschool may be available for observational research on a regular basis; more often, research is limited to college sophomores dragooned into psychology experiments as subjects or exposed to studies with rats or pigeons. Even such limited opportunities can be provided to only a small proportion of students in most institutions of higher learning.

In principle, the Fifth Dimension–UC Links program provides an inexpensive solution to the problems facing both institutions in any given partnership program. The community organization gets many hours a week of flexibly deployable help from motivated undergraduates, who are supervised in their implementation of the Fifth Dimension by a college instructor throughout the academic year. The college or university gets the use of a unique, real-life laboratory environment that is largely equipped and maintained by the community organization. The additional costs to each institution of collaboration in a Fifth Dimension, while not negligible, are a small fraction of the cost of running the program.

Obstacles to Institutional Collaboration

Because we are dealing with a form of innovation that requires collaboration between institutions, a careful examination of challenges to its sustainability must include a look at both sides of the arrangement, as well as at the relationship between them.

Difficulties on the Community Side of the Program   Two kinds of difficulties have predominated on the community side of the relationship. The first is staff turnover. Although it is customary for the university partner to provide, or support the training of, a site coordinator in the early stages of a Fifth Dimension program, in the long run the community partner is expected to provide a staff person to fill this role. This expectation is not routinely achievable. Running a Fifth Dimension can be learned through participation for a period of a month or so, but the salary of most after-school workers, just slightly over the minimum wage, leads to high turnover. Moreover, a staff member's training in a Fifth Dimension idioculture is unlikely to be spread throughout the organization before that staff member leaves. Additional training time for more staff is possible (and in fact is routinely offered), but the realities of everyday routines at most after-school institutions make it difficult to arrange additional time for training. Nor is this problem automatically solvable by raising wages for the person who runs the Fifth Dimension. The local institution has its own norms of staff pay, and to pay significant extra wages to a site implementer often runs against institutional policy.

The problems when a community organization forms de novo to run a Fifth Dimension, such as occurred at La Clase Mágica, are slightly different and potentially more resistant to solution. In this case, space may be easier to provide than ongoing staff support, the cost of which is likely to be a major issue even if the staff are parents from the community.

Beyond the narrow issue of training, high staff turnover also makes it difficult to maintain the agreed-upon arrangements that provide common ground for the two institutions. This impact is particularly noticeable when supervisory staff leave—as happens often—and it becomes necessary to build up a common reservoir of assumptions about the partnership from scratch, with no guarantee that new leaders will be interested in arrangements made by their predecessors.

The second kind of difficulty is the upkeep of the facilities. Fifth Dimensions generally make extensive use of computers and, where available, computer networks. Provision of computers can be a problem, but this problem is often solvable by small grants and donations. What is not easily solvable is the challenge of routine equipment maintenance. Even new computers break, and old computers, subjected to the rough-and-tumble of an after-school site, are particularly vulnerable. Either a maintenance contract must be supported or some kind of computer-repair support organization must be created. With computers, the maintenance problem is multiplied by rapid changes in hardware and software. Most Fifth Dimension–UC Links sites make do nicely with outdated equipment, but new software often cannot be implemented without newer equipment. Solutions to the issues of maintaining computers and upgrading software can be both time-consuming and expensive.

Difficulties on the University Side of the Program   The difficulties on the university side arise in connection with providing for a relatively small, laboratory-style course during an entire academic year and maintaining a steady flow of students. This problem has two major components.

The first is academic-year provision of instructional support. Most colleges and universities advertise their commitment to their local communities and to the very best education for their students. However, these institutions are also under great pressure to offer *large* courses in order to accommodate large numbers of students with limited faculty. When the good intentions of community outreach conflict with teaching requirements, teaching requirements win, hands down. This problem is exacerbated by the fact that the structure of a Fifth Dimension–UC Links program prevents it from being turned on and off at will by one of the partners. Colleges and universities are accustomed to offering upper-division courses on a flexible schedule: some courses may not be offered when the instructor is on leave or is needed to teach other classes. The inflexible need to provide the course continuously is a demand that requires special efforts on the part of a college or university.

Steady provision of a Fifth Dimension course also challenges the research obligations of faculty. The members of the Distributed Literacy Consortium were all interested in their Fifth Dimension–UC Links programs not only as opportunities for research and teaching but as excellent venues for community service through their impact on the children and community members involved. However, a requirement of academic research is that it be *original*. Originality is, of course, a slippery notion, and a good deal of the research published monthly in our scholarly journals is questionable in this regard. But with the Fifth Dimension, a junior faculty member who might be tempted to begin collaborating with a more senior colleague is naturally concerned about being seen as simply following in the older faculty member's footsteps rather than setting out on an original line of research. This is not impossible within a Fifth Dimension–UC Links framework (several faculty have in fact followed this path), but neither is it easy. Consequently, finding junior faculty who are willing to enter into a preexisting program of teaching and research, even one that encourages diversity and individual initiative, faces real institutional difficulties.

The second difficulty for universities in providing small, laboratory-style courses for an entire academic year is the need to supply a steady flow of students. It might seem at first blush as if solving the problem of offering a course throughout the academic year would be sufficient to overcome any other problems of sustainability on the university side of a program, but our experience has taught us differently. An added requirement is that the course be positioned within the curriculum so that it is easily accessible to students as an option that forwards their academic careers. The almost essential need is that the course be at least an option for fulfilling a requirement for graduation from the program in which the student is enrolled. Such was the case at Appalachian State in its College of Education and in several other programs. But it was not invariably the case. At the Erikson Institute the Fifth Dimension was an optional research course that added to students' workload. At CSU San Marcos it was an optional course that did not contribute to the major. At UC Santa Barbara it was an exceptional course that students had to arrange to take well ahead of time. At Elon College the course could be offered only once a year. In all such marginal situations, sustainability becomes more difficult.

Challenges Arising from the Relationship Between the University and the Community Organization

Two major sources of difficulty arising from the relationship between the university and the community organization bear special discussion here owing to their prominent role in the demise of Fifth Dimension programs. The first arises from the impact of within-institution discontinuities on between-institution relations. The second arises from a gradual erosion of common goals and understandings that may or may not be the result of within-institution changes.

It is, of course, the norm to have a certain amount of discontinuity within institutions. Change, after all, is the only constant. Staff turnover is not a special problem, for example, in boys and girls clubs—it is a norm. The institution and its programming have evolved with this feature as one of its constants. At all institutions of higher learning, some faculty members are routinely on leave or assigned to cover an important course. However, even when matters are progressing satisfactorily from the perspective of one or both of the partners in a given Fifth Dimension–UC Links project, difficulties can arise because of the relationship between them.

It is especially dangerous to sustainability when discontinuities in personnel or decreases in other resources arise simultaneously on both sides of the partnership. If, for example, a faculty member is on leave but experienced partners are available at the community site, there might be a rough patch while the new faculty member put in charge of the course gets up to speed, but the program is likely to continue. Conversely, turnover in community staff can be compensated for by someone from the university side stepping in to make sure things run smoothly while a new site coordinator is trained. If two such discontinuities occur at once, however, the quality of the program is compromised, and it can easily die. Similarly, if the community usually provides equipment but runs out of funding for a while, arrangements can be made with the university partner to pick up the slack. But if both institutions are hit with financial woes at the same time, a break in the program is more likely to occur.

Subtler, and more pervasive, is a slow erosion of support from one or the other side of the program that imperceptibly leads to an acute situation that cannot be bridged. For example, Miriam Schustack responded to the research criteria needed for tenure by limiting attendance at her Fifth Dimension to the number of undergraduates available to ensure strict supervision for purposes of data recording, a restriction that improved her ability to evaluate the project. The effects of this limitation were amplified by norms in her department that made her Fifth Dimension course marginal within the curriculum and limited the number of students who could attend the site regularly. (Note that Schustack's university went out of its way, owing to its commitment to the Fifth Dimension program, to allow her to teach smaller-than-normal courses, so class size was not a problem.)

However, after the program had been running at the boys and girls club for several years, a new director arrived who was not a party to the initial arrangements for conducting the program, and he wanted to see a lot more children using the facilities. Meanwhile, increased student enrollments had added to the pressure in Schustack's department to teach large classes, and the marginality of her class became a problem. When she obtained tenure, she was asked to become head of the local academic senate, a time-consuming task that made it impossible for her to devote time to the course. No substitute was available. In these circumstances, both institutions "returned to form." The course was terminated, large numbers of children flooded the computer room, and the Fifth Dimension came to an end.

Sometimes as the partners get to know each other in the process of implementing the program, increased familiarity reveals deeply buried institutional presuppositions that, when publicly acknowledged, combine with the discoordinations arising from institutional factors to end the program. This was the case at the Erikson Institute, where the local community's fear of domination by the alien language and cultural practices of mainstream academic culture became more and more articulated while the impossibility of finding a place for a Fifth Dimension course became more and more evident. The outcome was similar at Elon College. The child-rearing philosophy of the YMCA staff came into articulated conflict with the pedagogical philosophy of the Fifth Dimension more and more frequently; the resulting tensions might have been dealt with over time, but the situation coincided with the reluctance of college administrators to devote two full courses per year to the collaborative effort, despite their strong commitment to community outreach. Both the course and the faculty consortium member were thus undermined, and the course was abandoned.

In sum, it appears that the virtues of the Fifth Dimension program do not remove its vulnerabilities. It offers an inexpensive way to provide educational opportunities to both university and community partners, but it also makes it more difficult for those partners to agree on what constitutes worthwhile educational opportunities, and it imposes demands for coordination that carry a hidden cost of their own. In those communities where there is agreement on educational values, a strong commitment to university-community partnerships, a high value on providing college students with laboratory experiences, and respect for the social science research provided by community-based activity systems, the programs have prospered and continue to do so. Insofar as one or more of these desiderata are not present, the activity is put at risk.

THE FIFTH DIMENSION–UC LINKS PROJECT TODAY

As we noted in chapter 1, our research follows up on a long history of efforts to create after-school activities that promote the development of children, especially children from families and neighborhoods with relatively few resources who are forced to spend the hours after school either home alone or on streets that are inhospitable, if not dangerous. In fact, as citizens and parents ourselves, our motives are not so different from those of the legendary ladies from Hartford who invited a group of boys in for a tasty snack and ended up starting an after-school program. Moreover, all of us have witnessed the youth gang activities in our neighborhoods that inspire the promoters of after-school centers to "fight crime" and provide a supervisorial bridge between home and school and, of course, an environment where children can accrue resources to deal with the increasingly rigid demands of the public school system and modern workplaces.

In the years since this line of research was initiated, the issue of latchkey children has not gone away, but after-school programs have become dramatically more available. As Robert Granger and Thomas Kane (2004, 72) note, "Over the last half-decade [1998 to 2004], after-school programs have moved from the periphery to the center of the national education policy debate. It happened very quickly."

This rapid change in the national focus on the after-school hours—and particularly the shift in orientation toward academic goals—sets the context for assessing what might be learned from our own efforts.

Suggestions from Contemporary Evaluation Studies

Despite variations in emphasis, there is now a reasonable consensus on the characteristics of after-school programs that are likely to improve children's academic performance while decreasing their involvement in social behavior that puts them at risk. The National Research Council Committee on Community-Level Programs for Youth (Eccles and Gootman 2002) lists a number of these features:

1. Physical and psychological safety

2. A social structure with clear and consistent rules, clear boundaries, and age-appropriate monitoring

3. Warm, supportive relationships with adults who provide caring guidance

4. Broad inclusion regardless of the child's background

5. Positive social norms, including the expectation that the child will help others

6. Support for developing feelings of self-efficacy, accepting responsibility, and being taken seriously

7. Opportunities for acquiring a broad range of intellectual skills and social and emotional competence, and an intentional learning experience that includes "cultural literacies," the ability to communicate effectively, and other socially valued capital

Robert Halpern (2003, 115ff), on the basis of his long involvement in the evaluation of after-school programs, provides a similar list of desirable characteristics and argues that after-school programs ought to be well suited to provide just these kinds of experiences. Similar views can be found in several contributions to a recent collection of essays on organized out-of-school activities as contexts of development (Mahoney et al. 2005).

However, current evidence indicates that while such positive environments and subsequent positive developmental outcomes are attainable, they are by no means an automatic consequence of providing after-school care. This conclusion is clearly illustrated by Deborah Vandell, Lee Shumow, and Jill Posner (2005) in a longitudinal comparison of third-, fourth, and fifth-graders in two programs in the same inner-city neighborhood. A significantly higher level of the properties identified by the NRC report characterized the first program, and the academic outcomes mirrored the quality of the programming (as measured by a combination of interviews and observations). Elsewhere, Vandell and Pierce (2003) have identified a number of characteristics—including high child-adult ratios, a restricted range of activities, and coercive adult socialization practices—that lead to negative developmental outcomes.

In sum, positive developmental outcomes are simply not possible at an after-school site that cannot routinely and reliably create the environmental properties associated with those outcomes. Here financial resources are unquestionably an issue: it is more likely that well-trained staff who are paid a living wage and work in an environment that allows for a range of structures will engage in "social capital–building" activities. But financial support is no guarantee that a program will embody the principles of the NRC report.

It is here that the broader lessons of the Fifth Dimension appear most relevant. Even though the specific curricular values embedded in the Fifth Dimension (which map clearly onto the NRC report's recommendations) were not valued in some communities (a problem certainly faced by many implementers of other programs), every single implementation of the Fifth Dimension program did succeed in creating the kind of environment associated with the NRC's criteria for positive developmental outcomes. Moreover, in every such environment where "scientifically sound" evaluation was feasible, the program produced positive results, and it did so at very low relative cost across a wide range of populations defined in socioeconomic, ethnic, and gender terms.

A FINAL WORD

A skeptic might grant us our claim that the Fifth Dimension–UC Links model is a fine way to organize after-school care in those socio-ecological circumstances where it can be implemented. But isn't that socio-ecological niche too small to be significant? We offer two responses to this question.

First, there are 2,200 colleges and universities in the United States. If every such institution made participation in a Fifth Dimension course a requirement for graduation (a suggestion made by the former governor of California before an energy crisis and economic downturn got him thrown out of office, and by his successor, who made universal provision of after-school programming the launching pad of his political career), there would be two major consequences, according to our data: American undergraduate education would be improved across the board, and education in the K–12 pipeline leading into those institutions of higher learning would be improved as well.

Second, even programs implemented on a smaller scale—focused, for instance, on social science students planning careers in social services or education—would provide a massive number of "educational extension stations" in many parts of the country where people concerned about improving after-school care and professors concerned about their students receiving a superficial education would come in contact with professionals who could provide on-site support for the implementation and development of similar activities.

We began many years ago with the goal of demonstrating the effectiveness of a particular model of education during the after-school hours, solving the technical problems of evaluation, and exploring the process by which successful innovations fail. As we conclude this report, it would seem that our efforts, unbeknownst to us, have been part of a larger zeitgeist, one that has spawned a plethora of sophisticated programs. Not only do they share many of our theoretical principles, but these other programs have attracted the involvement of many communities both inside and outside the academy. They have also shown that such efforts are generalizable to older children and youth for whom work and community involvement, not play, are the leading activities.

In the beginning, we expected our small group of Fifth Dimension programs to disappear quietly in a few years so that we could write up our reports and get on with our lives. Instead, we find that we have created a program that spreads globally faster than it dies locally. Although it has been but one effort among many, we hope that our experiences with the Fifth Dimension make a worthwhile contribution to that zeitgeist of concern for the development of children and the productiveness of their after-school lives.

Notes

CHAPTER 1

1. Prime examples include the After-School Foundation located in New York City, which opened in 1998 and has raised over $360 million from private and government resources. In 2003 this foundation was supporting over 240 centers and expected to keep expanding its support (TASC 2003). The Mott Foundation has supported a variety of after-school initiatives, including money for evaluation of the 21st Century Community Learning Centers programs.

CHAPTER 2

1. For alternative formulations of this kind of perspective, see the recent monograph on after-school programs edited by Mahoney, Larson, and Eccles (2005).
2. In fact, the Fifth Dimension has been implemented in schools during the school day. We report briefly on such extensions of the program in chapter 8, but for present purposes we focus on the after-school efforts that have received the lion's share of our attention.
3. It is not unusual to encounter such reward systems in purportedly educational software. For example, the educational game "Oregon Trails" uses hunting for animals as a "relief" from the problem-solving goals of the game.
4. For a general discussion of the notion of sociogenesis of cognitive development, see Valsiner (1998).
5. Russian, French, and a number of other languages differ from English in that they contain a concept that means *both* teaching and learning (for instance, "obuchenie" in Russian). This idea, which emphasizes the double-sided nature of ideal educational interactions, may not be encountered very often in classrooms but is characteristic of the teaching and learning interactions in Fifth Dimension programs.
6. When we began this work, the World Wide Web did not yet exist, and our community partners had not yet begun to use email and listservs on a daily basis. At present, the use of the Web and the Internet plays a larger role in everyday practice within Fifth Dimensions than it did during the period when this work was funded as a research project.

CHAPTER 3

1. For one discussion of the ubiquitous nature of this problem, see Pittman, Tolman, and Yohalem (2005).
2. As we have noted elsewhere (Cole 1996), this failure was not for lack of effort. Many highly dedicated Latino students labored to involve local Latino children, but without success.
3. With the advent of a new club administration, a wide variety of well-organized activities has been developed.
4. Whittier College's enrollment is consistently between 30 and 35 percent Latino, and most come from Spanish-speaking homes in the Los Angeles area.

CHAPTER 4

1. Because year 1 was devoted to planning, the program was implemented in year 2.
2. Analysis of the regimes of control at private after-school educational centers, such as SCORE, tells the same story. Children's attendance is required by their parents, not representatives of the state, but since the parents are paying significant fees, they expect significant test score changes in their children. As a result, children are heavily policed by paid tutors working with structured drill-and-practice computer programs and systems of rewards for points scored (Dahl 2002).

CHAPTER 6

1. Pseudonyms are used for participants throughout this chapter. The text taken from participants' writings—the undergraduates' field notes and the children's letters—is used without revisions for diction or orthography.
2. Two separate videotapes were made of the session: a camera captured the interaction of the two participants while a scan converter recorded the output on the computer's display screen. The two videotapes were later "piped," or edited into one videotape, and timed such that participants' interaction and movement on the computer screen were displayed simultaneously. This interaction is available for inspection on the Web site for this book: http://communication.ucsd.edu/5thd.manual.
3. Peg Griffin designed these partially "precooked" games of graded difficulty.
4. The hints book is an artifact used in this Fifth Dimension. As part of fulfilling task card assignments, children write down in the book hints about useful strategies, which are collected and categorized for use by later players.

CHAPTER 7

1. For all of the Whittier sessions studied, two videotapes were available: one taken by a camera showing the interaction of the college student, the child,

and the artifacts throughout the hour-and-a-half session; and a second made simultaneously through a scan converter showing action on the computer screen throughout the session.

CHAPTER 8

1. All such commitments are more transient than permanent. Funding was suspended for a while in 2004 owing to a budget crisis. It has since been restored, but at a reduced level and on a temporary basis.

CHAPTER 9

1. This periodization is not intended to be culturally universal (see Goncü 1993), but it does provide useful guidelines for the societies in which the Fifth Dimension has been implemented.
2. Similarly, and on a larger scale, the use of voucher programs that allowed families from inner-city housing projects to resettle in different kinds of neighborhoods in Chicago provided the opportunity for one of the most persuasive demonstrations of the impact of neighborhoods on developmental outcomes (Rubinowitz and Rosenbaum 2000).
3. For a critique, see the statement issued by the 21st Century Community Learning Center Evaluation Advisory Board (Bissel et al. 2003) and the Forum for Youth Investment (2002).
4. Todd Oppenheimer (2003) tells a similar story about in-school uses of computers. In programs across the country, he has documented the failure of many programs owing to lack of technical support and ongoing repairs. In Oppenheimer's view, these programs were ill conceived in the first place and driven by the hand waving and wishful thinking of technophiles, by computer vendors, and by the fears of parents that their children would be left behind. In the schools that Oppenheimer visited, programs in the 1990s fared best where implementers knew that optimal learning environments require engaged people. Oppenheimer's recommendation that schools return to a program of "enlightened basics"—including an atmosphere of high expectation, sophisticated creative inquiry, well-paid, well-trained teachers, and a willingness to avoid equating the evaluation of learning outcomes with standardized tests (408)—echoes the core values of Fifth Dimension implementers working after school.
5. Gil Noam (2003) provides a stimulating discussion of different forms of partnerships that could, in principle, be applied to the Fifth Dimension–UC Links model. Especially relevant to our purposes is his emphasis on the need to focus on the sustainability of the *partnership* and not just its constituents.
6. Service learning classes substitute for laboratory-style classes in some institutions; others substitute work in classrooms as teacher's aides. The first ap-

proach lacks the rigorous academic training associated with laboratory research classes, while the second subordinates research to teacher training and is restricted to a highly bureaucratized setting. If implemented as practicum-style laboratory classes, service learning may provide the most promising venue for dissemination of the Fifth Dimension–UC Links approach.

References

Barab, Sasha A., and Tom M. Duffy. 2000. "From Practice Fields to Communities of Practice." In *Theoretical Foundations of Learning Environments*, edited by David H. Jonassen and Susan M. Land. Mahwah, N.J.: Lawrence Erlbaum.

Becker, Alton L. 1995. *Beyond Translation: Essays Toward a Modern Philology*. Ann Arbor: University of Michigan Press.

Belle, Deborah. 1999. *The After-School Lives of Children*. Mahwah, N.J.: Lawrence Erlbaum.

Bissell, Joan S., Christopher T. Cross, Karen Mapp, Elizabeth R. Reisner, Deborah L. Vandell, Constancia Warren, and Richard Weissbourd. 2003. Statement from members of the scientific advisory board for the 21st Century Community Learning Center evaluation (May 10).

Blanton, William E., Rita Menendez, Gary B. Moorman, and Linda C. Pacifici. 2003. "Learning to Comprehend Written Directions Through Participation in a Mixed Activity System." *Early Education and Development* (special issue: "Vygotskian Perspectives in Early Childhood Education") 14(3): 313–33.

Blanton, William E., Gary B. Moorman, Bobbie A. Hayes, and Mark L. Warner. 1997. "Effects of Participation in the Fifth Dimension on Far Transfer." *Journal of Educational Computing Research* 16(4): 371–96.

Blanton, William E., and Erin Simmons. 1997. "Understanding Learning Systems and Development in the Fifth Dimension: Model Systems and Microgenetic Methodology." Paper presented to the meeting of the American Educational Research Association. Chicago (March).

———. 1998a. "The Application of Microgenesis to Study Learning in the Fifth Dimension." Paper presented to the Fourth International Congress on Activity Theory, Aarhus, Denmark (June 7–11).

———. 1998b. "Cultural-Historical Activity Theory: Application to a Mixed Activity Learning System." Paper presented to the annual meeting of the American Educational Research Association. San Diego (April).

Bormuth, John R. 1969. "Factor Validity of Cloze Tests as a Measure of Reading Comprehension Ability." *Reading Research Quarterly* 4: 358–67.

Bronfenbrenner, Urie, and Pamela A. Morris. 1998. "The Ecology of Developmental Processes." In *Handbook of Child Psychology*, 5th ed., edited by William Damon, vol. 1, *Theoretical Models of Human Development*. New York: Wiley.

Brown, Ann L., and Joseph C. Campione. 1998. "Designing a Community of Young

Learners: Theoretical and Practical Lessons." In *How Students Learn: Reforming Schools Through Learner-Centered Education*, edited by Nadine Lambert and Barbara L. McCombs. Washington, D.C.: American Psychological Association.

Brown, John S., Allan Collins, and Paul Duguid. 1989. "Situated Cognition and the Culture of Learning." *Educational Researcher* 18(1): 32–42.

Chaiklin, Seth, and Jean Lave, eds. 1993. *Understanding Practice: Perspectives on Activity and Context*. Cambridge: Cambridge University Press.

Chi, Michelene T. H., and Randy D. Koeske. 1983. "Network Representations of a Child's Dinosaur Knowledge." *Developmental Psychology* 19: 29–39.

Cognition and Technology Group at Vanderbilt University. 1996. "Looking at Technology in Context: A Framework for Understanding Technology and Education Research." In *Handbook of Educational Psychology*, edited by David C. Berliner and Robert C. Calfee. New York: Macmillan.

Cole, Michael. 1986. "Reconfiguring Contexts of Education." Grant proposal for the Spencer Foundation.

———. 1988. "Cross-cultural Research in the Sociohistorical Tradition." *Human Development* 31(3): 137–52.

———. 1994. *The Velikhov-Hamburg Project 1985–1994: An Experiment in Computer Mediated Communication Between Nations in Conflict*. San Diego: University of California, Laboratory of Comparative Human Cognition.

———. 1996. *Cultural Psychology: A Once and Future Discipline*. Cambridge, Mass.: Belknap Press of Harvard University Press.

Cole, Michael, Sheila Cole, and Cynthia Lightfoot. 2005. *The Development of Children*. 5th ed. New York: Worth.

Cole, Michael, and Yrjö Engeström. 1997. "A Cultural-Historical Approach to Distributed Cognition." In *Distributed Cognitions: Psychological and Educational Considerations*, edited by Gavriel Salomon. New York: Cambridge University Press.

Cole, Michael, and Eugene Subbotsky. 1993. "The Fate of Stages Past: Reflections on the Heterogeneity of Thinking from the Perspective of Cultural-Historical Psychology." *Schweizerische Zeitschrift fuer Psychologie* 52(3): 103–13.

Corrigan, Dean. 2000. "The Changing Role of Schools and Higher Education Institutions with Respect to Community-Based Interagency Collaboration and Interprofessional Partnerships." *Peabody Journal of Education* 75(3): 175–95.

Cuban, Larry. 1986. *Teachers and Machines: The Classroom Use of Technology Since 1920*. New York: Teachers College Press.

———. 2004. "Answering Tough Questions About Sustainability." Keynote address at TERC First Virtual Conference on Local Systemic Change. Cambridge, Mass. (May 13–22).

Dahl, Bianca. 2002. "Profit, Learning, and Ideology: A Comparative Study of Institutional Structure and Idioculture in Two After-School Child Enrichment Programs." Honors thesis, University of California at San Diego.

Davidson & Associates. 1994. "Grammar Games" (computer game). Torrance, Calif.: Davidson & Associates.

Davydov, Vasilii V. 1988. "Problems of Developmental Teaching," pts. I–III. *Soviet Education* 30(8–10): entire issues.

———. 1990. *Types of Generalization in Instruction*. Reston, Va.: National Council of Teachers of Mathematics.

Duranti, Alessandro, and Charles Goodwin. 1992. *Rethinking Context: Language as an Interactive Phenomenon*. Cambridge: Cambridge University Press.

Eccles, Jacquelynne, and Jennifer A. Gootman, eds. 2002. *Community Programs to Promote Youth Development: Committee on Community-Level Programs for Youth*. Washington, D.C.: National Academy Press.

El'konin, Daniil B. 1977. "Toward the Problem of Stages in the Mental Development of the Child." In *Soviet Developmental Psychology*, edited by Michael Cole. White Plains, N.Y.: Sharpe.

Engeström, Yrjö, Reijo Miettinen, and Raija-Leena Punamaki, eds. 1999. *Perspectives on Activity Theory*. Cambridge: Cambridge University Press.

Fine, Gary Alan. 1987. *With the Boys*. Chicago: University of Chicago Press.

Forum for Youth Investment. 2002. "Out-of-School Research Meets After-School Policy." *Out-of-School Time Policy Commentary* 1(October). Available online at: http://www.forumfyi.org/Files//ostpc1.pdf.

Gallego, Margaret A., and Michael Cole. 2000. "Success Is Not Enough: Challenges to Sustaining New Forms of Educational Activity." *Computers in Human Behavior* 16: 271–86.

Goncü, Artin, ed. 1993. *Children's Engagement in the World: Sociocultural Perspectives*. New York: Cambridge University Press.

Granger, Robert C., and Thomas Kane. 2004. "Improving the Quality of After-School Programs." *Education Week* 23(23): 76.

Greeno, James G. 1998. "The Situativity of Knowing, Learning, and Research." *American Psychologist* 53: 5–17.

Griffin, Peg, and Michael Cole. 1984. "Current Activity for the Future: The Zo-ped." In *Children's Learning in the Zone of Proximal Development: New Directions for Child Development*, no. 23, edited by Barbara Rogoff and James V. Wertsch. San Francisco: Jossey-Bass.

Halpern, Robert. 2002. "A Different Kind of Child Development Institution: The History of After-School Programs for Low-Income Children." *Teachers College Record* 104(2): 178–211.

———. 2003. *Making Play Work: The Promise of After-School Programs for Low-Income Children*. New York: Teachers College Press.

Hammill, Donald D., and Stephen C. Larsen. 1988. *TOWL-2: Test of Written Language 2*. Austin, Tex.: PRO-ED, Inc.

Harton, Helen C., and Martin J. Bourgeois. 2004. "Cultural Elements Emerge from Dynamic Social Impact." In *The Psychological Foundation of Culture*, edited by Mark Schaller and Christian S. Crandall. Mahwah, N.J.: Lawrence Erlbaum.

Heath, Shirley B. 1994. "Learning for Anything Everyday (Learning to Learn)." *Journal of Curriculum Studies* 26: 471–89.

Honig, Meredith I., and Morva A. McDonald. 2005. "From Promise to Participation: After-School Programs Through the Lens of Sociocultural Learning Theory." *After-School Matters* 5(Fall): 1–26.

Karmiloff-Smith, Annette. 1992. *Beyond Modularity: A Developmental Perspective on Cognitive Science.* Cambridge, Mass.: MIT Press.

Körkel, Joachim, and Wolfgang Schneider. 1991. "Domain-Specific Versus Metacognitive Knowledge Effects on Text Recall and Comprehension." In *Learning and Instruction: European Research in an International Context,* vol. 3, edited by Mario Carretero, Maureen Pope, P. Robert-Jan Simons, and Juan Ignacío Pozo. Oxford: Pergamon.

Kozulin, Alex. 1998. *Psychological Tools: A Sociocultural Approach to Education.* Cambridge, Mass.: Harvard University Press.

Laboratory of Comparative Human Cognition (LCHC). 1982. "A Model System for the Study of Learning Difficulties." *Quarterly Newsletter of the Laboratory of Comparative Human Cognition* 4(3): 39–66.

———. 1989. "Kids and Computers: A Positive Vision for the Future." *Harvard Educational Review* 59: 73–86.

Larson, Reed, and Suman Verma. 1999. "How Children and Adolescents Spend Time Across the World: Work, Play, and Developmental Opportunities." *Psychological Bulletin* 125(6): 701–36.

Lauer, Patricia A., Motoko Akiba, Stephanie B. Wilkerson, Helen S. Apthorp, David Snow, and Mya Martin-Glenn. 2004. *The Effectiveness of Out-of-School-Time Strategies in Assisting Low-Achieving Students in Reading and Mathematics: A Research Synthesis,* updated ed. Aurora, Colo.: Mid-continent Research for Education and Learning.

Lave, Jean. 1988. *Cognition in Practice: Mind, Mathematics, and Culture in Everyday Life.* New York: Cambridge University Press.

Lave, Jean, and Étienne Wenger. 1991. *Situated Learning: Legitimate Peripheral Participation.* Cambridge: Cambridge University Press.

Lemke, Jay. 1997. "Cognition, Context, and Learning: A Social Semiotic Perspective." In *Situated Cognition: Social, Semiotic, and Psychological Perspectives,* edited by David Kirshner and James A. Whitson. Hillsdale, N.J.: Lawrence Erlbaum.

Leontiev, Aleksei N. 1978. *Activity, Consciousness, and Personality.* Englewood Cliffs, N.J.: Prentice-Hall.

———. 1981. *Problems of the Development of the Mind.* Moscow: Progress.

Levin, James, Margaret Riel, Naomi Miyake, and Moises Cohen. 1987. "Education on the Electronic Frontier: Teleapprentices in Globally Distributed Educational Contexts." *Contemporary Educational Psychology* 12(3): 254–60.

Lobato, Joanne. 2003. "How Design Experiments Can Inform a Rethinking of Transfer and Vice Versa." *Educational Researcher* 32(1): 17–20.

Luchins, A. S. 1942. "Mechanization in Problem Solving: The Effect of Einstellung." *Psychological Monographs* 54(6): 95.

Luria, Alexander. 1932. *The Nature of Human Conflicts.* New York: Liveright.

Lyon, G. Reid. 1999. "In Celebration of Science in the Study of Reading Development, Reading Difficulties, and Reading Instruction: The NICHD Perspective." *Issues in Education: Contributions from Educational Psychology* 5: 85–115.

Mahoney, Joseph L., Reed W. Larson, and Jacquelynne S. Eccles, eds. 2005. *Organized Activities as Contexts of Development: Extracurricular Activities, After-School and Community Programs*. Mahwah, N.J.: Lawrence Erlbaum.

Mariage, Troy, and Arthur Garmon. 2003. "A Case of Educational Change: Improving Student Achievement Through a School-University Partnership." *Remedial and Special Education* 24(4): 215–34.

Mathematica Policy Research Institute. 2003. *When Schools Stay Open Late: The National Evaluation of the 21st Century Community Learning Centers Program: First Year Findings* (December 2002). Report prepared for the U.S. Department of Education. Available at: http://www.ed.gov/pubs/21cent/firstyear/index.html.

Matusov, Eugene, and Renee Hayes. 2000. "Sociocultural Critique of Piaget and Vygotsky." *New Ideas in Psychology* 18: 215–39.

Mayer, Richard E., ed. 1988. *Teaching and Learning Computer Programming*. Hillsdale, N.J.: Lawrence Erlbaum.

———. 1999. "Instructional Technology." In *Handbook of Applied Cognition*, edited by Francis T. Durso. Chichester, Eng.: Wiley.

Mayer, Richard E., Jennifer Dyck, and William Vilberg. 1986. "Learning to Program and Learning to Think: What's the Connection?" *Communications of the Association for Computing Machinery* 29: 605–10.

Mayer, Richard E., Jill H. Quilici, and Roxana Moreno. 1999. "What Is Learned in an After-School Computer Club?" *Journal of Educational Computing Research* 20(3): 223–35.

Mayer, Richard E., Jill H. Quilici, Roxana Moreno, Richard Duran, Scott Woodbridge, Rebecca Simon, David Sanchez, and Amy Lavezzo. 1997. "Cognitive Consequences of Participation in a 'Fifth Dimension' After-School Computer Club." *Journal of Educational Computing Research* 4: 353–70.

Mayer, Richard E., and Merlin Wittrock. 1996. "Problem-Solving Transfer." In *Handbook of Educational Psychology*, edited by David Berliner and Robert C. Calfee. New York: Macmillan.

McKenna, Michael C., and Richard D. Robinson. 1980. *An Introduction to the Cloze Procedure: An Annotated Bibliography*. Newark, Del.: International Reading Association.

Mehan, Hugh. 1979. *Learning Lessons*. Cambridge, Mass.: Harvard University Press.

Moll, Luis C., Cathy Amanti, Deborah Neff, and Norman González. 1992. "Funds of Knowledge for Teaching: Using a Qualitative Approach to Connect Homes and Classrooms." *Theory into Practice* 31(1): 132–41.

———. 1999. "Writing as Communication: Creating Strategic Learning Environments for Students." In *Pathways to Success in School: Culturally Responsive Teaching*, edited by Etta R. Hollins and Eileen I. Oliver. Mahwah, N.J.: Lawrence Erlbaum.

Murolo, Priscilla. 1997. *The Common Ground of Womanhood: Class, Gender, and Working Girls' Clubs, 1884–1928*. Champaign: University of Illinois Press.

Naylor, Alice, and Mark Evans. 2003. "A Qualitative Study of Sustainability Factors in the Fifth Dimension Program (5-D) of Appalachian State University." Unpublished paper. Boone, N.C.: Appalachian State University.

Newman, Denis, Peg Griffin, and Michael Cole. 1989. *The Construction Zone*. Cambridge: Cambridge University Press.

Newman, Sanford, T. Berry Brazelton, Edward Zigler, Lawrence W. Sherman, William Bratton, Jerry Sanders, and William Christeson. 2000. "America's Child Care Crisis: A Crime Prevention Tragedy." Washington, D.C.: Fight Crime: Invest in Kids.

Newman, Sanford, James A. Fox, Edward A. Flynn, and William Christeson. 2000. "America's After-School Choice: The Prime Time for Juvenile Crime or Youth Enrichment and Achievement." Washington, D.C.: Fight Crime: Invest in Kids.

Nicolopoulou, Ageliki, and Michael Cole. 1993. "The Fifth Dimension, Its Play-World, and Its Institutional Context: Generation and Transmission of Shared Knowledge in the Culture of Collaborative Learning." In *Context for Learning: Sociocultural Dynamics in Children's Development*, edited by Ellice A. Forman, Norris Minick, and C. Addison Stone. New York: Oxford University Press.

Noam, Gil G. 2003. "After-School Education: What Principals Should Know." *Principal, Beyond the Bell* 82(5, May–June): 19–21.

Nocon, Honorine D. 2004. "Sustainability as Process: Community Education and Expansive Collaborative Activity." *Educational Policy* 18(5): 729.

North Carolina Department of Public Instruction. 1994. *North Carolina End-of-Grade Tests*. Raleigh: Accountability Services, Department of Public Instruction.

Olt, Amy, Michael Cole, and Scott Woodbridge. 1994. "Documenting Children's Problem-Solving Behaviors Using Field Notes of Participant Observers." Paper presented to the annual meeting of the American Educational Research Association. New Orleans (April 4–8).

Oppenheimer, Todd. 2003. *The Flickering Mind: The False Promise of Technology in the Classroom and How Learning Can Be Saved*. New York: Random House.

Padilla, Mary Lou, and Garry L. Landreth. 1989. "Latchkey Children: A Review of the Literature." *Child Welfare* 68(4): 445–54.

Patton, Q. M. 1997. *Utilization-Focused Evaluation*. London: Sage.

Piaget, Jean. 1970. "Piaget's Theory." In *Carmichael's Manual of Child Psychology*, 3rd ed., vol. 1, edited by Paul H. Mussen. New York: Wiley.

Pittman, Karen, Joel Tolman, and Nichole Yohalem. 2005. "Developing a Comprehensive Agenda for Out-of-School Hours: Lessons and Challenges Across Cities." In *Organized Activities as Contexts of Development: Extracurricular Activities, After-School, and Community Programs*, edited by Joseph L. Mahoney, Reed W. Larson, and Jacquelynne S. Eccles. Mahwah, N.J.: Lawrence Erlbaum.

Polman, Joseph K. 2004. "Perils and Promise: After-School Programs on School Territory." *After-School Matters* 4: 5–14.

Rankin, Earl F., and Joseph Culhane. 1969. "Comparable Cloze and Multiple-Choice Comprehension Test Scores." *Journal of Reading Behavior* 13: 193–98.

Raygor, Alton. 1977. "The Raynor Readability Estimate. A Quick and Easy Way to Determine Difficulty." In *Twenty-Sixth Yearbook of the National Reading Conference*, edited by P.D. Pearson. Clemson, S.C.: National Reading Conference.

Reyna, Valerie. 2002. *Proven Methods of Scientifically Based Research*. Washington: U.S. Department of Education. Available at: http://www.ed.gov/nclb/methods/whatworks/research/index.html.

Riel, Margaret. 1985. "The Computer Chronicles Newswire: A Functional Learning Environment for Acquiring Literacy Skills." *Journal of Educational Computing Research* 1(3): 317–37.

Rogers, Everett M. 1983. *Diffusion of Innovations*, 3rd ed. New York: Free Press.

———. 1995. *Diffusion of Innovations*, 4th ed. New York: Free Press.

———. 2002. "Diffusion of Preventative Innovations." *Addictive Behaviors* 27: 989–93.

Rogoff, Barbara. 1990. *Apprenticeship in Thinking: Cognitive Development in Social Context*. Oxford: Oxford University Press.

———. 1994. "Developing Understanding of the Idea of Communities of Learners." *Mind, Culture, and Activity* 1(4): 209–29.

———. 2003. *The Cultural Nature of Human Development*. London: Oxford University Press.

Rose, Edward, and William Felton. 1955. "Experimental Studies of Culture." *American Sociological Review* 20: 383–92.

Rossi, Peter H., Howard E. Freeman, and Mark W. Lipsey. 1999. *Evaluation: A Systematic Approach*, 6th ed. Thousand Oaks, Calif.: Sage Publications.

Rubinowitz, Leonard, and James Rosenbaum. 2000. *Crossing the Class and Color Lines: From Public Housing to White Suburbia*. Chicago: University of Chicago Press.

Sarason, Seymour. 1982. *The Culture of the School and the Problem of Change*. Boston: Allyn and Bacon.

———. 1988. *The Creation of Settings and the Future Societies*. Cambridge, Mass.: Brookline Books.

———. 1991. *The Predictable Failure of Educational Reform*. San Francisco: Jossey-Bass.

———. 1997. "Revisiting the Creation of Settings." *Mind, Culture, and Activity* 4(3): 175–82.

Saxe, Geoffrey. 1994. "Studying Cognitive Development in Sociocultural Context: The Development of a Practice-Based Approach." *Mind, Culture, and Activity* 1(3): 135–57.

Schustack, Miriam W. 1997. "Evaluating a Voluntary Participation Program:

Who's the Control Group?" Paper presented to the annual meeting of the American Educational Research Association. Chicago (April 8–11).

Schustack, Miriam W., Rachelle Strauss, and Patricia E. Worden. 1997. "Learning About Technology in a Non-instructional Environment." *Journal of Educational Computing Research* 16(4): 337–51.

Schustack, Miriam W., Patricia E. Worden, K. Swaine, E. Willett, Catherine King, and Gillian McNamee. 1994. "Assessing the Impact of After-School Activity on Children's Computer Knowledge." Paper presented to the annual meeting of the American Educational Research Association. New Orleans (April 4–8).

Slavin, Robert E. 2003. "A Reader's Guide to Scientifically Based Research." *Educational Leadership* 60(5): 12–16.

Strauss, Anselm, and Juliet M. Corbin. 1990. *Basics of Qualitative Research: Grounded Theory Procedures and Techniques*. Thousand Oaks, Calif.: Sage Publications.

Sunburst Software. 1996. "Puzzle Tanks" (computer game). Pleasantville, N.Y.: Sunburst Software.

Taylor, Wilson L. 1953. "Cloze Procedure: A New Tool for Measuring Readability." *Journalism Quarterly* 30: 415–33.

———. 1957. "'Cloze' Readability Scores as Indices of Individual Differences in Comprehension and Aptitude." *Journal of Applied Psychology* 41: 19–26.

Tharp, Roland G., and Ronald Gallimore. 1988. *Rousing Minds to Life: Teaching, Learning, and Schooling in Social Context*. New York: Cambridge University Press.

The After-School Corporation (TASC). 2003. *The After-School Corporation Fifth Year Report*. New York: TASC.

Tuomi-Gröhn, Terttu, and Yrjö Engeström. 2003. "Conceptualizing Transfer: From Standard Notions to Developmental Perspectives." In *Between School and Work: New Perspectives on Transfer and Boundary-Crossing*, edited by Terttu Tuomi-Gröhn and Yrjö Engeström. Oxford: Elsevier Science.

U.S. Bureau of Labor Statistics. 2003. "Employment Characteristics of Families Summary (table 4)." Washington: U.S. Department of Labor.

Valsiner, Jaan. 1998. *The Guided Mind: A Sociogenetic Approach to Personality*. Cambridge, Mass.: Harvard University Press.

Vandell, Deborah L., and Kim M. Pierce. 2003. "Child Care Quality and Children's Success at School." In *Early Childhood Programs for a New Century*, edited by Arthur J. Reynolds, Margaret C. Wang, and Herbert J. Walberg. University of Illinois at Chicago Series on Children and Youth: Issues in Children's and Families' Lives. Washington, D.C.: Child Welfare League of America.

Vandell, Deborah L., Lee Shumow, and Jill Posner. 2005. "After-School Programs for Low-Income Children: Differences in Program Quality." In *Organized Activities as Contexts of Development: Extracurricular Activities, After-School, and Community Programs*, edited by Joseph L. Mahoney, Reed W. Larson, and Jacquelynne S. Eccles. Mahwah, N.J.: Lawrence Erlbaum.

Varenne, Hervé, and Ray McDermott. 1998. *Successful Failure: The School America Builds*. Boulder, Colo.: Westview.

Vásquez, Olga. 1994. "The Magic of La Clase Mágica: Enhancing the Learning Potential of Bilingual Children." *Australian Journal of Language and Literacy* 17(2): 120–28.

———. 2003. *La Clase Mágica: Imagining Optimal Possibilities in a Bilingual Community of Learners*. Mahwah, N.J.: Lawrence Erlbaum.

Vygotsky, Lev S. 1978. *Mind in Society*. Cambridge, Mass.: Harvard University Press.

———. 1987. *Problems of General Psychology*, vol. 1, *The Collected Works of L. S. Vygotsky*, edited by Robert W. Rieber and Aaron S. Carton. New York: Plenum. (Orig. pub. in 1934.)

Wertsch, James V. 1985. *Vygotsky and the Social Formation of Mind*. Cambridge, Mass.: Harvard University Press.

———. 1991. *Voices of the Mind: A Sociocultural Approach to Mediated Action*. Cambridge, Mass.: Harvard University Press.

———. 1997. *Mind as Action*. New York: Oxford University Press.

Williams, Raymond. 1976. *Keywords: A Vocabulary of Culture and Society*. New York: Oxford University Press.

About the Authors

Michael Cole is University Professor of Communication and Psychology at the University of California, San Diego.

William Blanton is professor in the Department of Teaching and Learning at the University of Miami.

Donald Bremme is professor of education at Whittier College.

Mary E. Brenner is associate professor in the Education Department at the University of California, Santa Barbara.

Katherine Brown is assistant professor in the Department of Communication at California State University, San Marcos.

Richard Duran is professor in Gevirtz Graduate School of Education at the University of California, Santa Barbara.

Lucy N. Friedman is president of The After-School Corporation in New York City, co-chair of the New York State Afterschool Network, and chair of the Executive Committee of the Coalition for Science After School.

Margaret Gallego is professor in the Teacher Education Department at San Diego State University.

Catherine King is associate professor in the Department of Education at Elon College.

Richard Mayer is professor of psychology at the University of California, Santa Barbara.

Ray McDermott is professor of education and (by courtesy) anthropology at Stanford University.

Gillian McNamee is professor and director of teacher education at the Erikson Institute Graduate School of Child Development.

Luis C. Moll is professor of education and associate dean of the College of Education at the University of Arizona, Tucson.

Honorine Nocon is assistant professor at the School of Education and Human Development, University of Colorado at Denver and Health Sciences Center.

Robert Rueda is professor of psychology in education in Rossier School of Education at the University of Southern California.

Miriam Schustack is professor of psychology at California State University, San Marcos.

Olga Vásquez is professor in the Department of Communication at the University of California, San Diego.

Scott Woodbridge is coordinator of public programs at the University of California, Berkeley, Graduate School of Education, UC Links Program.

Index

Boldface numbers refer to figures and tables.

evaluating after-school programs (*cont.*)
80; desirable characteristics of after-
school programs, consensus on,
198–200; in difficult circumstances,
181–82; at the institutional level,
82–83; problem-solving transfer, the
problem of demonstrating, 74–75;
qualitative studies of children's
learning (process evaluation), 73,
79–83, 178–79 (*see also* social dynamics); quantitative strategies for cognitive and academic evaluation of children, 73–79, 179–81 (*see also*
cognitive and academic skills); questions for Fifth Dimension programs,
66; revisiting issues of, 178–84; science foiled by reality: the initial
plan, 67–72; timing of, 76
Evans, Mark, 191

faculty: Fifth Dimension, reasons for
participation in, 1, 5–7; research foci
at the implementation sites, 36, 40,
43, 46, 49, 51, 52–53, 55, 58, 61
Felton, William, 32
"Fifth Dimension: Local Learning
Communities in a Global World,"
165
Fifth Dimension Clearinghouse,
167–68
Fifth Dimension programs: benefits of,
1–2, 187–88; cognitive and academic
skills, development of (*see* cognitive
and academic skills); design of (*see*
design of Fifth Dimension programs); diffusion of (*see* diffusion of
the Fifth Dimension); evaluation of
(*see* evaluating after-school programs); goals of, 1–2, 5–6; as a heterogeneous system, 111–12; hybrid
character of, 108; implementation, issues and questions raised by, 64,
177–78; implementation sites of (*see*

implementation sites); as a model
for after-school programs, xv–xvii,
200–201; prototype system of, 6–8;
the social dynamics of learning in
(*see* social dynamics); sustainability
of (*see* sustainability); theories of
learning and development underlying (*see* theories of learning and development); undergraduate participants, impact on (*see*
undergraduates)
Fifth Dimension—UC Links program,
1, 6, 192–93. *See also* Fifth Dimension
programs; UC Links project
Fight Crime: Invest in Kids California,
3
Fine, Gary Alan, 32
Finland, 164
Friedman, Lucy, xv

Gallego, Margaret, 43–45
Gallimore, Ronald, 145
general law of social development, 22
girls: computer technologies in after-
school programs, use of to invite the
inclusion of, 5; nineteenth-century
programs for, 3
goal formation, importance of, 28–29,
153–54
Golem. *See* mythical figurehead, the
Gootman, Jennifer, 4–5
Granger, Robert, 4, 198
Griffin, Peg, 204*n*3
guided participation, 22–23

Halpern, Robert, 2–3, 17–18, 199
Harvard University, 4
heterogeneous system, the Fifth Dimension as, 111–12
higher learning, institutions of: college
courses linked to the Fifth Dimension offered by, 9, 176; diversity of,
significance of, 10–12; evaluation

through continued support of programs, 183; sustainability difficulties confronted by, 194–98; UC Links Project, participation in, 1, 7, 9; in the UC Links structure, 10–12. *See also* faculty; undergraduates

ICT. *See* information and communication technologies
idioculture, 31–32
implementation, questions of, 64, 177–78
implementation sites: diversity and local adaptation at, 34–35, 64–65; historical expansion of, 35–36; overview of, **10–11**; partnership between California State University at San Marcos and the Boys and Girls Club, 55–57, 77, 87–93, 95–96, 101–3; partnership between Elon College and the YMCA, 51–52; partnership between Erikson Institute and Le Claire—Hearst Community Center, 46–48; partnership between Michigan State University and the Cristo Rey Community Center, 43–45, 153–55; partnership between the University of California at San Diego and La Clase Mágica (*see* La Clase Mágica); partnership between the University of California at San Diego and the Boys and Girls Club, 36–39, 78–79, 121–27; partnership between the University of California at Santa Barbara and the Boys and Girls Club, 57–61, 74, 77, 94–95; partnership between the University of New Orleans and the Claiborne School, 49–51; partnership between Whittier College and the Boys and Girls Club (*see* Whittier College); partnerships of Appalachian State University (*see* Appalachian State University); program evaluation at, 76–79. *See also* diffusion of the Fifth Dimension
information and communication technologies (ICT), 162–65, 167–70. *See also* technology
institutional hybrid, the Fifth Dimension as, 108
intergenerational community of learners, 22–24, 112–13
interinstitutional collaborations, designing the, 177
"Island Survivors," 121–27

Kane, Thomas, 4, 198
Karmiloff-Smith, Annette, 28
King, Catherine, 35, 49–52

Laboratory of Comparative Human Cognition (LCHC), 36–38
La Clase Mágica (LCM): community staff, benefits for, 187–88; computers available at, 25; culture integrated into, 32; Fifth Dimension program at, 10; heterogeneous players in the activity system of, 112–20; partnership with the University of California at San Diego, 39–42; program evaluation at, 74, 77–78; undergraduates, impact of Fifth Dimension participation on, 157
La Clase Mágica Midwest (LCMM), 43–45
"Language Explorer," 112–19
La Red Mágica, 167
latchkey children, 2
Latinos, 40–42
Lave, Jean, 15, 22–23
LCHC. *See* Laboratory of Comparative Human Cognition
LCM. *See* La Clase Mágica
LCMM. *See* La Clase Mágica Midwest
leading activities, 21–22, 173–74
learning: and development, theories of